Free to Worship

Creating transcendent worship today

MICHAEL MARSHALL

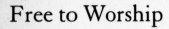 Marshall Pickering
An Imprint of HarperCollins*Publishers*

The Power of God is the worship he inspires.
A. N. Whitehead

Marshall Pickering is an Imprint of
HarperCollins*Religious*
Part of HarperCollins*Publishers*
77–85 Fulham Palace Road, London W6 8JB

First published in Great Britain
in 1982 by Marshall Morgan & Scott
under the title *Renewal In Worship*
Revised American edition published in 1985 by Morehouse-Barlow
Co. Inc., Connecticut
This revised edition published in 1996 by Marshall Pickering

1 3 5 7 9 10 8 6 4 2

A catalogue record for this book is
available from the British Library

0 551 02975 7

Printed and bound in Great Britain by
Caledonian International Book Manufacturing Ltd, Glasgow

Contents

Acknowledgements

I once read, from a source long since forgotten, some words which have stayed with me throughout a long ministry: 'There are no lone rangers in the Kingdom.' If that is true – and I'm sure it is – then it is equally true that there are no soloists in publishing. Publishing a book is a team effort, and blessed is an author who is fortunate enough to have a team of colleagues who will assist without necessarily agreeing with much of what is written – or indeed any of it! I have been abundantly blessed in this regard. Christine Smith of HarperCollins invited me to write this brand new edition of a former book – *Renewal in Worship* – and continued to encourage me in the undertaking from start to finish.

Every author needs a technological 'wordsmith' who will exercise great skill in producing the manuscript and all the other paraphernalia associated with 'floppy disks' and the rest! Rita Almond has exercised these skills with much patience and for that hard work I wish to express my deep gratitude. The book would not have been produced without her. The Reverend Paul Atherton not only read the penultimate version of the manuscript, but offered substantial input into the text. Several parts owe a great deal to his contributions, both at the level of content and of style.

I am heavily indebted for the encouragement and input of Canon Richard Giles, one of the church's leading architectural advisers on the reordering of church buildings. I am grateful to him for the trouble he took to scrutinize Chapter 10 and for the suggestions he made. I dedicate this book to him and the congregation at St Thomas', Huddersfield – a church renewed through transcendent worship, in a building gloriously reordered for service in the wider community.

Foreword

'When people return to the Church . . . what will they find in the worship that is being offered Sunday by Sunday?' This is the question that has prompted Michael Marshall to write this book, because he believes that what they find frequently falls short of the very best that we can offer to God.

Why does worship matter so much? Because worship expresses the heart of our faith – that we are most fully ourselves when we are giving not getting; because it is worship – assembling for common prayer – that identifies and sustains us as believers, and makes the Church visible; because worship in a church which has no confessional statements to define the boundaries of belief is what carries and shapes doctrine; because worship is what holds together before God the realities of our existence – the potential and the pain of being a human being – and the possibility of transformation.

Is that what people experience? Do they expect to meet the living God in worship and to be transformed by it? What if a surreptitious video were made of our normal Sunday service: What would we see? In an age of short sound bytes and polished presentation, there is an understandable pressure to opt for entertainment rather than worship. We have come a long way from the days when possession of the *Book of Common Prayer* and a clear reading voice were the only attributes thought necessary for leading worship. There is more to it than what Parson Woodforde called 'reading prayers'. Those who prepare and lead our worship need to make discriminating choices – not only between different language styles, but also between the many alternative services now authorized.

We are gradually learning to shape a liturgy on the basis of our understanding that worship carries us from where we are to where we ought to be, and so has a natural dynamic of its own. We are gradually learning to let that worship reflect a particular and perhaps changing understanding of ourselves as a local community. We are gradually learning that the way the building is ordered, or the way in which the whole act of worship is presented, may powerfully affirm – or equally powerfully contradict – the theology that liturgy is trying to express. To focus on just one aspect – whether it is word, or sacrament, or music or ritual – and not to integrate all of these with a sense of the continuity of the worshipping community embodied in the way in which the building has been ordered, is to run the risk of posing contradictions which merely confuse and baffle the worshipper.

Yet that is often what people experience, and because it is in church, we somehow put up with muddle and sloppiness which would never be tolerated in other areas. Bishop Michael is passionate about getting our worship better ordered, and realizes that much of the difficulty is that those who lead worship are often ill informed. His vivid presentation and wide experience will carry his readers with him, and catch them up into his enthusiastic and integrated vision of what worship can be – a window into heaven.

David Sarum
Bishop of Salisbury
Epiphany 1996

Introduction

For the past four years I have worked as a bishop with a roving commission as the Archbishops' Adviser in Evangelism. Happily, there appear to be modest signs that people are returning to Christian life and commitment. As they do, what will they find in the worship being offered Sunday by Sunday? Will they discover a living faith and a lively spirituality in and through the worship offered? Unfortunately, those questions would often have to be answered in the negative, in every tradition or denomination, whether catholic, evangelical, charismatic or liberal. In other words, this book is directed – hopefully with humility – to practitioners of worship right across the ecclesiastical spectrum.

As I visit dioceses and parishes and try to discern the climates and cultures in which the gospel needs to be proclaimed and heard, I am increasingly convinced that Word and sacrament, proclamation and celebration need to go hand in hand. I want to press further on this point today than I would have done ten years ago. Many people are 'word weary' in this age of more information and less communication. It is in worship that we can interiorize the Word of the Gospel and make it our own in heart and head (and ultimately in the will). Many people who would not go near a church have been wonderfully moved by the Taizé experience in worship. In an age of television and sophisticated entertainment, the presentation of our worship in churches is, by comparison, often slipshod, distracting rather than engaging, opting for entertainment at one extreme or for therapy at the other.

How has this situation come about? Several factors have had their part to play. The liturgical revolution of recent years is most certainly still with us, and parish clergy and laity have yet to find their feet in its lengthy, necessarily evolving, yet equally disturbing process. Furthermore, many clergy who are in senior, responsible positions were trained at theological colleges or seminaries at a time when worship was fairly low on the list of curriculum priorities. In those days, pastoral counselling was top of the agenda and few of us were trained either for cooperative ministry (involving laity leading worship) or in the use of innovative liturgies, which at that stage were only just beginning. There was the almost unquestioned assumption that to be too concerned with the details of worship was to be too concerned with matters which interested the more high-church brethren, or to be turning one's back on the more compelling issues of contemporary society. Concern about worship was seen as the somewhat academic, anti-quarian interest of the liturgical scholar or the 'churchy' Christian, while for the rugged and 'real' apostolate of the Church there would be more pressing concerns.

All this has combined to bring about a situation in many of the churches today in which the faithful are seriously underfed. 'The sheep look up and are no longer fed' might be reversed to express this current 'famine' in the phrase, 'The sheep are fed up and are no longer looking' to the mainstream churches for spiritual awakening and renewal. So perhaps rightly, this book is written with a note of urgency, the sort that is inevitable when hunger and famine are in the air.

There is also a second reason why there is a note of urgency about this book. The good news is that many churches now are struggling to recover forms of worship which will speak to, and engage with, the unchurched and especially the young. Those experiments need all our support and encouragement. The bad news, however, is that in recent years, some of those experiments have gone wildly, even dangerously awry. History has proved again and again that 'DIY ritual' can be hazardous to our spiritual health. Little wonder that in the case of the church in Corinth in the first century as well as the Church of England in the sixteenth century, wise leaders from Paul to Cranmer have persistently issued spiritual health warnings, emphasizing that everything must be done 'decently and in order'.

Nevertheless, God forbid that in the name of 'safety first' we should revert to the dry worship of the quite wrongly termed 'good old days' of the quiet service! Even so, there is a real need for a word of caution. We need to bring ritual order out of potential chaos, and to benefit from the experience of the Church in handling the awesome fire of the Spirit. All hell can be let loose when fired by worship that is more of an entertainment and therapy than a call to repentance and renewal. There is something very dangerous about worship that does not issue in discipleship and service.

I hope that this book constitutes the right kind of challenge and invitation, if it is received in the spirit in which it is written. I would not wish to give the impression that my colleagues in the gospel, especially those in parishes, are careless or indifferent about worship. Rather, I am certain that they are hard-pressed on every side, and have little time for serious study of their stock in trade, nor the opportunity to go and see what is happening in other parishes, or other parts of the Church. My first concern is for them, linked with the hope that this book may be for them a useful resource, offering lots of ideas and practices for contemporary worship in a reasonably accessible form. I hope above all else that it might provide strong encouragement by holding out the great possibilities for contemporary forms of worship, at a time when we all need strong mutual encouragement in seeking to bring meaning, purpose and transcendence into a weary, disillusioned world.

So quite unashamedly and in the spirit I have just outlined, I would wish that this book might primarily be addressed to 'professionals' (in the best sense) – to all ministers of religion and especially to those called to and charged with the ministry of Word and sacrament.

Also, I hope that this book might be used by those currently in training for the ordained ministry. If this particular ministry is to be their distinctive and particular calling, nothing should be spared in trying to make certain that for *all* those who come to Church, nothing less than a banquet of Word and worship is carefully prepared for each successive Sunday, or whenever and wherever God's people meet for worship. All this requires skill and a serious commitment costly both in time and energy. Yet in addition to all this, there will always be the *sine qua non* of the gift of the Holy Spirit to anoint and to drive our worship Godward. I truly believe that even a modest improvement in the standards of worship and preaching in parishes throughout the country will promote renewal and spiritual awakening on a huge scale. If we get this right, a great deal else will follow. The renewal of the churches today converges *inwards* on worship, preaching and discipleship, and simultaneously breaks open *outwards* in evangelism, service and a proper concern for God's world.

Finally, I hope that this book will be helpful for the laity. In an age when a serious cut-back in the number of those being ordained to the ministry of Word and sacrament is likely, it must follow that very soon the laity will be more and not less involved in leading worship. However, all this should be seen not as a problem but rather as an opportunity for rediscovering ministry, in all its varied forms, as being the concern and calling of the whole people of God. Simon Tugwell OP, writes these encouraging words:

> It is to be hoped that we shall see a general revival in the church of all the various ministries and offices listed by St Paul: for too long, the priest has had to shoulder the lot, and he is most unlikely to be naturally or supernaturally equipped for it. He needs the prophets and healers, and those gifted with supernatural wisdom and knowledge. If all those charismatic ministries are revived this will probably constitute more than anything else to the revival of the true charism of the priesthood, which will be free of other burdens to be itself.[1]

Those trained as readers or for lay ministry will hopefully also find this book helpful, both to update themselves with the growing range of worship resources, and to pick up some useful hints about the leadership skills needed so that there is maximum participation, as well as minimum hindrances to transcendent and authentic worship.

Michael Marshall
Epiphany, 1996

I

Worship and the human condition

I worship therefore I am!

'Why was I created?' That question in the Scottish Catechism constitutes ultimately the most fundamental of all human enquiries. Without an answer to that question, all human striving is pointless, or in the words of the book of Ecclesiastes, 'All is vanity and a striving after wind' (Eccl. 1:14).

'I was created in order to worship God and to enjoy him for ever,' is the reply in that same Scottish Catechism, and that constitutes the basic thesis of this book. For if that reply is true, then it strikes at the whole basis of the human condition and cautions us that until we discover true and authentic worship we shall be less than human. Every man, woman and child was created for worship. That bold statement in the Scottish Catechism is universal in its application and is not restricted simply to people who go to church or who happen to like that sort of thing. Worship is the basic, fundamental instinct within every creature, an instinct more basic and more lasting than our sexual instincts, and yet an instinct largely ignored or scarcely heeded in the ordinary daily conversation and concerns of the twentieth century – to say nothing of its studied neglect in the syllabus of contemporary education.

'If you don't worship you'll shrink: it's as brutal as that,' explodes the psychiatrist in the play *Equus*.[1] In other words, like all basic human instincts, if it is neglected it does not evaporate or just go away; neglected or misdirected worship retains the power to corrupt and even to destroy, since humanity, which was made for worship, will demand ways of expressing this compulsive drive in one form or another – for good or ill.

From our early childhood, all of us have experienced the strange power and release of worship in one form or another. So fundamental is the experience of and instinct for worship that it even predates verbal expression and all rational processes, for it transcends even the most sophisticated vocabulary. Autistic children, to say nothing of the mentally handicapped, are not excluded from the experience of worship. Hence, children and illiterate people are not excluded from its power or its claims. Indeed, we can go further and say that for those who have not yet reached the age when they are restricted by the inhibition of words, the doors to worship are more easily opened and the checks and brakes of rationalism are not so easily applied. One writer has commented:

> For all praying begins with desire. Desire comes in many forms. At its best, desire in prayer is what Augustine calls an 'affectionate reaching out' to God. We long for contact, for connection at the centre, that grounding that brings full hearted peace of mind and soul.[2]

It is the tyranny of rationalism in the wake of the Enlightenment which has led to the contemporary mistrust of worship and therefore, perversely, to the contemporary curiosity, bordering on obsession, with mystical and transcendental experiences, induced by drugs and erotomania. In our day, we are paying dearly in many and varying ways for the reductionist claims of Descartes, Freud, Darwin and Marx. Reductionism by definition writes off the claims of the higher and explains them away in terms of the lowest common denominator. So when Descartes claimed in a dangerous half-truth, 'I think, therefore I am' (*'Cogito, ergo sum'*), he struck at the very foundations on which Western culture was based – art, music, poetry and supremely worship. He made claims about the integrity of the whole educational system which had brought him and our culture to where it was. All our deepest experiences would require from that point onwards to be justified and proved at the bar of reason and reason alone. The self-destructive process of reductionism had begun, and it has continued to our own day in differing keys and in many variations and guises.

Hence, 'I am what I do' (functionalism – little wonder people do not know who they are when they have lost their job); 'I am what I own' (materialism, fostering greed, which in turn feeds the credit industry in an over-heating economy); 'I am my sexuality' (Freudianism run amok – siring the destructive aspects of feminism as well as some of the more counter-productive claims of gay and lesbian rights); or 'I shop, therefore I am' – and all, of course, in those temples to Mammon we so pretentiously refer to as shopping malls.

Of course, there is some truth in all of these reductionist assertations, including that original claim of Descartes, but the whole truth is something bigger than all these put together and then much more besides.

It's not good enough to ask a person what they do for a living – and certainly not in an age of redundancy. It might be much more instructive, in fact, to enquire about their hobbies or what they do in their leisure time, and supremely what they do (or never do, as the case may be) on Sundays! Is there to be no place for corporate leisure in the modern world, a time just for being and being together at that; a time just to look and stare; to stand still, to listen and just to *be* without any apologies for inactivity? Even holidays, won as of right at great cost for working people, are now termed 'vacations', with the implication of empty space in the diary, only to be bartered for by ever-more persuasive tourist agencies on the understanding that every moment will be filled with worthwhile activity.

And whatever has happened to Sunday? It is now simply an adjective to describe trading – 'Sunday trading'. The leisurely Sunday has been sacrificed on the altar of the reductionism of the last decade – 'I shop, therefore I am' ('Tesco, *ergo sum*', as Robert Warren so humorously and perceptively reminds us). For surely, according to Genesis, we are most godlike when we rest, when we enjoy being together (for God has revealed himself as three persons in community), just looking with joy and pleasure upon the face of God, both in his creation and beyond in his new creation – the glory of God in the face of Jesus.

So, 'I worship, therefore I am' is the necessary rejoinder to Descartes and to all the rest of the reductionists. The ultimate joker in this whole pack of half-truths is the awesome reality that we become what we worship. That is why, presumably, we are sometimes aware that dogs begin to look a little like their masters, or conversely (and even more disturbing), that masters sometimes begin to look a little like their dogs!

'We are God's children now; it does not yet appear what we shall be, but we know that when he appears, we shall be like him, for we shall see him as he is' (1 John 3:2). In the meantime we must refuse to settle for any of the reductionist alternatives, living with the mystery of our identity and entering that mystery daily through the door of worship and adoration.

The capacity for wonder

Perhaps the highest price we have paid for all this reductionism has been the precious human capacity for wonder – the ability to stand and stare, the sense of expectation, the awareness of the numinous in the world around us as well as in the world within us. 'I am fearfully and wonderfully made,' says the psalmist (Ps. 139).

There is an urgent need today to reclaim this capacity for wonder, within the total understanding of what it is to be truly human. To gain the whole technological world at the expense of our ability to stop and wonder would reduce the human race to an all-time low level of poverty. So Dag Hammarskjöld, the United Nations Secretary General who was killed in a plane crash in 1961, wrote these prophetic words in his personal journal:

> God does not die on the day when we cease to believe in a personal deity, but we die on the day when our lives cease to be illumined by the steady radiance, renewed daily, of a wonder, the source of which is beyond all reason.[3]

Clearly, just one look into the eyes of many children tells you that on first entering this world we all experienced 'the new-minted wonder of childhood'.[4] In his book *This Sunrise of Wonder* (taking its title from a phrase of the writer G. K. Chesterton), Michael Mayne addresses 24 letters to his grandchildren, urging them to cherish and if need be to protect their capacity to wonder. It's not insignificant that John Wesley saw the three ingredients, 'wonder, love and praise' as a package deal, and all acting as trailers for their ultimate expression in full-blooded worship and adoration.

So G. K. Chesterton wrote: 'At the back of our brains, so to speak, there is a forgotten blaze or burst of astonishment at our own existence. The object of the artistic and spiritual life is to dig for this sunrise of wonder.'[5] Thomas Traherne (1636–74) turned continually to the theme of our creation. The glories of the visible world, he said, were wonders more readily understood by those with eyes to see them:

> Will you see the infancy of this sublime and celestial greatness? . . . I was a stranger, which at my entrance into the world was saluted and surrounded with innumerable joys: my knowledge was divine. I was entertained like an Angel with the works of God in their splendour and glory.[6]

While words can sometimes help to express our wonder, they can also equally be at other times a hindrance or even a real blockage. The preface to the *Alternative Service Book* of the Church of England (1980) says that

> even agreed words are only the beginning of worship. Those who use them do well to recognize their transience and imperfection; to treat them as a ladder, not a goal; to acknowledge their power in shaping faith and kindling devotion, without claiming that they are fully adequate to the task.

Hence the importance of other carriers for worship – not least music, and that much-neglected common language of the human race, supremely the language of all lovers – namely, silence. It is not incidental to note the recent popularity of plainsong – even hitting the top of the pops – for evoking wonder and worship. Significantly, of course, it is the high proportion of silence in the worship of the Taizé community which has drawn thousands of young people across the face of Europe just to wonder and worship. We need to make certain in this society of the information super-highway that the capacity to wonder is safeguarded. We must not put all our resources for communicating the gospel into words addressed primarily to the intellectual or information department of the brain. It is this failure to draw out and open up human experience in and through worship which is compelling many of our young people to drop out of the mainstream, to open the doors of perception through drug-induced experiences. Perhaps many are saying something like, 'There has to be more to life than a mortgage and two point four children.' Evangelism should not rely exclusively on the preached Word, but should also trail the coat of the gospel way of life as being a fuller, richer life, through the experience of rich (not necessarily complicated) and deep worship. If the services of the Church can connect with this frustrated capacity for worship and wonder, it will be meeting people where they are and helping to bring them to that place which God has prepared for them.

The power of the numinous

However, in making all these claims for the power of the numinous – the divine other – and for worship to transcend our human limitations, we should be under no illusions about the potential dangers of worship. For by definition, the power of the numinous is awesome and capable of the greatest motivation of the human will. (It is not incidental that at the climax of Christ's temptations, the devil invites Jesus to worship him, for the devil would claim his charismatics also!)

The so-called Toronto Blessing and indeed the whole charismatic movement, which has brought so many blessings to the churches, was surely for such a time as this – a time of intellectual aridity. 'The madman is not the man who has lost his reason, but rather the man who has lost everything except his reason,' wrote G. K. Chesterton. The madness of the post-Enlightenment era needed to be released into something deeper and less rigid. We need to learn to laugh again and indeed to cry again, to give to the emotions and the expressions of the heart their proper place. W. H. Auden wrote:

> In the deserts of the heart
> Let the healing fountain start
> In the prison of his days
> Teach the free man how to praise.[7]

There is a sense perhaps in which 'heart disease' is symbolic of the sickness of the late twentieth century. To such an age 'let go and let God' could constitute good news, but not if the tyranny of the intellect is replaced by a mindless religion which claims in effect nothing better than 'I experience, therefore I am!'

Worship, ecstasy and the numinous open the human race to a minefield of highly charged and potentially destructive experiences, and not least when everything is done in the name of the Spirit. For worship describes necessarily that moment when we no longer retain the initiative: we are laid wide open to being taken over for good or evil. The word 'numinous' indicates a moment or a place when the world around me *beckons* me. I no longer stick to the facts; rather, a strange and even bewildering experience begins when it would seem as though reality is the other way round – the facts seem to stick to me! We can never be totally safe from the invasion of such moments, for they necessarily take us unawares. It can be that moment when the sun is setting or the moon is rising. It can be the occasion of a familiar and frequently heard piece of music, a work of art, or the presence of a particular person. Such numinous moments begin to draw me and take me out of myself. For a moment, I am lost.

> 'And man, the marvel seeing,
> Forgets his selfish being
> For joy of beauty not his own.'[8]

A moment or a place of worship demands that we transcend ourselves – 'lost in wonder, love and praise'.[9] Such moments and places can arise out of a particular discipline – like art, music or poetry – that is deliberately calculated to evoke adoration. An otherwise 'perfectly ordinary' place or person, or a common, everyday sound or sight, can suddenly be endowed with a *significance*, and a complex may be formed around that experience which may not disappear for the rest of our lives. Suddenly it is not so much that I see a different world, but rather that I see the same old, rather tired and jaded world very differently in a new light. A whole new perspective opens out in front of me. We frequently speak of such moments as moments of inspiration, when we catch our breath. These are times of illumination, which tempt us to suppose that we must have been blind before: 'There it was, staring me in the face, and I couldn't see it.' 'My God, now I see!' Sometimes the result brings great joy, great sorrow or a sense of deep disillusionment. What is quite clear is that we can never go back again to seeing things as we used to see them. We are initiated into a totally new perspective, with a new outlook as a result of this devastating new insight.

The New Testament word for this is *metanoia* – generally translated by the word 'repentance', but perhaps more accurately understood as a change of outlook because of a new insight. Worship and repentance at their best belong together, as we shall see later in our discussion. Where worship does not issue in repentance, there is a strong probability that all kinds of complexes, 'hang-ups' and difficulties will arise. For it is the strange ability of a scene, a smell, a touch or a sound – or even architecture – to take to itself something special that sets it aside, rendering it in some sense holy and different. We are suddenly aware, as surely as Jacob in the Old Testament, that we are on holy ground. Instincts are aroused that our cautious intellect may have told us were safely hidden beneath the veneer of sophistication and rationalization.

The dangers and perversions of worship

So we need to know from the outset that we are handling fire which has a disturbing ability to backfire in all kinds of bizarre and potentially destructive ways. The power of worship can bind together in a totally irrational way a particular substance with a particular impression, a particular place with a never-to-be forgotten experience. We can become prisoners, even fetishists, through this experience of worship, through this bondage of association. Not all worship sets us free, and we need to be reminded frequently that even the devil has his contemplatives. We need the discipline of repentance to realign the world of our experience so that the experience and context find their true perspective in our world-view. It is not for nothing that Christ cautions us that true worship is both 'in truth' as well as 'in Spirit' (John 4:24).

Not all worship is good or true; we need to *learn* to worship as surely as we have to learn to do properly what at first came to us by instinct. What a child at first does by nature has to be relearned if it is to 'stand up' in the adult world. The instinct to worship, as surely as any other instinct in our lives, needs to be directed if it is not to become corrupted. Every political tyrant since the dawn of history has known the power of worship and the compulsive need within every human being to express this instinct and to find objects for that worship. When the instinct to worship is wrongly directed, there are scarcely any limits to the depravity to which the human race can sink. The twentieth century is strewn with the wreckage of what happens when religion goes wrong: from the crimes of Nazism to the mass suicide of the People's Temple in Guyana in 1979; from the events at Waco, Texas, in 1994 to the subway chemical warfare in Tokyo in 1995 – and there will be yet more to come in the build-up to the millennium hysteria which will inevitably be fired by mindless worship. In all of this we can see the power and the persuasiveness of worship when it has gone wrong and has been perverted. Colin Dunlop comments:

> A man may divert his powers of worship away from God and set it upon himself or even upon the State. For people who know nothing about the true God, or who, though knowing God, are not interested in him, may still worship. For the fact that such worship is not directed to its true end does not prevent it being real worship. But worship of what is less than God, or opposed to God, though real, is harmful. Therefore it is essential that man shall learn to worship the true God and to give his homage where it rightly belongs. For to worship is to acknowledge with every part of one's being the worthship of what is worshipped, to acknowledge with the mind, the affections and the will its utter perfection. To commit oneself *thus* towards what is imperfect or perishable is to engender the lie in the soul: while *thus* to render homage to what objectively claims it, namely Almighty God, is to take one's appointed place in the universe and to do what each of us was born to do.[10]

Precisely because it is so powerful and so able to transcend the rationalizing processes, embracing the whole personality in every way, worship needs to be disciplined and sanctified if it is not to destroy its practitioners.

In spite, therefore, of the reductionism of the Enlightenment diagnosis, we are coming to see in our own age that the human condition is one of compulsive worship: hence the perennial perversion of idolatry. Religion and its accompanying expression through worship is persistent in every age, and refuses to go away, least of all under persecution.

Worship and freedom

Throughout the whole of the Old Testament the consistent caution to God's people is against idolatry. There is always the temptation to worship false gods. If the true God is not available to worship (as was the case for Aaron and the children of Israel at the foot of Mount Sinai), then mankind will fashion gods of their own making. The golden calf is never very far away and is always ready to masquerade as an alternative possibility for compulsive worshippers. The home-spun gods of Isaiah, taking different forms in different ages, are always turning their worshippers into slaves and condemning them to life-long bondage (Isa. 33:9–20). The tin gods of our own making are easily recognizable, for they always enslave those who worship them. It is the distinctive mark of the worship of the one true and living God that he is the only God who risks giving back to his worshippers an ever-increasing freedom. All other gods are the gods of the Egyptians, so to speak, and belong to our immaturity and the chapters of bondage in our lives. It is only the living God who repeats again and again: 'Let my people go' (Exod. 7:16; 8:1).

We were not born to be free; we were born to be possessed! Either we shall be possessed by our possessions (like the rich young ruler, who wasn't in reality, of course, anything of the kind, but just a rather poor old thing, longing to belong and yet ending up belonging to his belongings) or we shall be possessed by ourselves in the prevailing narcissistic tendencies of our own age, worshipping our own image and reflection. We shall be possessed by something like alcohol or drug abuse or compulsive shopping or gambling or the like; or we might end up possessed by the evil one, who all too easily seduces us with promises of power and wealth which he only fails to produce at the very last. Idolatry – or worship of those things and people that are not worth that sort of unconditional bartering – is truly at the root of all our contemporary ills. No, we were most certainly not created to be free; paradoxically, we are created to be possessed, and the only difference between being possessed by the one true God and all the false gods and substitutes is that when we are possessed by the one true God he gives us back our freedom as best we are able to bear it.

That, of course, is the basic thesis of Paul in his epistle to the Romans: humanity has 'exchanged the truth about God for a lie and worshipped and served the creature rather than the Creator' (Rom. 1:25). So the opposite of sin is not virtue, but rather true worship of the one true God, for sin is misdirected worship and virtue is the worship of God in and above all things.

Now perhaps we can see even more clearly why Jesus demands in the New Testament that our worship shall be 'in Spirit and in truth' (John 4:24). We must learn to transfer all our instincts for worship to the one true and living God: 'To love him in all things and above all things.'[11] In true worship we lose ourselves – our old selves – but in turn, the living God gives us back our true and new selves. 'For freedom has Christ set us free' (Gal. 5:1). Every other liberator so often leaves us 'hung up', as we say, on the very objects of our worship. An age hungry for kicks will always be dangerously open to the call to let go and let God! But this hysterical and enthusiastic statement presupposes the very question with which the Bible is rightly concerned from cover to cover – namely, which God? 'Let go' may well be very important in an age indoctrinated for too long by the tyranny of the intellect, but it is far more important to ask into what we are letting ourselves go. Of course, worship brings release, and people who have been starved of the opportunity to worship or strongly cautioned to be suspicious of the inexplicable will soon begin to search for such a release. 'Let go', however, could presumably have been the call to those Gadarene swine as they chorused together 'And so say all of us,' heading disastrously towards the precipice! For there will always be great dangers in a quest that demands an unquestioning attitude. The unquestioning compulsive worshipper knows he is right; he is on the 'right wavelength', and that is a very dangerous place to be!

It was Teilhard de Chardin who said that in the end there were only two alternatives for mankind: adoration and annihilation. It is a strong statement, but it is profoundly true. Adoration is the superlative of love, yet love frustrated is never very far from hatred. The Church's task – to teach men and women to worship the true and living God – is an awesome and terrifying responsibility.

Worship and education

There was a time when religion and learning were joined together: our ancient universities were all known originally as foundations of religion and learning, for they are at their best when they are together. The layout of an Oxford or Cambridge college still resembles that of a Benedictine monastery, and the very architectural plan of the building spells out what it requires for humanity to be truly human. Eating and drinking together in the great hall; living in collegiality around a garden and frequently beside a river; tutorials conducted domestically; and at the heart of it all, the worship of the chapel. In such places and in such an environment, education and discernment – the mind, the heart and the spirit – are all pursued together, and all this is set within a community in which belonging, believing and behaving are nurtured in daily worship. In such places, worshippers met in buildings where architecture and design invited the healthy experience of the transcendent. In such environments heart and mind could grow together. Worship was informed by truth and moral commitment; scholarship was lifted beyond itself into the fuller environment of adoration.

Contrast this with the contemporary scene of education. In many of our schools and universities in many parts of the so-called Christian world, worship has no place whatever in the timetable. Religion, insofar as it is taught, is the poor relation of all the other disciplines in the curriculum and lingers a long way behind them as just another subject imparted only through the intellect. Not surprisingly, therefore, modern man is wide open to every false god and the claims that false gods make. We are all too easily duped once we enter the sanctuary of worship, where we are not at home and for which we have not been trained. Our experience of the numinous and the inevitable quest for the transcendent easily deteriorate into a dangerous and morbid curiosity. It is precisely this that feeds the ever-increasing market at the present time for white and black magic. The cult of the occult is not going to disappear in an age that is hungry for kicks and needs to break loose from the prison of the intellect. Witches' covens have not disappeared with the Middle Ages. They are back with us again, populated so often by the sophisticated and those who have the spiritual age and discernment of a new-born baby.

Furthermore, we are told on good authority that by the end of the century, among young people, those who do not use drugs will be in a minority. It was Richard Rolle in the fourteenth century who diagnosed the human problem in this way: 'Since the human soul is capable of receiving God alone, nothing less than God can fill it; which explains why lovers of earthly things are never satisfied.'[12] This contemporary dissociation between religion and learning may well be responsible for many of the ills of our present time.

It is now a truism to speak of the importance of addressing both sides of the brain: the left-hand side is concerned more with functions, intellectual pursuits and the grammar of life, while the right-hand side is more concerned with art and music, the intuitive and poetic, with the spiritual and with worship. Our contemporary educational programmes are failing to address both sides of the brain and are therefore producing maimed robots rather than human beings fully alive. It was Irenaeus, writing at the end of the second century, who wrote, 'The glory of God is a human being fully alive, and the life of humanity consists in the vision of God.'[13]

In all of this it should be all too self-evident that all ministers of religion need to be recalled to their primary task of ministering to the religious needs of people and to the worshipping instinct within mankind. Such ministry is a skill as well as a charism. It has to be learned – everything from Christian formation and spiritual direction, to how to conduct worship in ways that will open doors and windows for ordinary people as well as feeding folk with the Word and with the sacraments. For lost in a labyrinth of false alternatives, our own age is crying out to be shown a route to the truth and the warmth of the sunshine. Moonshine is no substitute! (Incidentally, it is perhaps no accident that lunacy and the moon are powerfully and emotively connected in popular understanding.)

The release of transcendent worship

Yet the route is hazardous, precisely because it is best found in those very areas of human experience most often neglected or, worse still, just abandoned to an uncharted instinct, uninformed by reason or truth. The call to the Christian minister of religion is to school others in a worship that is both 'Spirit-filled' and a revelation of the truth. It is that elusive and yet vastly important enterprise that is the activity and responsibility of the Church in its daily life and in its services of public worship week by week. When worship really comes alive, it is a very intoxicating and a very dangerous and powerful experience.

It is not an accident that at the first Pentecost the Spirit-filled apostles were mistakenly regarded by many as drunk (Acts 2:15). In all ecstatic experiences, and whenever and wherever men and women are released through the transcendence of worship, there is always the possibility of confusing and overlapping phenomena. This is hardly surprising. For a finite creature to experience and to 'take on' something of what, by definition, is infinite is not unlike trying to transcribe an orchestral symphony for piano or to reproduce a three-dimensional scene on a two-dimensional piece of paper. In the former case one note on the piano would have to represent several sounds (flute, oboes and strings); in the latter case a diagonal line would sometimes signify a diagonal line and sometimes a line in depth that can be reproduced in no other way. So with many intensely deep and even dramatic responses to worship.

Of course, laughing, crying, tongues, falling flat on the floor and so on can all be explained in a reductionist way as 'merely' laughing (irreverence), or 'merely' hysterical behaviour (tears or tongues). Indeed, in some, if not in many cases, that may be the explanation. Nevertheless, the same experience may be better explained in a totally different way. A fit of the giggles (like Sarah in the Old Testament), or baptism with tears, or release in tongues (Hannah in the temple) are well attested religious phenomena and can occur whenever finite men and women are faced with the transcendent and the infinite. Discernment, therefore, is required if we are to distinguish between two very different causes of the same symptom. It is not by chance that we seem to have toppled at this point into medical language. A minister of religion must be also a physician of the soul, able to exercise discernment wherever renewal is occurring, and not least in places where the power of worship is released.

For too long many churches in the West, and especially the Reformed churches, have placed worship low on the list of priorities. At best it has become a means to an end. It has been there to edify, to exhort, and to aid the good life. It was William Temple who used to say that most people thought that the end of human life was the good life, with worship as the means to that end. In fact, as he so rightly commented, the reverse is the truth: the end of man is to worship and the good life is one of the means to that end:

> People are always thinking that conduct is supremely important, and that because prayer helps it, therefore prayer is good. That is true as far as it goes: still truer is it to say that worship is of supreme importance and conduct tests it.[14]

So if the quotation with which this chapter began is true, then it will be worship that continues when all else has ceased:

> After this I looked, and behold, a great multitude which no man could number, from every nation, from all tribes and peoples and tongues, standing before the throne and before the Lamb . . . [They] fell on their faces before the throne and worshipped God (Rev. 7:9–11).

The Bible begins with creation and ends with worship. That is the direction in which we must all move. The social gospel, commitment to the concerns of the Third World, care for the environment, the right ordering of our resources – all these are important concerns for the churches at the present time, but they will only find their true perspective in the total picture of Christian discipleship if they flow from and are transcended by the true purpose and goal of all creation – worship and adoration. The purpose and peace of mankind is only to be found ultimately in the worship of the One who created us for such an end.

Untune that string,
And, hark! what discord follows.[15]

So from the outset let us be under no illusion about the importance of our subject. Worship is vital; worship is crucial to man's survival and sanity; worship is powerful and dangerous, demanding direction; it is most certainly 'not a rule of safety – it is an adventure of the spirit'. Those words from a larger statement by A. N. Whitehead leave no doubt about the importance which that great Cambridge mathematician and philosopher attached to worship. He wrote:

Religion is the vision of something which stands beyond, behind, and within, the passing flux of immediate things; something which is real, and yet waiting to be realized; something which is a remote possibility, and yet the greatest of present facts; something that gives meaning to all that passes, and yet eludes apprehension; something whose possession is the final good, and yet is beyond all reach . . . The immediate reaction of human nature to the religious vision is worship . . . and worship is a surrender to the claim for assimilation, urged with the motive force of mutual love. The vision never over-rules. It is always there, and it has the power of love presenting the one purpose whose fulfilment is eternal harmony. The power of God is the worship he inspires. That religion is strong which in its ritual and its modes of thought evokes an apprehension of the commanding vision. The worship of God is not a rule of safety – it is an adventure of the spirit, a flight after the unattainable. The death of religion comes with the repression of the high hope of adventure.[16]

2

The nature and characteristics of Christian worship

All is worship!

We have seen how worship is the universal instinct rooted deeply within our human make-up and that it is therefore neither restricted to the activity of a particular religion, nor is it only to be found in buildings specifically set aside for it. Worship is at the heart of all that it means to be truly human. Therefore, not surprisingly, worship is at the heart of all world religions, addressing, focusing and harnessing this deeply ingrained instinct that is so powerfully latent in all human beings, whether they would care to call themselves religious or not. However, it also follows, as we have briefly indicated in the previous chapter, that not all worship – however sincere or instinctive – is good, and furthermore that this human drive – like all that is human – is wide open to misuse, abuse and perversion. So when religion goes wrong it does not go just a little wrong. Rather, as the perversion of all that is best rapidly degenerates to become the worst, so with religion and with its most characteristic expression, worship. An ordinary nutter is bad enough, but a religious nutter has to be the very worst!

Hence true worship must be taught as well as caught. So Christian teaching about worship seeks to purge and redirect this natural urge to worship, for in this area as in so many, speculation will not be enough, unless it is matched and corrected by the breaking in of revelation, as 'the wise men' of old learned to their cost. All their philosophy, skills and religious drive brought them to the wrong address, to that king who demanded worship without being worthy of it. For it was ultimately the leading of that star and not their natural hunches (however convincingly informed by philosophy) that finally redirected them to the right place of worship. It brought them to the real King, perceived only by the eyes of faith; revelation corrected their own speculations and ultimately brought them to the One who never demands compulsive worship, but who, on the contrary, graciously accepts worship freely given from a heart set free in wonder, for love, praise and thanksgiving. As we see from that same account of the pilgrimage of those wise men, all learning and education are a pilgrimage culminating in worship. That pilgrim-way takes us beyond the intellect and the powers of reasoning into the real presence of God, where the only appropriate response is 'to fall down and worship him' (Matt. 2:11).

It is wholly appropriate, therefore, that the last word of the Bible in the book of Revelation should give us a glimpse of the worship of heaven. Do not forget, however, that the Bible starts also with a picture of worship in the opening chapter of the book of Genesis. In Genesis we see a picture of God enjoying and delighting in what he has made – his creation. In Revelation we catch a glimpse of humanity enjoying and delighting in the One who made us – our Creator. Properly understood, these two pictures of worship belong together and are mutually complementary. For if it is right to say that 'we love because he first loved us' (1 John 4:19), might it not also be true to say that we delight in God, adore and worship him, because he first delighted in us – and worshipped us? Dare we say that?

Yes, in some sense we dare and we must. For worship means also 'worth-ship', and in those opening chapters of Genesis we see God endowing his creation with its true worth. The human race, in comparison with the rest of creation, has little value, significance or worth: compared with the hills and the mountains we are transient, here today and gone tomorrow; compared with the sea and other natural elements we are weak and ineffective. It is only in our relationship with God – our capacity to know him, to worship, love and adore him – that we find our significance and worth. So our lasting value as human beings can only truly be derived from the One who created us and supremely from the One who redeemed us. The price of Calvary is our true worth – in other words, we are priceless!

The flaw, however, in what should be a purely natural response to God's love for us and his adoration of us before the

Fall, is that we have lost our hearts to the wrong things, creating a topsy-turvy world of false values with false gods. These false gods rapidly became rival gods with price tags around their necks out of all proportion to their real and lasting value. It may not be stretching a point too far to say that it is no accident that ours is an age of economic chaos, for if we do not know where we are going we can hardly be expected to know what is a fair price for the journey! We are unable to identify objects worthy of our worship, as God, in his turn, is no longer able to recognize the work of his hand and his image in his creation.

It is only in Jesus Christ that God once again comes to take delight in his creation, and both at the baptism as well as at the transfiguration of Jesus, the cry of *déjà vu* is repeated: 'You are my well beloved Son in whom once again I come to take delight' (Mark 1:11; 9:7). God the Father recognizes again in Christ's humanity the glory which they both enjoyed together before the world began (see John 17:5). By our baptism into Christ, God sees us in Christ and once again comes to take delight in us, his fallen creatures – fallen, but restored not only in the image but also in the likeness of God. That is our glory – God's delight in us, his creatures – a glory which we enjoyed quite naturally before we started playing God and so caused all the problems which issued out of that.

So all is worship from start to finish – but it is a two-way street, with the transparent Christ showing us the glory of the Father and showing to the Father our restored humanity. In and through Christ the way of worship is opened up once again, and from both ends, at that: the Son glorifies the Father, the Father glorifies the Son, and those who are in the Son become once again acceptable and recognizable by the God and Father who first created them in both his likeness and his image.

So we can see how the Bible, from cover to cover, is the story of worship and how God's people in the Old and New Testaments alike are essentially a worshipping people. We shall not be surprised to find at the outset many crude expressions of worship, with all the dangers that pertain to such immature insights. Nevertheless, slowly that worship is purified, not developing in a straightforward way nor progressing smoothly, but rather lurching unsteadily – now going back again to earlier patterns and now

reaching forward to refined and more God-centred worship –
until at last it is perfected in the One who is himself alone the only
true, perfect, sufficient sacrifice, offering and oblation acceptable
to God – Jesus Christ, our Lord and Saviour. In Jesus, all ingredients of inadequate and unacceptable worship are focused,
redeemed and redirected to create 'a sweet smelling savour' (Eph.
5:2) acceptable to God.

Worship and the Old Israel of God

Now we need, however briefly and inadequately, to trace the
course of the history of worship in the Bible. We will see how it
has evolved,with all the elements common to all forms of worship,
and yet at the same time with the distinctive features of biblical
worship belonging uniquely to the redemption and reorientation
of worship in Christ.

In the Old Testament we read of sacred places, sacred objects
and sacred persons, the sanctuary, the ark, altars, priests, sacred
times (feasts and the sabbath) and general acts of worship such as
purifications, consecrations, sacrifices, prayer in all its forms,
fasting and prohibitions. These are the ingredients common to
worship in all major religions. Naturally enough, therefore, in
earlier times, much of this worship expresses itself in little more
than pantheism (God penetrates and is coterminous with the
universe) and animism (the belief that certain material objects –
e.g. stones and trees – are possessed by spirits). The Creator and the
creation are inseparable and confused; and therefore fertility gods,
the gods of the harvest and the fruits of the earth are worshipped.

The great 'showdown' between Jehovah and Baal-worship in
the time of Elijah is no isolated occasion (1 Kings 18:20–40), for the
Bible is the story of a long process during which the God of history
is unravelled from all the other gods of nature. Also we see how
true worship and the distinctive worship of Jehovah deliberately
distanced itself from the characteristics of worship that belonged to
other peoples and the surrounding tribes with whom God's people
were daily involved. Essentially, the God of the Old Testament
distinguishes himself from other gods by his historical activity, his
saving deeds, and his mighty acts. So William Temple writes:

On the biblical view the locus, the sphere, the area of revelation, is primarily the historic event, not thoughts in men's minds at all, but the thing that happens – the deliverance from Egypt, the retreat of Sennacherib, the exile, and the return. In these things we are to read the action of God, his purpose, his judgment.[1]

For the God of the Old Testament is not the invention of the human mind, born from reflection and speculation, but rather he is the God of revelation, delighting to reveal himself in hard-edged historical events in which he shows his hand, his purpose, and something of his person. The challenge put by Elijah to the Baal gods is that they also should show their hand in an equally unambivalent event of incontrovertible disclosure. Only by such an act can the true God distinguish himself from the false gods who have neither hands nor noses, who smell not, who walk not and who even have to be carried about (Isa. 44:9–12; 46:5–7). It is this God, the true and living God, who alone is faithful to his people through these mighty acts: a people who in their turn must be faithful to God in giving to him – and to him alone – their worship, adoration and commitment.

So it is a long – and sometimes tedious – story, in which the people of the Old Israel learn that not everything that passes for worship is acceptable to God – the true and living God, and also that creation does not in fact reflect truthfully the person and features of its Creator, but rather must be clearly distinguished from him.

C. S. Lewis speaks of this, for it is not just an ancient problem, but rather it is a recurring and ever-present misconception. We are always to some extent in danger of mistaking the creature for the Creator, and we are always ready to turn the icon of creation in all its forms into an idol to which we will surrender a worship which properly is due to God alone. Lewis writes:

These things, if they are mistaken for the thing itself, turn into dumb idols, breaking the hearts of their worshippers. For they are not the thing itself; they are only the scent of a flower we have not found, the echo of a tune we have not heard, news from a country we have never yet visited.[2]

The creation, even at its best, is but that 'cracked mirror' which St Paul writes about (1 Cor. 13:12) and which offers us, at best, only ambivalent evidence about the nature of the God who created it. Our own human contribution in God's continuing creative activity persistently distorts his handiwork, so that the creation presents a flawed and therefore unreliable image, deceiving those who are tempted to use it as a vehicle for worshipping its Creator. If we follow that road all the way, it will lead us to the wrong kind of king and the wrong kind of kingdom, as it did at first for the wise men in Matthew's Gospel.

For it is the existence of God, beyond and apart from his creation, which demands a worship that does not confuse him with his creation, so that pantheism, animism and idolatry must first be teased out of all worship if such worship is to be acceptable to God – worship 'in Spirit and in truth'. Idolatry is never far below the surface wherever the instinct for worship is at its strongest: in art, music, poetry, in beautiful High Church ceremonial. The challenge at the end of the contest between Jehovah and Baal is still the challenge that we need to hear wherever we are drawn most strongly to worshipping the created order: 'How long will you go limping with two different opinions? If the Lord is God, follow him; but if Baal, then follow him' (1 Kings 18:21).

The confusion between the Creator and his creation is, however, but one of many hazards facing worshippers. For holy places have the continuing and perverse habit of becoming 'high places' – to use the terminology of the Old Testament – with their own cults. The local shrines and local cultic worship, with their associations of human sacrifice and ritual prostitution, appear frequently in the Old Testament.

The story of Jacob's ladder is of course one of the Bible's many memorable stories – memorable because it rings many bells with our own religious experience. Jacob sets up an altar after his dream and vision and names the place with a special name (Gen. 28:10–22). How very true that is for all worshippers, for we all have our places that are sacred alone to us, where we have experienced the presence of God in some possibly spectacular way. We may well even have our own 'nicknames' for them or return to them in pilgrimage whenever we need to recall with thankfulness all that God has done for us and all that he has given to us.

Nevertheless, the Old Testament contains a strong warning against such powerful experiences, and certainly against ecstasy, with the dangerous desire to replicate and conjure up again and again such experiences. If we do so, we fall prey to the dark side of our religion or even to the occult, which is never far away whenever religious experience is at its strongest. Old Testament customs that may seem to us barbaric and totally alien can still play tricks with us. For sanitized sophistication is always a 'pushover' for superstition, and we need to remember that human sacrifice, ritual prostitution and the occult are ever present in any age – including our own – and do not automatically disappear in the name of progress or at the bidding of the intellect.

The religious seeker in every age must be reminded that Jacob's vision was a given moment from a giving and gracious God. Such moments of ecstasy and spiritual awareness in worship are gifts. Gifts are made to be received and not achieved, repeated or manipulated, nor contrived for their own sake or for the sake of 'kicks' associated with them.

So from early and primitive forms of folk religion the distinctive elements of Hebrew worship slowly emerged. The focus of this worship was at first the Ark as the symbol of God's presence among his people. It was a sign of God's redemptive acts in delivering the chosen people from their enemies. At first movable, the Ark rested in various sanctuaries (for example, at Shiloh), and for a pilgrim people without stable geographical territory this was a living and sacramental sign of God's love and presence in their midst.

In that whole experience of pilgrimage God was intent upon teaching his people that continuing lesson of the difference between icon and idol. So in the book of Numbers we read:

On the day that the tabernacle was set up, the cloud covered the tabernacle, the tent of the testimony, and at evening it was over the tabernacle like the appearance of fire until morning. So it was continually, the cloud covered it by day, and the appearance of fire by night. And whenever the cloud was taken up from over the tent, after that the people of Israel set out; and in the place where the cloud settled down, there the people of Israel encamped . . . Sometimes the cloud was a few days over the tabernacle, and according to the command of the Lord they remained in camp; then according to the command of the Lord they set out. And sometimes the cloud remained from evening to morning, and when the cloud was taken up in the morning, they set out, or if it continued for a day and a night, when the cloud was taken up they set out. Whether it was two days, or a month, or a longer time, that the cloud continued over the tabernacle, abiding there, the people of Israel remained in camp and did not set out; but when it was taken up they set out (Num. 9:15–22).

That somewhat tedious account hammers home the basic lesson that a pilgrim people needed to learn: God's presence is *in* his world, but also *beyond* it. To locate permanently the presence of God in a partlcular place – *in* any icon – is to commit idolatry. That is why in the discipline of iconography you are not invited to look *at* the icon, but rather to look *through* and *beyond* it. Hence the reluctance of Jehovah for either David or Solomon to build a permanent temple: to set this whole worship business, as we say, in stone. Tents and a tent of meeting were far more appropriate for a people on the move, as God's people must always be if they are to be a truly pilgrim people.

So the story of Solomon's desire to build a substantial temple as a 'resting place' for God, although natural enough and a most telling account of religious desire and fervour, nevertheless uncovers many of the pitfalls associated with the religious drive in humanity and our compulsive need to get this whole worship business buttoned up and tied down!

There is a note of impatience in the reply of Jesus to the question of the Samaritan woman about which temple is the proper place to worship. 'The time is coming,' says Jesus hopefully, 'when we shall not be worshipping God in either of those two man-made temples you have referred to!' Indeed, the consistent theme throughout the whole of the Johannine writings is that a temple not made with hands will replace all temples made with hands. Temples by definition must necessarily have a proper note of provisionality about them, since in the new Jerusalem, there is no temple, at least according to the book of Revelation.

But back to Solomon's temple. The temple was to be the only place for sacrificial worship (see Deut. 12), and this is clearly a strong counter-attack upon localized 'high places', shrines and altars. It's not difficult to see how sacrifice at local shrines was always in danger of becoming so indigenous that it merely reflected the local folk religion and before long would all too easily become syncretistic and indistinguishable from the pagan worship of the surrounding area. On the other hand, we can see how the establishment of a kingdom under David and the territorial settlement of David's victories gave to God's wandering people a sense of national identity – a king, a capital, and therefore a temple – rather than a pilgrim identity related to one God who was always one step ahead of his people, continually calling them out – an ecclesia in that sense.

All worship in the life of the Church needs to have about it this tension between what is local and therefore close to degenerating into folk religion on the one hand, and what is catholic and universal worship on the other hand. Our worship must be both local and universal. It must certainly reflect what is local and belongs to the community. (There really is a place for harvest festivals, after all!) So often Christian missionaries have made the mistake of trying to export the gospel wrapped up in language, music and a style that is utterly alien to the culture of the missionary field. We need to meet folk religion and embrace it before we can redirect it. In our own day in many areas of the inner city a sophisticated middle class with a largely cerebral religion has failed to incarnate faith and worship in the culture of the local community, with devastating results. A really incarnational religion for a pilgrim people will wish to reaffirm what is local, passing and even contemporary and therefore temporary in language, music and style, for only in this way will it be free from the equal dangers of the cultic, centralized and formalized worship of 'the temple'. Nevertheless, if the life and worship of the Church are only local and contemporary, then they reflect only half the story. Worship must have about it the wider claims of what is universal, 'for all people, at all times' – in other words, what is truly catholic. Local and universal, contemporary and ageless; these should form two sides of the same coin in a worship that is of the Spirit and yet also committed to truth. We shall be looking at the practical outworking of this later in the book.

But back to the Old Testament. In all the Old Testament

discussions about worship, perhaps the strongest note of caution and the most earnest plea to seek redirection came from the prophets. They proclaimed a total loyalty to Israel's God, linked with obedience to his will, and for them this was the overriding precondition for authentic and acceptable worship. So the psalmist insists: 'The sacrifice of God is a troubled spirit: a broken and contrite heart God will not despise' (Ps. 51). The saving God of the Exodus and of the Ten Commandments is a holy God who demands that the people whom he would mould into a priestly nation shall also be holy: 'Say to the congregation of the people of Israel, "You shall be holy; for I the Lord your God am holy" ' (Lev. 19:2).

Worship and prophecy

Worship, however moving and 'correctly' done, is no substitute for obedience and morality – 'Christianity goes disastrously and dangerously wrong when Jesus is worshipped but not followed.'[3] The refusal to separate acceptable worship from a righteous life is a note struck from the earliest times in the words of Samuel the prophet:

> Has the Lord as great delight in burnt offerings and sacrifices as in obeying the voice of the Lord? Behold, to obey is better than sacrifice, and to hearken than the fat of rams. For rebellion is as the sin of divination, and stubbornness is as iniquity and idolatry (1 Sam. 15:22–23).

This must surely be a recurring reminder in every age to would-be worshippers. Worship and service belong together, and both are directed first and foremost to God in a life of discipleship. This theme is continuous throughout the Old Testament. The later prophets of the eighth century are so adamant about the priority of obedience that we could sometimes be forgiven for supposing that they really do not see much place for worship at all. That, of course, is not so. They base their prophecy on the presupposition that worship is the basis of all religious observance. Nevertheless, they do wish to emphasize that such worship must issue from an obedient heart if it is to be authentic. So Amos pronounces without equivocation:

> I hate, I despise your feasts [says the Lord], and I take no delight in your solemn assemblies. Even though you offer me your burnt offerings and cereal offerings, I will not accept them, and the peace offerings of your fatted beasts I will not look upon. Take away from me the noise of your songs; to the melody of your harps I will not listen. But let justice roll down like waters, an righteousness like an ever-flowing stream (Amos 5:21–24).

So again with Isaiah:

> When you come to appear before me, who requires of you this trampling of my courts? Bring no more vain oblations; incense is an abomination to me. New moon and sabbath and the calling of assemblies – I cannot endure iniquity and solemn assembly. Your new moons and your appointed feasts my soul hates; they have become a burden to me, I am weary of bearing them. When you spread forth your hands, I will hide my eyes from you; even though you make your many prayers, I will not listen; your hands are full of blood. Wash yourselves; make yourselves clean; remove the evil of your doings from before my eyes; cease to do evil, learn to do good; seek justice, correct oppression; defend the fatherless, plead for the widow (Isa. 1:12–17).

Ben Sira in the book of Ecclesiasticus is just as insistent when he writes: 'The Most High is not pleased with the offerings of the ungodly; and he is not propitiated for sins by a multitude of sacrifices' (Ecclus. 34:19). And again: 'The offering of a righteous man anoints the altar and its pleasing odour rises before the Most High' (Ecclus. 35:6).

Worship and the Word belong together

So this relationship of works to worship is a constant theme of renewal in worship in the Old Testament. The words of the prophets are intended to inform and reform the life of the temple.

Throughout religious history there has always been a tension between the cult of the temple and the call of the prophets. The cult, without prophecy and the Word, rapidly degenerates into mere ceremonial obsession, with every detail of sanctuary drill as the only priority. Equally, prophecy and the Word without worship and sacraments are in serious danger of becoming merely cerebral and moralistic. The Word and the worship need each other and each is corrected by the other.

Ironically, the reaction against a cultic and degenerate Catholicism (the cult of the mass) in the Middle Ages was the moralistic, wordy, and cerebral religion of the Reformation – out of the frying pan of priestcraft and into the fire of the preacher and the pulpit. Happily, renewal in the Church today has brought prophecy and the cult of the temple together. As we shall see in Chapter 11, renewal demands that a renewed life be fed and sustained in worship and sacrament, and that worship, in its turn, overflows into a proper concern for justice, the poor and for any in need: when the worship is ended the service begins!

The history of the Old Testament is a long tug-of-war between the two, in which – in the end – both lost! For it is only in the life and witness of Jesus that both worship and obedience come together and are acceptable to the Father. In that sense Jesus is both the Word made flesh, doing the will of the Father, and his body is the temple, destroyed by religion gone awry but rebuilt in three days (John 2:19).

Worship and mission in Isaiah

Perhaps the place in the Old Testament where we see the richest and fullest agenda for all the implications of acceptable worship is in Isaiah 6, the well-known passage dealing with the prophet's vision. It begins, as all worship must, when the prophet enters into a realization of the presence, the holiness, and the glory of God. That moment is the given moment of the numinous, with all the power that is latent within such religious experience. It is a moment of vision and insight. It is a moment when the doors of perception, normally closed by man's cerebral censorship, are flung wide open. Ears, which had previously seemed deaf, begin at last to hear. Eyes, which must have been blind in the past, are opened at last. It is a definite moment in time (the year of King Uzziah's death), yet its significance breaks through the limits of time and the finite into the realms of eternity and the infinite. It is localized in the temple, yet its message not only strikes at the heart of the nation but also has spoken most eloquently to men and women of every age and every culture ever since. The vision speaks at the same time of the glory of God and the holiness of God. Here is no religious 'kick' for its own sake, but rather a demanding clarion call originating in eternity yet speaking directly to men and women in history, calling the nation to repentance and its citizens to service within the community. The impact, reverberating with glory from the heart of heaven, powerfully evokes a sense of sin. Worship and a sense of unworthiness come in the same breath. True worship always demands repentance, renewal and rededication. The ecstatic had brought about a dislodging of perspective for Isaiah as real as the physical dislodging suffered by Jacob when he was lamed in his wrestling match with God. The prophet finds himself seeing things now from a very different viewpoint, and a very uncomfortable viewpoint at that. There can be nothing cheap about such a gracious and given moment; it will issue in nothing less than costly commitment to the voice and purposes of God – renewal of life and a new obedience in service.

So, those eight verses of Isaiah spell out all that is meant by true worship offered to the true and living God: vision, repentance, service, and ministry and mission. Yet such an answer begs all the questions. As the Old Testament grew increasingly conscious of the scope of true worship, so it began increasingly to realize that man is ultimately utterly incapable of such an offering. The height of his religious consciousness was also the moment of his greater religious torment. Such is the dilemma of the Old Testament writers. At the highest point of their insight into the nature of true worship, they discovered their human frailty and impotence. This is set out perhaps at its most poetic by the psalmist:

Sacrifice, and meat-offering, thou wouldst not: but mine eyes hast
thou opened
Burnt offerings, and sacrifice for sin, hast thou not required: then
said I, Lo I come,

In the volume of the book it is written of me, that I should fulfil
thy will, O my God: I am content to do it; yea, thy law is within my
heart (Ps. 40:6–8).[4]

The fulfilment of all worship in the perfect offering of Christ

Here is the religious consciousness of the Old Testament at its
highest, with its understanding at last opened fully by God, reaching out to the One who was to come, who would do precisely what
true worship demanded – namely, the sacrifice of an obedient life.
In his heart would be the law of God and in his life and vocation
God's will for mankind would be fulfilled even to the point of
'sacrifice for sin'. In him, and in him alone, worship would achieve
its integrity. Christians recognize in Jesus Christ the answer to the
questions posed in the Old Testament about authentic worship and
see all their worship and oblation in the one great perfect offering
of Christ in his incarnation, passion, death, resurrection, ascension
and glorification. This unrepeatable and yet all-sufficient activity is
continually recalled and filled with the prayer, worship and intercession of the Church in every age (Col. 1:24). Christ is our worship. Wherever this one great offering of Christ is remembered by
his people, there is the 'temple', whether it be in a small village
church, at a house communion for the elderly and the housebound
together with two or three neighbours, or at a glorious act of
worship in some vast and beautiful cathedral. Jesus Christ defines
both the proportions and content of Christian worship, drawing
together all the conflicting strands of insight from Old Testament
worship, and indeed the worship of all religions and faiths, refin-
ing (though never emasculating or falsely spiritualizing) even the
earliest and most primitive urges for worship known to the Old
Testament world and to all other world religions.

Since this is so, Christian worship belongs within the strong
framework of Christian spirituality and Christian doctrine – *lex
orandi, lex credendi*. It should not be inhibited either by spirituality
or doctrine, but it always needs to be informed by them. With so
many changes in the ordering of worship throughout all the
churches in recent years, many people – not only the faithful laity
– find themselves confused, irritated and distracted by what can so

often appear to be either change for change's sake or just the vicar's latest fad and whim: 'He likes doing it this way!' But, if worship is to play a proper place in the renewal of the Church, it must be seen as the outward and visible sign of our spirituality and our belief about God, Christ, his world and his Church. For we shall not get the worship of the Church right simply by looking at the reordering of the Church – either in its buildings or its common life. All eyes must be on the coming Kingdom, from which we take all our cues for renewal, right across the board from start to finish.

In other words, renewal in worship is only the tip of the iceberg; it requires a secure and massive undergirding with teaching, teaching and more teaching. If, as we have claimed, Jesus Christ defines the proportions and content of our worship, then what we do when we come together as the Body of Christ should have about it the features of Christ and what we know of him in his saving work. The doctrines of his incarnation and baptism as well as of his passion, death and resurrection should all take to themselves the flesh and blood of worship, not only expounded through the words of Scripture but acted out in the shape of the liturgy and made explicit in the contours of our prayer. The worship of the Orthodox Churches of the East at first always appears complicated to Western Christians. If, however, we see it for what it is – a sacrament of God's activity in creation and redemption – then we may see that such rich worship makes explicit in the most effective way possible a living doctrine and a deep and yet far-reaching spirituality. Although it must not set out simply and only to be didactic, worship must nevertheless relate always to what is taught as well as to what is believed.

Pope Paul VI wrote in October 1957:

To link the sacred and the secular
in such rapport
that the first is not deformed or contaminated,
and the second
is not altered but sanctified:
this is the mystery
of the Incarnation of God made Man
which liturgy prolongs.

You could scarcely find a better summary of true Christian worship. Precisely because the Word of God has enfleshed himself in all that is human and of this world, by and through worship, all that is of this world can now be redirected and reformed (without being deformed or contaminated) and be lifted to the presence of the holy. The hinge on which all this turns is Christ and all who are in him. Just as the psalmist of old delighted to recall the mighty acts of God in the history of Israel and to see this as the central activity of praise and worship (Ps. 136), so the Christian of the new Israel delights to recall and re-enact the saving acts of God in Christ, to remember and to give thanks.

But there must be a real sense of rapport between the sacred and secular. We can have a worship so heavenly minded that it does not touch us, let alone move us, or, as Coleridge would say, 'find us'. Such worship springs from a wrong doctrine of Christ and his Incarnation. Our worship will give the clue to the inadequacy of our belief. In a full doctrine of the Incarnation there must be real contact between the God of heaven and the flesh of earth. That is what we mean by the Incarnation. In the same way as we can speak of some worship being so heavenly minded that it does not even touch the earth, so there can be the opposite disease of a church worship which is so 'relevant' that it never even gets off the ground. Here again this will reflect a wrong belief about the person of Christ. A church with worship of that kind will be a church not really living the full doctrine of the nature of Christ – two natures in one person. For in true Christian worship there is a living link between heaven and earth, between the sacred and the secular, between spirit and flesh. That link is Jesus Christ. Perhaps most of the time we prefer in fact to preserve our schizophrenia and to live between two worlds – generally getting the worst of both!

True worship lifts us and summons us to leave the no-man's-land in which we spend most of our time and to enter one man's world – the world of Christ. For that world is the world of heaven *and* earth, of God *and* man, spirit *and* flesh, in which glory fills all and all is glory. In Isaiah's vision, the startled prophet was shown one world in which both heaven and earth were filled with glory. Like Isaiah of old, we also will require new eyes, new ears, and new senses to apprehend it all, for it is a 'brave new world' for brave, new men and women. We shall need repentance, *metanoia,* and a totally new outlook if we are to enter the Kingdom of heaven, for flesh and blood cannot enter unless it is first re-ordered in Christ. This was the significance in the Early Church of the custom of anointing the eyes and ears of the new Christians during the Lenten season before their baptism at Easter. It was to prepare their senses for the impact of the Kingdom.

True worship cannot end in anything that is churchy. By the *anaphora* (the eucharistic prayer in which we solemnly recall God's mighty acts) we are lifted up as the Church, into the King-dom where the Church fulfils its deepest yearnings. So our worship must never just leave us where we started, but rather lift us to where we belong – the Kingdom of heaven. In his portrait of the saintly Bishop King, Henry Scott-Holland tells of an incident in which the bishop was instructing a shepherd in a village in the wolds of Lincolnshire:

> He loved one of them, who had slowly learned that the candles on the altar were lighted in broad daylight, because they had no utilitar-ian purpose. They were not there to give light but to bear witness. 'Eh! Then yours is a Yon-side religion, I see, Sir.' It appeals, he meant, to something beyond this world.[5]

There is a sense in which all our religion should be 'yon-side' because Christ is 'yon-side'. There is also a sense in which Christ-ian worship should start at *this* side, where Christ's redemptive work began. In living Christian worship we are moved from one side to the other, as we enter ever more fully into the mystery of Christ's journey – his 'passage' or passover. Nothing less than this – the closest of all possible associations between the Christian and Christ's saving activity – was St Paul's vision of the Christian life. Nothing less than this is the scope of full, living, renewed and authentic Christian worship. The doors of the Kingdom are stormed at every cry of 'lift up your hearts', and wherever two or three are gathered together in Christ. Christmas and Ascension are no longer isolated feasts in the Church's calendar, but rather markers at the two extremes of the total spectrum of worship and adoration. God is let loose on earth; humanity is released into the environment of heaven.

The privilege of daily worship is that as ordinary, confused, weak and sinful Christians we already begin to live the life of heaven here on earth – 'the end in the middle', as Bishop John Robinson used to say. We pray the prayer of the Kingdom daily in order to live the life of that Kingdom here and now. There is apparently good evidence that the word which Jesus used in the Lord's Prayer for 'daily' (as in 'daily bread') would be better translated not 'daily' but 'of the coming day', so that we would pray something like, 'Give us tomorrow's bread today' – not unlike that man in the parable who insisted upon pestering his neighbour in the middle of the night for some bread rather than waiting patiently like any other sensible person for the bakery to open tomorrow morning. Worship is intended to change our perspective in just that kind of radical way, so that we are living God's tomorrow now, right in the midst of a confused and undirected world.

For ultimately, nothing less than that is the mandate given to the Church in the ordering of its worship, and that is our business every Sunday and 'seven whole days, not one in seven'.[6] The Church is a school for this, the most vital, yet most natural yearning of mankind – the desire to worship and adore; to enjoy God forever; to enter the Kingdom of heaven, even now on earth; and to begin to learn, while we are still pilgrims in a passing age, the 'conversation' of heaven (Phil. 3:20).

3

Worship and the Church today

Making the connection

The specifically Christian worship of the Church in every generation must be related to that instinct for worship which is common
to all humanity. It must connect with the aspirations for worship
which are latent in every human being, of all ages and in every age
and every culture. Although the worship of the Church's liturgy
must necessarily reorder that instinct in Christ, in a worship that
is acceptable to the Father and in the Spirit, nevertheless the
Church's worship must never become so elevated, clinical or
stereotyped – or even so well ordered – that it fails to pick up what
is basic and universal within the human psyche.

This means that the Church must have a positive approach to
all that we call 'folk religion', which is still prevalent even in our
Western and apparently sophisticated culture. All too easily, we
tend to speak of our own culture as being secular, when in fact we
live at a time of all kinds of religious revival! Throughout history
– and not least towards the end of a century, or even more especially towards the end of a millennium – in times of change and
instability, religion in one form or another always raises its ugly
head. 'Jesus came to save us from religion,' said Paul Tillich, but
that implies not that we can ignore religion but rather that we
should follow the ways in which Christ redirects this basic human
urge which, to use the phrase of Andrew Greeley, is perennially
'persistent'.[1] He summarizes his thesis in rather startling words at
the outset of his book:

> The thesis of the book, bluntly, is that the basic human religious
> needs and the basic religious functions have not changed very

notably since the late Ice Age; what changes have occurred make religious questions more critical rather than less critical in the contemporary world.[2]

Christian worship, therefore, cannot, just because it is distinctively Christian, bypass this innate religious drive to worship expressed through the folk religion of every society. Yet to redirect anything you must first make a connection with it. Put another way, in the words of Thomas Aquinas, 'Grace perfects nature, it does not annihilate it.'

So when Augustine of Canterbury came to the shores of England in AD 597, he found all kinds of religious practices, some more obviously Christian than others, already in place in shrines and buildings throughout the country. Pope Gregory, who had first sent Augustine on the mission, gave him good advice about how he should proceed. In one letter to another bishop (Bishop Mellitus), the Pope asks him to hand on to Augustine advice about his approach to the shrines and temples of worship – many of which were clearly far from orthodox in their practices. Pope Gregory tells Bishop Mellitus to tell Augustine

> that the temples of the idols in that nation ought not to be destroyed. Let holy water be made and sprinkled in the said temples, let altars be erected, and relics placed. For if those temples are well built, it is requisite that they be converted from the worship of devils to the service of the true God; that the nation, seeing that their temples are not destroyed may remove error from their hearts, and knowing and adoring the true God, may the more familiarly resort to the places to which they have been accustomed.

Good advice indeed!

Perhaps one of the main failings of the Church today is its inability to 'baptize' the folk religion (albeit a folk religion in grave need of redirection and redemption and at times, perilously bordering on pantheism and sycretism). So much of our worship in church does not make the connection with what we might term the 'religiosity' that many people in this nation still claim to practise.

For example, on many surveys of popular attitudes to religion and faith, 60–80 per cent of the people in Britain still claim that they pray – many of them, every day. So, for example, just supposing that all the churches in the North of England had held a day of prayer (as we did in wartime) during the trauma issuing for many people out of the Jamie Bulger murder in 1994, we might well have found that our churches were crowded to the doors. To put all this somewhat crudely, good worship will scratch people where they itch.

In this sense, the worship of the Church must first be natural – in the best sense of the word – before it can ever hope to be truly supernatural. Otherwise it generally ends up being just blatantly unnatural, churchy, pious and, even worse, supremely self-conscious. In the words of Pope Paul VI, quoted in the previous chapter, while the sacred must not be 'contaminated' by the secular, nevertheless at the same time the secular must not first be so churchified, rarefied and 'altered' to the point of being deformed, unnatural, and unrecognizable that it fails to make this vital connection. The principle of the Incarnation is a continuing principle, always at work at the heart of the Church as an unending process throughout its whole history. Perhaps it is nowhere more in evidence than in the worship and liturgy of God's people in every age.

Anywhere, everywhere or somewhere?

However, in recent debates within the life of all the churches there have been some prior questions that demand our serious consideration if we are to proceed later in this chapter with some detailed discussion about the conduct of worship and the shape and form of its contemporary renewal. We shall need to begin by applying and testing some of the principles of Christian worship we have discussed above. For there are those (strangely enough, both from within the ranks of Christians, as well as outside) who will contest that as God is everywhere there is no need for specific acts of worship specially constructed and located in specific buildings. This conviction has expressed itself in two ways.

In the first place there has been the more general and naïve assertion (admittedly largely among non-churchgoers, and perhaps in an attempt to excuse themselves from commitment to regular worship at church services) that a God who is everywhere can therefore be worshipped anywhere, not requiring specifically to be worshipped somewhere. However contemporary this sentiment may be in its expression, it is an old chestnut! God *is* everywhere, but I am not. God is infinite, but I am finite. Always, therefore, for the finite creature, the opening on to the universal is necessarily through the specific. People who start by trying to recognize God and worship him *everywhere* generally end up knowing him *nowhere*. In order to recognize God *everywhere* we must first start by coming to know him *somewhere*. As creatures of habit and institutional animals, in order to be nourished at all times, we have specific mealtimes, and although all rooms in a house may be used for all purposes (in an emergency, for example), nevertheless some rooms are designated to be used for some particular things at certain times.

Perhaps a more homely analogy might be drawn from those people who fall in love with love! They set out to love everybody, but fail to recognize the need to start by loving somebody if they are to avoid the pitfall of ending up by loving nobody – except perhaps themselves! It is the same pitfall and paradox. We may desire to love *everybody* (and a proper desire it most certainly is). Nevertheless, we best achieve that end and ideal by giving our specific commitment to *somebody*. The lesson of universal love is best learned by starting right on my doorstep, where the most uncomfortable and demanding love always begins – indeed, 'Charity begins at home,' as we frequently say. So it is with our love of God and our adoration of him. He is everywhere, if only we had 'eyes to see' and 'ears to hear', for indeed 'heaven and earth are full of his glory'. If I am to recognize him everywhere, however, I must start where I am. If I am to pray at all times, I must certainly begin by praying at specific times and in specific places. Of course, it must not end there, but then we must not in any case suppose that worship either begins or ends with the church service timetable. That is a further question we shall need to address later.

The place of buildings

The second contemporary debate, which often follows from the assumptions of the first discussion above, is more subtle and perhaps more insidious. There is a contention abroad (admittedly, it was more strongly expressed in the fifties and sixties among many churchgoing Christians and even church leaders) the substance of which is dangerous precisely because it is partly true. It relates to church buildings and to their place in the life of the Church.

Rightly, much stress in recent years has been laid upon an understanding of the Church as the people of God and as the Body of Christ. We have certainly talked for far too long about 'going to church' rather than 'being the Church'. For when we speak of the Church, first and foremost we should be alluding to the people of God rather than to the building in which they meet for worship. The Church in a village or town is surely primarily the local congregation: they use a building for the purpose of their corporate worship. So in the Fourth Gospel, the temple made with stones falls under the strongly iconoclastic condemnation of Jesus, unless it gives way to the temple 'not made with hands' – those living stones that are the members of Christ's Body, the Church. The First Epistle of St Peter is equally adamant when it urges Christians to 'Come to him, to that living stone, rejected by men but in God's sight chosen and precious, and like living stones be yourselves built into a spiritual house' (1 Pet. 2:4f.).

However, it does not follow from that important theological principle that church buildings – and especially expensive ones – can or should be dispensed with altogether. It is, of course, undeniably true that, in the first two centuries, church buildings were not high on the priority list of a persecuted Church. Furthermore, throughout history, wherever Christians have been forced 'underground' they have found it perfectly possible to meet for prayer and worship without a building specifically and totally set aside for that purpose. Yet it is equally a historical fact that whenever Christianity has been able to come 'above ground' it has swiftly built large, numinous and beautiful buildings in and through which to express corporate worship.

We need to reflect upon this indisputable fact, because it tells us something about the nature of Christian worship that remains an abiding ingredient in any theology and fuller understanding of Christian liturgy. It was Archbishop William Temple who used to remind us that 'Christianity is of all religions the most materialistic.' For Christianity is an incarnational and a sacramental religion and not a purely spiritual religion – indeed, in that sense it is not really a religion at all. Our apprehension of the infinite and transcendent God is *through* the incarnate Christ – man and God, born of a woman, bone of our bone and flesh of our flesh. Therefore Christian theology resolutely sets its face firmly against any attempt to bypass our physical world of flesh and blood – bricks, stones and mortar – in order to leap into the higher realm of the spirit. (We can safely leave that to the New Age followers in our own day, as Augustine of Hippo left it to the Gnostics and Manicheans in the fourth and fifth centuries.) For the realm of the spirit is not split off in Christian spirituality – or it should not be – from the realm of the flesh. Rather, the flesh is the very vehicle of the spirit and is picked up into the realm of the spirit where it attains its true and lasting significance and glory.

'I no longer desired a better world,' wrote Augustine on leaving Manicheism for Catholicism, 'because I was thinking of creation as a whole: and in the light of this more balanced discernment, I had come to see that higher things are better than the lower, but that the sum of all creation is better than the higher things alone.'[3]

It follows, therefore, that in the Christian view of things – essentially an incarnational and sacramental view – the meeting point for humanity with all that is spiritual is necessarily located right here and now, within the realm of time and space, in the bread and the wine and most conspicuously and particularly in the Incarnate Christ (the Word made flesh). But the work of the Incarnation is an ongoing process, picking up all that lies in its path apart from sin – what one writer calls the 'slow consecration of the universe'.[4] This means that spiritual worship is always clothed in matter and expressed in and through the world of flesh and blood. Artists, architects, musicians, poets and dancers have seen the raw material of their craft immeasurably enhanced through worship. The inevitable result is that since the very beginning of the Church's life, all offering, while spiritual in its goal, has never been ashamed to pick up and reshape the raw material that is at hand along the way, bending it exclusively to the glory of the spiritual and unseen God.

In other words, if you were to pull down every religious building set aside for worship and start again, there would always be artists and stonemasons bent on erecting again some very similar buildings (equally glorious) that would point beyond themselves in what, for want of a better word, we would have to call worship. It began with Mary, the mother of the Lord, in her *Fiat mihi* – her great 'Amen' – when she offered her body as the ark and temple of the Word. The tradition continued with the other Mary (possibly of Magdala), who worshipped Jesus with the best that she had to offer: 'oil of spikenard, very precious'. Furthermore, we are told that the first 'church building' (the cenacle in many ways of all future church buildings) was an offering by the 'good man of the house' who, when asked by Jesus for the smallest room in his house for the Passover celebration (and for the institution of the Eucharist), in fact offered his 'large upper room, well furnished' – the very best that he had to offer. And so it has been ever since. Worshippers have instinctively offered only the best 'the cream of all my heart' (in the words of George Herbert) – and that has also frequently been the costliest and the most sacrificial. So we rightly sing:

> Were the whole realm of nature mine,
> That were an offering far too small
> Love so amazing, so divine,
> Demands my soul, my life, my all.[5]

At the heart of true worship is that sacrificial offering, supremely once and for all at Calvary, yet imitated and reflected in the infinitely less sacrificial offerings of our lives, in all that we have and are, to God – offerings made acceptable in the one perfect offering of Christ. So in the words of the old Prayer Book, 'And here we offer and present unto thee ourselves, our souls and bodies to be a reasonable, holy and living sacrifice.'

King David in the Old Testament is certainly part of that prodigal tradition. When he was offered the threshing floor for his altar 'on the cheap', he pointedly refused the offer with the words: 'I will not offer to the Lord that which costs me nothing' (2 Sam. 24:24). Worshippers like the woman in the house of Simon the Pharisee in the New Testament have frequently embarrassed more cautious souls with their positively prodigal and seemingly wasteful excesses in this realm of worship, and all this with their deep desire to give to God only the best for the best.

It is not surprising, therefore, that for a truly worshipping Church there is the perennial problem of how to avoid becoming indecently and decadently rich! For the Church has naturally been the recipient, or perhaps more accurately, the custodian and steward of the world's greatest gifts, given to the glory of God, whether in compositions of music or as the paintings of a Michelangelo on the ceiling of the Sistine Chapel.

All this is an inevitable by-product of worship. Perhaps we need to press the advocates of a spiritual and invisible Church (the doctrine of the real absence, as we might term it!) a little further, for there is a good deal that is not only theologically wrong in their arguments but also not a little that might even be misleading .

Of course, in many places the local congregation is best housed in a simple and purpose-built church building. Often, such churches are the best precisely because they are small churches built in the shape of a box. That is fine. Yet the argument begins to look a little less convincing when we see that God's house is made of 'wood' while the houses of the congregation are made of 'stone'. (That is what affronted King David when God's people finally settled down after all their wanderings, living in well-constructed houses and no longer in tents.) It is not unusual to hear congregations who own their own houses of not inconsiderable value, and not exactly inadequately furnished, claiming that God's house should just be simple and, by inference, cheap. What sort of religion and worship is it that can contest for such a glaring dichotomy? It could be, quite frankly, just some convenient double thinking: spiritual (and cheap) for God; material and substantial (and the best and most expensive) for self.

This is not to say, though, that we should become slaves to buildings or relegate ministry to forming an antiquarian society for the maintenance of ancient buildings. If Hitler had not destroyed many churches (at least in London) during the war years, then responsible church planners would have had a very large headache indeed in the years following 1945. For the truth is that the church building (like the music and everything else that is done in it) must be the servant of the gospel and not the master. The structural tail must not wag the mystical dog – the mystical Body of Christ of which all worshipping Christians are members.

Many large buildings can be and should be sensitively and

imaginatively reordered to enable greater use for more hours, by more people, for more purposes. In recent years we have seen many good examples of this up and down the country in all the denominations. Of course, some buildings simply must go – not least in areas of shrinking population. Nevertheless, recent experience and research have taught us that a church building in any area (even where there is only minimal church attendance) makes a significant and eloquent statement about the soul of that community and should never be lightly dismissed as redundant. Whenever and wherever we close a church building, we need to remember that we are making a very flesh-and-blood – even a very gutsy – statement and comment, not only about the gospel, but also about the whole of the surrounding community, and our care for that community which that particular church was first erected to serve.

A Church without any buildings at all may well be a very spiritual Church and might indeed go a long way to meet the spiritual ideals of the young and some of the enthusiastic religious sentiments of our present day, but it would have very little to do with the Church which Jesus Christ came to found. Because, in fact, God does not deal with us in a 'spiritual' way. When God wanted to express his love for us, he did it in a way that ensured that it would show up on the pages of the history and geography books. He sent his Son, born of a woman, to live at an address and to enter into history as well as to transcend it. Such must always be the double thrust of a church and of the Christian presence in a city or in a nation. If God is to have a place in urban society, at least for the present, he must be visible on the skyline, with an address and telephone number! The Church must be visibly and tangibly present (as everything else is present and tangible) in order to create a place of meeting *within* the consciousness of society. W. H. Vanstone writes:

> Man aspires to present an offering of love ... This offering is something that actually is. It belongs to the same level of concrete actuality as the stones and trees and stars in which the creativity of God is expressed and completed. As the creativity of the artist is nothing until, through struggle and discipline, it discovers itself in the emergence of a work of art, so the responsive creativity of man to the love of God is nothing until it discovers itself in the emergence of the

concrete actuality of the church. The church is not 'the cause which the church serves' or 'the spirit in which the church lives': the church is the service of the cause and the actualization of that spirit in words spoken, in bodies in a certain place or posture, in feet walking up a certain hill: in stone placed upon stone to build a church, in wood carved into the fashion of a cross: in music composed or practised, played or sung: in the doing of certain things upon a particular day and the giving up of certain things during a particular season: in the fashioning, out of time and care and skill, of something beautiful, and in the maintaining, out of time and care and labour, of the beauty of it: in the gathering and training of others so that they may contribute to and continue and enlarge the offering: in the going out to others so that they may share the offering: in the struggle of brain and pen to find expression and interpretation for the love of God: in the event of worship which celebrates the love of God: in hands stretched out for the receiving of Bread and in the lips raised for the touch of Wine. Here, at this level of concrete actuality is the response of recognition to the love of God: here is the work of art, the offering of love, which is the church.[6]

So the Church must never be ashamed to begin (like a tree's roots) low enough and deep enough, if (also like a tree's branches) it is to reach far enough and high enough into the sky. However, as we have seen, it has so often been the fate of the Church to fall between both worlds and then to end up by connecting with neither. Worship must either be natural or supernatural, but it should have no place in the world of the unnatural and the self-conscious. It is hardly surprising that we have erred in giving a proper priority to bricks and stones and buildings in our understanding of worship, since for far too long the Church has not really given a proper priority to the place of 'the flesh' – the outward and visible and tangible – in its understanding of spirituality in general as well as in worship and prayer in particular.

Wholistic worship

Worship is an activity that includes every aspect of the human awareness: heart and mind, senses and intellect. St Paul bids us to 'present' our 'bodies' as a living sacrifice, holy and acceptable to God, which is our *spiritual* worship (Rom. 12:1). We can see how he is using the word 'spiritual' here: not in contrast to the physical, but rather as a quality of worship that includes the physical and ultimately transcends it. Nothing in the human experience lies outside the scope of true Christian worship. So that great Anglican divine, priest and poet, George Herbert, could write for us to sing: 'Teach me my God and King in *all things* Thee to see; and what I do in *anything* to do it as for Thee.'

For too long by half, at least in the West, and perhaps especially among the Protestant churches of the Reformation, worship has been an activity primarily of the mind. It has been reduced to a process of edifying the mind and informing the intellect. Yet the scriptural commandments in the Old and New Testaments alike are as all-embracing as they possibly can be: to love God with all our heart, soul, mind, body, passions and strength. Perhaps it is not totally fatuous to say that if, in the days of Moses and the Ten Commandments we had understood the working of the brain as we do today, the law might well have exhorted us to love God 'with both sides of the brain'! Apparently, according to contemporary research, it is the left-hand side of the brain which makes us right-handed and dextrous – matter-of-fact, down-to-earth activists concerned with the straightforward grammar of life – while it is the right-hand side of the brain which makes us left-handed – dreamers, poets, musicians and people of intuition. Authentic worship speaks to both sides of the brain and, in our own day, is most likely to speak more easily to the right-hand side in reaction against an age when we have concentrated on the rational to the exclusion of the imaginative capacity for wonder and adoration, for the poetic and the intuitive. (We shall need to look further into this thesis later, when we come to address in detail the need for rich worship which goes beyond words – and especially the place of music in worship. See Chapter 6.)

Archbishop William Temple spoke of this wide-ranging appeal of worship when he wrote:

> To worship is to quicken the conscience by the holiness of God, to feed the mind with the truth of God, to purge the imagination by the beauty of God, to open the heart to the love of God, to devote the will

to the purpose of God. All this is gathered up in that emotion which most cleanses us from selfishness because it is the most selfless of all emotions – adoration.[7]

And again he insists:

> What worship means is the submission of the whole being to the object of worship. It is the opening of the heart to receive the love of God; it is the subjection of conscience to be directed by him; it is the declaration of need to be fulfilled by him; it is the subjection of desire to be controlled by him; and, as the result of all these together, it is the surrender of the whole being. It is the total giving of self.[8]

So we can clearly see that all Christian worship is intended to evoke and to educate all the ingredients within the human personality. But does it? So often worshippers in church are regimented in pews, restricted either to standing, sitting or kneeling, and we receive all that is going on largely, if not exclusively, through the ears. So much that passes for worship reflects the mentality of the lecture-room rather than the environment of the laboratory, the theatre, or the book of Revelation. For true worship is an activity involving the whole body – the Body of Christ, seen and unseen on earth and in heaven. The prayer and liturgy of the universal Church is explicit and unanimous at this point: 'Therefore with angels and archangels and with all the company of heaven . . .' Nothing less than such a cosmic vision is the context of Christian worship.

In practice, in all the traditions (perhaps with the exception of the Orthodox Churches of the East) worship has deteriorated into something 'conducted' by the ordained minister. This has been true in recent centuries, whether you have regard either to the Reformed traditions, where there is a monopoly of worship by the preacher with the emphasis on the Word, or in the more Catholic traditions, where much of the worship is a monologue recited by the priest alone. There is an urgent and pressing need to recover our understanding of worship as an event and as something *done,* rather than as an idea or primarily as something said. Something *happens* on Sunday mornings in our churches. So Jesus said, 'Do this . . .' (*poieite,* a plural verb). This means that the worship of the

Church is intended to be the total activity of the *whole* Body of Christ. That is precisely why, from the earliest times, the Church has spoken of worship as liturgy. We find the word is used in the days of the apostles and in the book of Acts (Acts 13:2). Clearly, from the outset the Church realized that it could borrow no better vocabulary than that which was at hand in the ancient Greco-Roman world, where in the Greek city-state each citizen performed his or her own *liturgia* – their job or function on behalf of the whole community. That would include anything and everything, from cleaning the drains to keeping the city treasury. Each citizen had their appointed task or 'liturgy' for which he or she was particularly responsible and also, presumably, best equipped. When this task was undertaken within the whole community and alongside the responsibilities of all other citizens, it completed the many and varying tasks essential to the maintenance of the city-state.

The nature of corporate worship

So we might say that liturgy, either in the Greek city-state or in the churches of the ancient world, was both personal as well as corporate – which, incidentally, is most certainly not the same thing as saying that it was individual and collective. In an age of individualism such as our own – which is itself a reaction against the threat of collectivism, centralization and depersonalization – in such an age we shall need to recover the proper relationship between personal prayer (which is not the same as private prayer) and corporate worship, which may not come quite so easily in an era which is rightly suspicious of crowds and the anonymity of large metropolitan areas.

We see a significant picture of healthy Christian worship in an early letter (c. AD 96) written by St Clement of Rome to that tiresome congregation of Christians in Corinth who gave such birth-pangs to Paul only half a century earlier in their over-enthusiastic and highly individualistic worship. Clement writes:

> Unto the high priest his special 'liturgies' have been appointed, and
> to the priests their special place is assigned, and on the Levites their
> special 'deaconings' are imposed; the layman is bound by the

ordinances for the laity. Let each of you, brethren, make eucharist to God according to his own order, keeping a good conscience and not transgressing the appointed rule of his 'liturgy' .'

For St Clement, properly ordered worship was an activity of the whole Body of Christ, with each member playing his or her part and with no individual member dominating the rest. There was no audience in that sense, for all were participants – though not in any democratic fashion, but rather in the most profound and mysterious image of corporate activity, namely the image of the human body, in which each member functions within an overriding unity. (The French have this concept clearly embedded in their language when they speak of the congregation – *assister à la messe* – meaning to be present, but also to help and participate fully in the total offering of the liturgy.)

So we can see from the Early Church that there was to be nothing of the one-man band about real liturgy. Rather, it was to be an orchestra. And notice the problem for the church in Corinth – a problem to which both St Paul and St Clement were compelled to address themselves – namely, the problem of over-participation with the resulting discord, rivalry and competition. Faced with a whole orchestra of ministries and witness, the problem would appear to have been the maintenance of harmony and unity. This healthy kind of ecumenical problem arises only when there is so much diversity that the necessity for unity becomes uppermost in the minds of those charged with the ministry of oversight – namely, the ordained ministry of the bishop and his representatives in the local clergy. But notice that you do not solve that problem by silencing or paralysing the orchestra; rather, you seek out that distinctive and subtle charism of oversight (an 'overseeing' that is not 'overbearing'; Acts 20:28; 1 Pet. 5:3) that encourages participation and diversification while 'preserving' the unity of the Spirit in the bond of peace (Eph. 4:3).

So worship, for the Corinthian church, was an activity in which all played their part. Renewal in the Church today is marked by a sense of corporate worship and similarly needs to preserve the unity of the Spirit, while at the same time encouraging diversities of charisms and gifts. Time and space do not permit a further development here of the relationship between the ordained ministry, which is essentially characterized by oversight (episcopacy), and all the other 'charismatic' ministries it presupposes. It is only when all the ministries are in evidence in any church, that the worship can be fully orchestrated. 'Clericalism' was first apparent in its domination over all the other ministries before it became evident in the 'conduct' (that ghastly word) of worship. Wherever there is genuine renewal in the life of the Church, it is evident both in its expression through shared ministry (a partnership in leadership) as well as in renewed worship. The two belong together.

Body language in spiritual worship

We need to take the concept of corporate worship further and understand our worship not only as an activity involving the whole Body of Christ and all its members but also as an activity involving the whole human body and all its members – mind, heart and spirit. We shall explore what this means more fully in Chapter 5, but at this point it is important to establish the principle. Miguel de Unamuno writes: 'There are people who appear to think only with the brain, or with whatever may be the specific thinking organ; while others think with all the body and all the soul, with the blood, with the marrow of the bones, with the belly, with the life.'[10] Such is the total process of worship. Perhaps it is not surprising that the worship which is most conspicuous for its renewal among young people all over the world is the worship of the Community at Taizé, a little village deep in the countryside of France, not many miles from the site of the medieval monastic foundation of Cluny. Each year, hundreds of thousands of 'fringe Christians' are drawn to this remote spot on the map of Europe by the sheer power and authenticity of its worship. It is out of that experience that the Prior of the Community, Roger Schultz, writes these words of advice about the place of the body in worship:

> Do not look for a solution that fails to take your humanity into account. Personally, without my body I should have no idea how to pray. I am no angel, and I have no complaint about that. At certain periods I sense that I pray more with my body than with my

49

understanding. Such prayer is at ground level – one's knees bent, prostrate, looking at the place where the Eucharist is celebrated, taking advantage of the silence and even of the sounds coming up from the village. The body is well and truly present to listen, grasp, love. It would be sheer folly to want to leave it out of account.[11]

Once again, it's a matter of the use of both sides of the brain – and not least with our young people. In the fifties and sixties we spilt much ink in liturgical commissions and other places, seeking to make the liturgy more easily understood and more immediately accessible. In some quarters this resulted in a lack of the sense of transcendence and mystery, and often this was deliberately done to make worship more 'attractive' to the much-abused and, incidentally, much-misunderstood man or woman in the street. In practice, our culture has moved on and is now seeking a reappraisal of the 'right-hand side of the brain', to use the contemporary jargon. For example, there is a reaction in our schools against technology, with an ever-increasing number of students wishing to study arts subjects. The charismatic movement offers new music, which facilitates prayer and the worship of the heart. We shall need to look at all this in much more detail later, but what is clear from the outset is that all those responsible for leading worship need to take on board a radical shift in our culture, which is hungry for the experience of worship in ways which transcend merely intellectual and rational responses.

In all this it is quite clear that we cannot and indeed must not exclude the body, with all its senses, in the totally involving activity of worship, for actions have always spoken louder than words in every walk of life, and there can be no exception to that rule in the realm of what is, at an instinctive level, the most natural of all human activities – worship. The use of the body is an outward and visible sign of the intentions of the heart and mind, as every ballet dancer and actor knows – or forgets at his or her peril. Yet, at a more mundane level, we also know that the use of the body for self-expression is true in the ordinary affairs of everyday life. If I am conducting an interview, the position of my body will indicate the level at which I intend to conduct that interview and will also say something of my relationship with the person I am interviewing. If I remain seated, behind a desk, and you are compelled to remain standing, I am implying that you are my inferior and you may well be on the carpet! If, on the other hand, you are seated and suddenly I stand up and begin to walk up and down the room, there is the chance that I shall be remonstrating and seeking to make a point or even to deliver myself of some lecture upon a topic that has become the burden of my soul. But if I come from behind the desk and pull up an armchair alongside you, the ice is broken and confidence and cordiality would perhaps be the name of the game. Truth to tell, the whole of our life is shot through with ceremonial, often unconsciously, but frequently quite consciously – as at dinner parties, for example. So it would be a strange fragmentation if, when we expressed ourselves before God, we suddenly affected a distaste for ceremonial. So Colin Dunlop rightly reminds us:

> Ceremonial is the contribution of body to the offering of the total man. You cannot really avoid using the body in any communal act of worship. You cannot for purposes of worship contract out of the material conditions in which you live, even if it were desirable to do so. You cannot demand with reason conditions of worship which are 'purely spiritual'. Even the Quaker must use the organs of speech and hearing. To employ also those of sight, smell and touch; to use arms and legs; all this adds no new principle, except it be the principle of 'wholeness'; the use of your entire being in the worship of the creator. Worship is giving to God what belongs to him: all our body, as well as mind and spirit are his.[12]

The use of the body in worship can be far more compelling and eloquent than many pious words. The liturgy of Good Friday in the Western Church begins with the three sacred ministers entering the derelict sanctuary in silence and prostrating themselves (flat out) on the bare floor of a stripped and desolate church. There they remain for several moments in silence, in an action that speaks volumes about all that could never be put into words concerning Good Friday, Christ's passion and dereliction, his crucifixion and death. So in the Early Church (as in the book of Revelation) corporate prayer by the whole priesthood of all believers was always undertaken standing. You knelt to plead;

you extended your hands to receive; you raised them in blessing or praising. So worship (not unlike a dance) has movement, shape, poise and rhythm: an excellent cure for the most characteristic disease of worship – the wandering of the mind. Of course, your mind will wander if it is supposed to be doing or saying something totally out of step (literally) and unconnected with what the rest of your body is trying to say. Like a good oarsman (to use another image), the eye, the body and the mind must all be saying the same thing, each bringing a discipline to bear upon all the others, if the boat is to move forward swiftly, most easily and seemingly, with the least self-conscious effort.

Clearly, if the principle stated here is accepted, then there will have to be in the renewed Church with its renewed worship a refusal to attach party labels to various activities and attitudes or postures. Neither posture, gesture nor vesture should degenerate into party slogans within a renewed Church: each should be chosen because it is appropriate to the occasion and not for 'high-church' or 'low-church' demonstrations. Kneeling, a posture characteristic for so long of 'popish' practices, is now restricted among many of the churches (including the Roman Catholic Church) to only a small and penitential part of the liturgy, while standing and sitting are both encouraged as postures of prayer for all Christians. We do not seem to kneel as much as we used to do! Somehow it is all less fussy and yet more meaningful, and it is pointing all the churches to a unity in their worship representing a far fuller and richer understanding of worship than has existed in the past in any of the various traditions.

For the unity towards which all the churches are being drawn by the Holy Spirit is a unity of fullness and diversity. This should be nowhere more evident than in the renewal of worship sweeping through all the churches. It may not be too much of an exaggeration to say that unity will be more obvious and its cause forwarded more powerfully through worship than through any other aspect of the Church's life. In a renewed act of worship I am less conscious of churchmanship and party labels than at any other time. It will be in our renewed worship that we shall discover unity within plenitude rather than in pieces of paper, jigsaw ecumenism, or schemes and covenanting proposals. Although it is perhaps true to say that many outward postures with their accompanying ceremonial represent inward and hidden victories in past battles over doctrine and theology, it is equally true to say that the theological and doctrinal debate has now moved its ground and no longer bears the same relation to these attitudes and postures. There can even be a healthy pragmatism about our worship today, enabling us to experiment, as well as a promiscuous approach that is ready to beg, borrow or steal the best from all the traditions. The result should be a fuller expression of worship and, hopefully, an ever-increasing love and reverence for God – the experience of being constantly *lost* in 'wonder, love and praise'.

4

Unity and flexibility in worship

One of the continuing tensions in the whole of life at all levels is the tension between structure and spontaneity, between form and spirit, between what is organized and what is (or at least, what appears to be) spontaneous, immediate and 'off-the-cuff'. This tension is nowhere more evident than in Christian worship .

Our first responsibility is to believe that such a tension is healthy and therefore to resist the temptation to let go of either end. After all, in a good tug-of-war, the two extremes keep their feet firmly on the ground precisely because of the tension between the two contesting parties. Cut the rope – release the tension – and both parties will topple over backwards (incidentally and significantly, into even more extreme positions!). In any authentic and lasting renewal of the Church, this tension must be restored where it has been lost and maintained in all the traditions of the Church. For too long, parties have been formed among Christians that have hardened into denominations, championing and polarizing structure over against spontaneity, a rigid formalism versus the Spirit and a somewhat subjective enthusiasm. Perhaps the extremes of this polarization were most in evidence, on the one hand, in the Tridentine Mass, in which every movement of the priest's hands, down to the last detail, was prescribed by rubric, and on the other hand, in the totally spontaneous, spirit-filled worship of the Pentecostal churches.

In any recovery of health through spiritual renewal and especially in our worship, these two opposites must be brought back together, for, as in the case of a healthy human body, they belong together. It is precisely the *structure* of the spine which makes possible the maximum *flexibility*, enabling the body to respond spontaneously to each situation, whether it be to dance, run, walk, stoop and bend or just to sit. We cannot be either all bones or all sinew. Each relates to the other to give a maximum amount of structure and flexibility. So, we should not be surprised that an amoeba or a jellyfish cannot dance! Neither should we be surprised if we come to any lifting task in a rigid and resentful frame of mind, without putting our back freely and willingly *into* it, that our back is sooner or later put *out*, as we proverbially say.

What have been isolated and opposing factions in the churches over the centuries need to come together, for each needs the other. We are called to be one Body (2 Cor. 12:12–13f). These opposites need to be held together in tension in a new interdependence if the churches are to recover that plenitude of the gospel linked with authenticity in our corporate worship. The spontaneous needs what is structured and ordered to rescue it from the tyranny and even the anarchy of subjectivity and mere emotionalism. Likewise the structured worship of the more Catholic traditions needs the spontaneity of the Spirit to rescue it from deadly formalism.

Before we reflect upon the ways in which form and spontaneity have come together in recent revised orders of service and in many contemporary forms of worship, it might be worthwhile to gain an overview of the more far-reaching convergences of formerly opposing traditions. In recent years there has occurred a refreshing blending together of various practices, which in turn has given way to an enrichment and authenticity in the worship of the contemporary Church.

A threefold witness

'A threefold chord is not easily broken' (Eccl. 4:12). In practice it is possible to trace three main strands converging in the life and worship of the Church in the second half of the twentieth century: sacramental, scriptural and Spirit-led. The choice of these particular labels is deliberate. In the past, varying denominations and emphases have tended to lay claim to party labels and titles that by their very definitions should belong to the whole church. After all, no part of the church should want to be without its 'catholic' or its 'evangelical' emphasis, yet in the course of history these labels have been cornered by particular traditions and used as party slogans. It might be useful, therefore, initially at least, to cling rather carefully to the particular labelling chosen in this chapter.

The sacramental witness (often exclusively claiming the label of 'catholic') places its emphasis upon signs and symbols and, as we shall see in other parts of the book, this is valid and most certainly has its part to play in any form of corporate worship. We might want to suggest that in an age which is somewhat weary of words and all that goes with the information super-highway (as it is fondly called), signs and symbols may speak far more eloquently and dynamically.

Yet this emphasis, left exclusively to itself, is always in danger of degenerating into what is often designated as 'cultic', appealing only to the emotions and failing to edify and reach the mind and the will. Proper worship is intended to enlighten the mind, warm the heart and fire the will. So in isolation the sacramental emphasis is just not sufficient to communicate the full gospel. Indeed, one could go further and call to witness the decadence of the medieval Church, which promoted the 'cult' at the expense of the Word and renewal of life through a ministry almost exclusively focused upon the mass and the priest. It was not long before this gave way to the worst forms of priestcraft and medieval hocus pocus – as it somewhat unfairly came to be known by the reformers.

Incidentally, it is perhaps worth stopping briefly to give the origin of the phrase 'hocus pocus'. The English have a genius for corrupting language, since they affect indifference to and a total ineptitude for languages in general! So Rotten Row was the English version of *Rue de roi*, and so with 'hocus pocus', which was the English version of those words at the consecration of the bread in the Eucharist: '*Hoc est enim corpus meum.*'

Secondly, there is the scriptural witness of the Reformation, which was itself a reaction against the playing down of the Word, of preaching and of scriptural teaching in the late medieval Church. In architectural terms this manifested itself with the centrality of the pulpit and the marginalizing of the holy table in most Reformation church buildings. Here again, of course, this emphasis is valid as far as it goes, but once again, if it is left to itself, it is surely in danger, as history has proved, of being reduced to 'words, words and more words'; to a cerebral moralism, powerful in its moral challenge but failing to reach the heart and therefore to charge the affections and to challenge the will. To use contemporary jargon, it speaks only to one side of the brain, and to the side which has become somewhat overheated in recent years, at that.

The third witness we have called 'Spirit-led' quite deliberately, rather than using the over-emotive terms 'charismatic' or 'Pentecostal'; indeed, it might be even better to call this particular strand 'experiential'. Yet here again, in much popular talk those who would emphasize this particular strand have taken to themselves exclusively the label of 'charismatic', when, of course, that particular word, properly understood, must always be the property of all Christians. Whatever made us think there is any prayer or ministry which is not charismatic in the proper sense of that word – namely, 'given'? So St Paul would remind all those who want to make prayer a technique or to exercise a Pelagian spirit about their prayers that of course, 'it is not you who prays but the Holy Spirit who prays' (Rom. 8:26). Similarly, in the Anglican Church in the ordinal the bishop, when ordaining a priest, explicitly says: 'Receive the Holy Spirit for the office and work of a priest.' How on earth could we possibly envisage any ministry which was not charismatic in that sense?

For the experiential witness is surely a most important ingredient in all worship, not as the measure of how close we have drawn to God, or better still how closely he has drawn to us, but rather because full worship addresses the whole person at every level and not just as an attractive idea, floating somewhere between our two ears. So the experiential is certainly a most important ingredient in worship, emphasizing as it does the part played in our lives by the sense of release and the need to be moved (in every sense) and therefore often healed through worship, praise and prayer. In so much of the teaching work of the Church, we have often started at the wrong end and attempted to get people to 'swallow' doctrine and right belief. Would it not have been much better to start – say our confirmation course – by turning the 'class' (not the best word) into a prayer group, introducing the enquirers or seekers to the experience of God in prayer?

In a recently marketed language course, learning the French

language was promoted under the label, 'the French experience'. Lesson One took the student, with the aid of video, audio and a work-book, into a French restaurant, where the student was permitted to speak only French when ordering the wines and food. While doing all this, the various alternatives appeared on the video screen. Not unnaturally, one's mouth began to water, and all one's senses co-operated in an experience which was much more than a lesson. All the senses were, if you like, invaded and converged in an experience rather than in just an idea. As we shall see in a later chapter, worship needs to address all the senses, and not least at the level of signs, symbols, ceremonies and, of course, music. All can be seen as aids to worship in various forms for different people at different stages on the road of discipleship.

There was a time when many of us were taught to pray simply at the level of duty – almost as we were taught to clean our teeth: something that should happen preferably before breakfast and from which we were not particularly conscious of deriving any satisfaction. It was just 'good for you'! In the recent charismatic release, including the 'Toronto Blessing', as it has come to be known – a release which has manifested itself throughout all the various traditions of the Christian Church – many have come to experience a richer sense of worship, praise and adoration, and for this we must surely thank God. Nevertheless, here again, as with the other two strands, if this particular emphasis is exclusive and left in isolation, then the worship in those churches will soon degenerate into a slavish subjectivity – a perpetual taking of our own temperature, or worse still, the chasing after particular experiences and manifestations of the Spirit, such as tongues, ecstasy, prophesy, laughter, tears or being slain in the Spirit – in fact, into a worship which rapidly degenerates into either entertainment or into a blatant self-serving therapy.

So the joy of the whole renewal movement which has swept through all the traditions is to be found in the convergence, in our own age, of all three of these necessary ingredients, stripped now of the party labels which history has attached to them. For example, the use of oil or of incense in worship is not necessarily regarded today as being 'high church' or 'popish', as in the past. Icons have found their place again in many parts of the Church in the West and many Anglican cathedrals today (even those of a previously more 'evangelical persuasion') are using pricket stands and inviting pilgrims and visitors to light a candle and to offer a prayer. Equally, the emphasis upon Scripture, Bible study and the place and priority of preaching is no longer a party matter, as more and more Christians see the importance of worship that has within it a strongly scriptural element, both in the reading of the Bible and also in the expounding of the Word, either formally from the pulpit or even with a short homily at the early service of eight o'clock Holy Communion.

Many Christians today would wish to acknowledge the impact which the charismatic movement has had upon their own life of worship and prayer. While not necessarily being 'card-carrying' charismatics, they are in no doubt whatever that their sense of release in praise and prayer (accompanied or not by some of the familiar signs of tongues, tears and laughter) has brought to all the churches a deeper and more reflective – to say nothing of more loving and joyful – worship, and all this with a new sense of the love of God just for his own sake.

When we bind all three of these strands together – as is happening in many parts of the Church in our day – we begin to observe something of the richness and depths of the worship of God – a worship which can communicate through celebration the riches of the gospel just as powerfully as proclamation, if not more so. Sacramental, scriptural and spiritual belong together in a unity and plenitude which is most compelling and authentic for gospel communication. To emphasize the prime place of the Eucharist, for example, as the characteristic expression of Christian worship is no longer to make a divisive statement. The Eucharist is now accepted by many Christians of different persuasions as the characteristic, but not exclusive act of worship. Equally, the innovation in recent years of weekly prayer groups, or a monthly healing service with anointing and prayer, has wonderfully extended and enriched the opportunities for worship in many parishes up and down the country. Certainly, it is evident that many Christians are returning to the Scriptures and beginning to find in them a new authority and a refreshing source of 'daily bread' for their pilgrimage. To summarize, we might want to affirm that if you have the Scriptures without the Spirit you will *dry up*; if you have the Spirit without the Scriptures you will *blow up*; if you have the sacraments without the Spirit you will be *fed up*. Only with all three can you *grow up* into the fullness of the stature of Christ.

It is that kind of enrichment of worship through the convergence of formerly opposing strands which is bringing renewal in worship to all parts of all the churches. Much of this has been made possible through the work of liturgical reform in recent years, which has consistently built into the many and varying new prayer books a proper place both for structure as well as for spontaneity.

However, the unity and uniformity in our contemporary worship are to be found not so much in the words that are said as in the structure and in the flow of the worship. There is a new and refreshing agreement among all the traditions about what we should be doing in liturgy when we come before the throne of grace, and this in its turn has given Christians a new freedom to explore new verbal expressions of worship. It is this uniformity of action and structure that has made possible a new spontaneity at the heart of much of our worship, as our understanding of liturgy has recaptured something of that earlier and healthier appreciation that liturgy is primarily concerned with what is *done* before it is concerned with what is being *said*.

Paradoxically enough, there is therefore more uniformity today among Anglican churches in all the provinces of the Anglican Communion than ever there was with the Prayer Books of 1662 or 1928. It is true that there are many more alternatives and choices in these new books, but the alternatives belong to a pattern and structure of agreed activity. For example, the words of the various Eucharistic prayers are secondary to the fact that every congregation now knows what is going to *happen* after the celebrant has said or sung the words 'Lift up your hearts', even if they may not be certain which of the various Eucharistic prayers will be used. It was the new American Prayer Book of the Episcopal Church that perhaps most clearly drew the attention of all the churches to the primacy of structuring worship in what came to be rather unfortunately termed the 'Agenda Eucharist' (see pages 400–401). Here we have an agreed structure of activity in worship that enables and facilitates enormous flexibility in the words said and in the various prayers offered. All this endorses this underlying principle which remains true for all liturgical worship and not simply for the 'Agenda Eucharist'.

To grasp this is to offer to any sensitive pastor the real opportunity to 'tailor' the liturgy, in the best sense of that word, to the particular occasion in hand. It will be increasingly important to make a proper use of this freedom with genuine pastoral, liturgical and doctrinal sensitivity, paying due attention to the more timid spirits who will need, for a long time to come, a certain continuity with the familiar and traditional forms of worship inherited from the past if they are not to flounder and feel alienated by the 'new' and by an excessive amount of innovation, either in the language or the action of the liturgy.

'At all times and in all places'

Flexibility will be increasingly important as we seek in our own day to implement the ancient injunction of the Church that its worship should be available (as we say in the words of the earliest prayer books) 'at all times and in all places'. It is not 'high-church' practices that make our worship catholic, but rather that kind of flexibility in a worship programme for a parish where services are held at all sorts of times and in all sorts of places and styles, being accessible, therefore, to all sorts of people – men, women, children, the elderly, the infirm, those with unsociable hours of work, commuters, families, widows, singles and folk from the many and varied cultures living cheek by jowl in our multicultural and pluralist society.

By and large (though this has all the weaknesses of a sweeping generalization), most congregations in Britain today have a very long way to go before we can be seen to be taking full advantage of this 'catholic' injunction for differing times, places and styles of worship. 'At all times' – but it clearly is not. Worship in many places is still being offered at the 'sacred' and set hours that relate more to the milking habits of a rural community than to the travelling and working habits of an urban society over two and a half centuries into the industrial revolution, to say nothing of the contemporary technological revolution which is re-shaping life-styles in our own day.

What about the implications of the Sunday trading laws? Surely there really is no hidden virtue in summoning God's people together for their most important and characteristic activity – worship – at a time that is least convenient. Neither is there any point in consulting just those who already come to church about the best times for corporate Sunday worship: they are already conditioned and in any case are generally utterly unrepresentative as a group within the wider community of the parish or local community.

Worship should be at 'all times and in all places' precisely because it is intended to be for 'all sorts and conditions' of people, even for the lazy, laid-back or lapsed Christians, who might well be free and willing to attend the Eucharist on the Lord's Day (say at 5.30p.m.), for according at least to the New Testament, early or late, they all receive the same reward from the same generosity of the same gracious and bountiful master and Lord! There is no point in advocating that we upset the 'regulars' at 9.30a.m. by putting the service much later in the morning or even later in the day, in the evening. Rather, we need to be bold and to strike out with alternative opportunities for worship – eucharistic worship or non-eucharistic worship. Then we might well discover the truth of that old adage, 'The more pubs you open, the more beer you sell' – and it's beer, not pubs, we're in business for! Sunday evening worship – especially in the large cities – is returning again after nearly half a century of decline and demise. It may need to be a very different style of worship – a church for the non-churchgoers – and that will need imaginative tailoring and planning in more ways than one (see Chapter 9).

Yet thankfully, as renewal sweeps through all the churches, we are seeing a new willingness to break with the old patterns of time, place and style, moving away from one time (highly inconvenient), from one place (physically very cold, unwelcoming and frequently uncomfortable – at least from the perspective of the pew), and from one sort of person (i.e. someone who has become conditioned to the usual programme – a churchgoer). With contemporary work patterns (or lack of them) and with the increase of leisure patterns, the Church simply has to become far more flexible about times and places for its worship: Sunday morning for some people and Sunday evening for others; Tuesday afternoon for yet another group and Friday evening or Saturday evening for others still. For worship to be corporate, it is not necessary for everyone to be in the same place at the same time.

The 'Parish and People Movement' which grew up after the Second World War made some very important and positive points when it gave the mandate, 'All the Lord's people in the Lord's house for the Lord's own service on the Lord's day' – and implying also 'at the Lord's own sacred hour of 9.30a.m.' This movement focused the worship of the Church of England in the 'Corporate Communion' or 'Parish Communion' or 'Family Communion' as it was sometimes unfortunately called. Certainly there was much gain from the best side of that movement, and its achievements should not be minimized.

However, with the fragmentation of life in Britain today and indeed throughout the Western world, a rigid and unquestioning application of the principles of the Parish and People Movement will serve only to unchurch this nation. The corporate nature of the Church and of its worship is not at all like the corporate nature of any other body on earth, precisely because it derives its corporate nature from the one Body that is not on earth but which is in heaven – even the Body of the risen, ascended and gloried Lord, who ever lives to make intercession for us in the company 'of angels and archangels and all the company of heaven' – beyond time and beyond space. It is only as we experience our worship on earth being 'picked up' into the one great chorus of worship in heaven that we can truly begin to speak of our corporate worship. The light from that worship of heaven is necessarily refracted into many different aspects, colours, styles, languages and settings in the truly 'catholic' worship of the Church on earth.

Following through the breakthrough of the 'Parish and People Movement' should encourage all Christians to recover and to explore the opportunities for a new diversity along the lines I am suggesting above and also later in the book (see Chapter 9). For contemporary urban society is much more like a railway station than a parade ground. If you are to provide for the needs of passengers at a railway station, you need to be on the appropriate platform at the appropriate moment with the appropriate wares, and not standing in the station-master's office, expecting the travelling population to assemble there and to await further instructions! It will be much more a matter of 'meals on wheels', with a roving commission and a platform ticket for every platform in the station – and eighteen hours a day at that. For whenever and wherever a small group of Christians comes together, for whatever purpose (whether a meeting of the PCC or a harvest supper), appropriate worship should have its appropriate place.

Different dimensions of worship

Worship in a large cathedral, with perhaps several hundred people present, of course has its proper place in the overall life and witness of the whole Church, but there is certainly also room for worship on a much smaller and more informal scale, perhaps in a church hall, in an extended informal Eucharist before the church meeting; or in a field with a group of teenagers on a walking weekend or a pilgrimage; or in a home, as part of the weekly Bible study; or with just two or three people at the bedside of a sick or dying person. In these and in many similar 'small' occasions, what will constitute valid worship will be *an appropriate occasion, appropriately expressed*. In fact we would do well to take that phrase as the 'mission statement' of all our worship .

For surely it has to be admitted that it is so often at the level of the small and informal occasion that our worship is distorted and inappropriately styled: not because of the particular situation *per se* – because the numbers are too small or too great – but rather because we are striving to make a particular act of worship precisely what it is not and therefore *inappropriate*. So often our worship falls between all the various options and all the varying dimensions open to Christian worship today. Perhaps I can suggest that we think, roughly speaking, in terms of three categories for worship. We can talk of cathedral, church or cell, paralleling in a rough-and-ready way the three different categories for worship which we find in the Old Testament – the temple, the synagogue and the family.

In the old Israel these three categories were each validated in their own dimension. So on the eve of the sabbath, as soon as a minimum of seven stars could be seen in the sky, the father of the household led his family in a simple act of worship, for there is in Judaism a deeply rooted family spirituality for every day of the week, with prayers at table and for every occasion in work and leisure. You thank God not only for food but for every aspect of his creation, including the most earthy experiences of all – a motion of the bowels! (Our Victorian forebears shame us by their practice of family prayers and Bible readings at table and during the week. Hopefully in our own day this practice might well return in one form or another.) Then on the sabbath the devout Jew would attend the synagogue – the place where people gathered together, as the root word in Greek literally means. This did not have to be a large occasion. You could call together a synagogue with the minimum quorum of ten men. Jesus deliberately undercuts this number of ten when he says: 'Wherever two or three are gathered together ['synagogued'] in my name, there am I in the midst' (Matt. 18:20). Such a minimal gathering can, in the perspective of the New Testament, nevertheless constitute the gathered Church. Then at the great festivals of the Jewish year, the devout Jew would seek means and ways of going up to Jerusalem, to the temple, the unique place of sacrificial worship, where the priest and high priests performed all the Levitical and priestly acts of sacrificial worship.

So what might all this look like for the Christian in the new Israel when we speak of the cell, the congregation and the cathedral, which are partly paralleled by the temple, synagogue and family? For our ideal is to style worship which is *appropriate* in each situation and setting and which has an integrity about it from start to finish.

There is the big occasion of the cathedral or rally, when we are making a large statement about God's people and their response to his call in and through worship and service. Then there is the local church or congregation, which probably numbers only twenty or thirty, or a hundred or so in many of our rural and inner-city churches. There will be an appropriate expression of worship at that level also. But finally, there is also the cell – the building block of the local congregation – that New Testament quorum of 'two or three gathered together', and most certainly we need to recover and to discover a style of worship most fitted and suitable for such an occasion. At each level the worship will require skilful 'tailoring' if it is to be an *appropriate* act of worship, *appropriately* expressed. That is the challenge.

We shall undertake this exercise best if we are willing to go back in each case to the basic structure of the worship, with no decorations of any kind and then, and only then, consider the appropriate additions and externals and ways in which these need to reflect the occasion with its needs, its necessary restrictions and its unique opportunities. At that point this exercise will necessarily require a detailed consideration of vesture, gesture and posture, of ornaments, of music and its appropriate accompaniment or not, and all the other secondary ingredients of worship. They must, however, all *belong* to the particular occasion and should express that occasion fittingly and with integrity.

So often, however, this is simply not the case. Churches seem to be seeking to be an imitation of cathedral worship, without any or many of its resources for a particular kind of excellence. Inevitably this means that what is done is not done well, simply because the necessary and appropriate resources are not at hand. Everything then becomes a pale imitation of what it clearly is not. Yet God's worship at its best is never ashamed to take what is at hand, local and integral to the situation, and to turn it to the purposes of worship, whether it be the large stone water jars in the first 'sign' at Cana of Galilee or that young boy's 'packed lunch' at the feeding of the five thousand. It is only in this way that the 'connections' to which we have referred earlier in the book are likely to be made in the minds, but above all, in the imaginations of the worshippers – those connections between what is so often termed 'secular' and 'everyday' and what we like to keep separate under the Church's domestic title of 'sacred, holy and other'.

For in authentic and truly spiritual worship, the sparks fly between those two categories so that the barrier between sacred and secular is continually broken down as language, posture, signs, symbols and ceremonies 'pick up' all kinds of overtones and impressions and forge together a strong and awesome connection, so that we share in that primal vision of Isaiah, and discover the truth in the witness of the angels – namely that 'the whole earth is full of his glory' for those with eyes to see. In one sense good worship lures the worshipper down 'memory lane', evoking from the past, as well as blazing the path to new insights and to a deeper sense of awareness. The Bread is no longer just bread, only to be taken at its face value, so to speak.

Everything involved in our worship is there to represent and to stand for something greater than itself. It is representative in that sense as well as in many other senses – from the priest who represents the people of God as well as the incarnate priesthood of Christ, all the way across the board to the signs and symbols used in worship. For the aim of all our worship is surely nothing less than the slow consecration of the whole universe! In many ways, if the worship of our churches recovered its authenticity in the ways I am suggesting, then many of the 'ecclesiastical suppliers' would go out of business. We are not called to use 'altar breads' or 'altar wine' in our worship but rather the best of the bread and wine of our daily ('secular') lives, and to bring that as representative of the whole of our lives – our eating and drinking – for consecration on the altar of the acceptable worship of Christ to his Father and to ours. So perhaps it can almost go without saying that all self-consciousness must go if our worship is to speak with an authentic voice and with a power that can warm the heart, fire the imagination and drive the will through the emotions, bringing every part of our selves and our daily lives – 'our selves, our souls and bodies' – under the lordship of Christ and through him, therefore, into the presence of the Father, to whom all our worship is ultimately addressed.

Small can be beautiful

An inner-city bishop or a bishop with a significant number of missions and scattered congregations will frequently find himself visiting churches where the congregation is very small in number. The situation is similar in those dioceses which are predominantly rural, for it tends to be only in suburbia (and largely middle-class suburbia at that) where there are congregations in the three figures. This will be a challenge to the Church in the coming years, with less money and ordained ministers. Although there are special problems attached to the survival of small, far-flung congregations, there are also some advantages. The great temptation is to join up and to centralize for the sake of money and manpower. Beware – you cannot serve God and market forces! Rather, we need to find all kinds of ways for the redeployment of the ordained ministry. It will need to be imaginatively related to the supplementary ministry both of the non-stipendiary ministry

and the ministry of the laity, in a genuine partnership of leadership both in ministry and mission. There is no reason why we
should be defeated by the present situation and sell out to centralization, if we are prepared to be flexible in the times and places
and styles of our worship. Furthermore, our services, which will
be more rather than fewer, will not always need to be exclusively
eucharistic (see Chapter 8 on the Daily Office). The important
principle is that there should be the presence of the Body of Christ
at the heart of every community in our land, whether small or big,
praying and worshipping, interceding and caring for the wider
community, acting almost like a local neighbourhood watch committee, but concerned with the welfare of everybody in that vicin-
ity, irrespective of faith, religion, colour or background .

For surely what brings a sense of defeat and despair where the
congregations are fragile and small is not so much the numbers
game as the apparent inability of those responsible to order the
worship appropriately. So often everything about the worship in
such churches is borrowed and imported second-hand from a
faded and jaded form of worship that would have been more
appropriate in the setting of a cathedral church or 'in choirs and
places where they sing'.

Perhaps we can picture it for a moment. Possibly there might
be three women and a boy dressed in strange cassocks and surplices, standing apart (in what are supposed to be choir stalls),
accompanied by an incompetent organist playing on a very indifferent organ. The congregation (all 37 of them) are straggled all
over the place in the uncomfortable pews. The service begins with
a large and pretentious hymn, played to a large and pretentious
tune, pitched rather too high for most people who are present –
perhaps 'Nun Danket' (the well-known German tune to 'Now
thank we all our God'), which starts with three top Cs! There are
two and a half servers (or acolytes, as they are fondly known in the
United States), and one of them (the half one, who is the smallest)
is struggling to carry a cross at the head of what is parading as a
procession, while the vicar (given half the chance, arrayed in a
cope, because the bishop is present) is led in by the fragmented and
rather sad little choir, together with the 'team' of servers, all of
whom are entering the church as though it were the vast nave of a
European Gothic cathedral.

The sermon is preached from the tall pulpit (several feet above contradiction) in a style more appropriate to a state banquet or the opening of Parliament. The altar or holy table has been dressed with faded (though elaborate) hangings and a frontal with a rather over-large vase of flowers uneasily standing to one side. The collection during the hymn, which seems to be sung solely to 'cover up' the taking of the collection, is clearly a major operation, engaging the only two men from the congregation, carrying large, dusty, wooden plates in which a rather obviously small collection is pretentiously and even pompously being collected, presented and blessed. A bread-board bearing a loaf of bread and a bread-knife, together with a bottle of special 'sanctuary' wine, are rather uneasily, though self-consciously, carried down the central aisle in what is clearly intended to be an offertory procession in the fifties' style, although in reality the aisle is only 50 feet in length between the farthest seated member of the congregation at the back and the priest standing with hands extended at the holy table.

Everything from beginning to end is out of key and out of place and joint and, frankly, bordering on the absurd. There are all kinds of questions we need to ask. In the first place, why should the worship of the Church always have to be accompanied by an organ? Furthermore, is it appropriate to have a body of people who can act as a choir to support and boost the singing? Why should such a choir need to be dressed up and sitting away from the congregation, whose singing they are intended to lead and to encourage? Then again, why is it necessary or even desirable to 'preach' from a pulpit when it might be much more appropriate and 'immediate' and accessible for the congregational response to the preached Word if the priest or minister were to stand in the centre and body of the people, addressing them in a suitable tone of voice appropriate to the numbers who are there. It might be much more desirable, upon honest reflection, for the lectern used for the Scripture readings to be simply moved to the centre of the front, so that the address or homily is given in a face-to-face encounter (see Chapter 7 on 'Receiving the Word').

Please forgive this somewhat sharp criticism of many of our worshipping habits in the Church today. It might help both congregation and clergy if a frank and honest video recording were made of our weekly worship, and then to have a special meeting of the parish to critique it and to see something of what we look like when we are at worship. It does not need to be a cruel or negative appraisal, but it might hopefully underscore the point that is being made: namely, that everything will probably require retailoring if this small act of worship is to ring true and to lift those present into the one great act of worship in heaven.

For in many ways it is the small act of worship that demands the largest amount of work if it is to be authentic and appropriate. As in so much else, if we take care of the pennies then the pounds will possibly take care of themselves. Tailoring worship to the small occasion requires a ruthless eye for detail and the determination to start from scratch with few presuppositions and even fewer white elephants, and then only to add what is absolutely required and appropriate in a particular situation and setting. In that way the action of the liturgy will stand out clearly like a drama, instead of being lost in the claustrophobia of religiosity, which is perhaps the greatest enemy to true worship.

'Things old and new'

It is here and in this way that so many of the new prayer books, wisely used, can be such useful and flexible resource books for those whose task it is to celebrate and to lead worship. Note, however, that they are resource books and not handbooks, and that they are most certainly not books for the pews. *The Alternative Service Book* of the Church of England (1980) has no less than 1,292 pages! It cannot possibly be conceived as a pew book even for regular churchgoers, let alone for occasional visitors. The first requirement, therefore, for ministers of religion and for all those who are really concerned with the corporate worship of God is to sit down and to 'read, mark, learn and inwardly digest' these large and lengthy books from cover to cover. It is important to know what is available and what all the alternatives are, as well as to master the wide range and wealth of material they present.

In all this there is a rich flexibility precisely because there is a carefully designed sense of structure, shape and direction throughout all the various services that are suggested. Furthermore, closer inspection of the rubrics will reveal how very little of the material is mandatory. There is a real freedom for local colouring and styling at every turn. Yet this freedom is not given so that worship will degenerate into chaos and subjective enthusiasms, but rather in order to preserve a simple pattern and an obvious outline which serves to throw into high relief its own sense of things being done 'decently and in order'. Throughout this whole process of selection, we should not be too ready to add too much extra material (least of all hymns for their own sake) until we are very clear about the style which the worship demands for any particular occasion. Shape, structure, substance and style in worship should not compete with each other, but rather should belong together in a single integrity.

In addition to all these new orders of service and of worship, there is also now available a wealth of biblical material readily accessible and clearly available in the many and varied lectionaries in all the new prayer books. It will be time well spent to sit down and to make your own index of all the various services, readings and prayers so that they are readily available and accessible as options for worship for many and varying occasions. There are indeed today several computer programmes which put much of this material on disk – material which can be pulled up and selected very easily and swiftly. Happily, gone are the days of only some 30 or so years ago, when a priest or pastor could easily get by for a lifetime with just three books in the worship section of his library or study – a Bible, a hymn book and a prayer book! There is now an ever-increasing library of new material for worship, and a wise and sensitive pastor will value a detailed knowledge of these many and various prayer books from different traditions and from all parts of the world, together with hymn books, spiritual song books and lectionaries. The ministry – ordained or lay – will soon come to see that all this material constitutes important and necessary resources, essential for providing living and effective worship week by week.

Since a great deal of the new music is *not* best accompanied on the organ and as so much music suitable for singing in worship is comparatively new, keen church musicians should not be above taking the trouble to acquaint themselves with this ever-increasing musical repertoire. Much of this, of course, is third rate, as in any age, but much of it will have been found useful by those responsible for conducting worship in school assemblies and the like. We need to offer help and support in that area and to learn from their experience on the frontiers of faith in the secular world of Monday to Friday in a far from sympathetic environment.

All these ingredients require today from priest, people and musicians alike a vast working knowledge, as well as a readiness to experiment, to pick and choose, like a 'wise scribe' bringing out of our treasure 'things new and old'. For in good worship – as in good architecture – it is not only perfectly possible, but it is also even highly desirable to put various strands of material from differing periods and differing traditions alongside each other. They often make surprisingly good bedfellows. It should go without saying that each strand should be the very best of its kind and that there should certainly not be any hesitation to use material ancient and modern within the same service. A healthy and living tradition does not need to cut itself off from previous chapters of its tradition – chapters from the past which can nourish the present. Rather, past and present belong together helping us to reach out to the future and the shape of things to come.

Surely there will never be a generation that will not require the opportunity to sing that traditional hymn to the Holy Spirit, '*Veni Creator*'. At the same time we will also want to use as a prayer of the heart and as a spiritual song the lovely contemporary invocation, 'Spirit of the living God, fall afresh on me.' God's people need today many of the great prayers of the past, just as much as they were needed in the centuries in which they were composed and devised. There must be no doctrinaire or rigid cult of the 'neophiliacs', who so often appear to believe that renewal is all and solely to do with vogue, fashion and the latest thing. Of course worship must belong to the age in which it is rooted, but it must also reach beyond the limitations of that age by drawing upon deep and diverse resources which transcend that and indeed every age of history.

In conclusion

In conclusion, it might be helpful to rehearse a few basic underlying principles to guide us and also to release us into an authentic freedom, flexibility and unity in the Spirit in our worship. All authentic Christian worship should be Spirit-filled from start to finish. That lovely prayer so dear to Anglicans, the Collect for Purity, or some other such prayer invoking the Holy Spirit, needs to be used personally as well as corporately before all worship and not simply at the outset of the Eucharist. From first to last we must realize that worship will be authentic to the extent that it picks up the worshippers into self-transcendence, so that they are 'lost in wonder, love and praise'. Thomas Merton writes:

> Our destiny is not merely to be lost in God, as the traditional figures of speech would have it, like 'a drop of water in a barrel of wine or like iron in the fire' but rather found in God in all our individual and personal reality, tasting our eternal happiness not only in the fact that we have attained to the possession of his infinite goodness, but above all in the fact that we see his will done in us.[1]

Authentic worship is the means to that end – our true end, which can only be ultimately found in God, in whose heart and mind alone we have existed and continue to exist from eternity to eternity. In that sense worship must always be totally unself-conscious.

This does not mean that it must be spontaneous or unrehearsed any more than good dancing is necessarily spontaneous. Nevertheless, the difference between a rehearsal and a performance is precisely in this area of unself-consciousness. The rehearsal is necessarily calculating and calculated at every step: the performance has about it, of necessity, an element of 'givenness' which opens up as a gift (or charism) that whole dimension of the transcendent. No amount of preparation or natural skills can make up for the indispensable anointing of the Holy Spirit, for in that sense all authentic worship is gifted and anointed, or 'charismatic', as some Christians prefer to say. That vestry prayer before a service should be no perfunctory way of just blowing the whistle to get all the players on to the pitch. It needs to be a prayer which opens the hearts of all those responsible for the worship to great expectations of what God is about to do in and through their ministry.

Having said all this, however, it has to be admitted that so very much of our worship in church is blatantly self-conscious. From the moment people enter the church building in their 'Sunday best', there is this strong sense of religiosity which is the ultimate enemy of true worship and self-abandoned adoration. Paradoxically enough, it is Jewish worship and also perhaps the worship of the Orthodox Churches of the East which seem most able to achieve this blend of professional and well-rehearsed authentic worship with utterly natural postures and gestures and with the minimum of self-consciousness. You might say that they are truly supernatural because they are first and foremost natural. For, as St Paul is at pains to remind us, 'It is not the spiritual which is first, but the physical, and then the spiritual' (1 Cor. 15:46), and perhaps it is nowhere more important to remember this than in our times of worship.

Yet at this point we also need to enter a note of caution, for natural is not the same as cerebral, understandable, intelligible or relevant. For too long the churches have committed themselves to scaling down their worship (in time as well as in content) with what might be termed ceremonial and biblical 'filleting'! We have been doing this in the wrong ways and for the wrong reasons. The faulty reasoning behind this reductionism is the misguided assumption that unless worship is *understood* it is not authentic and appealing to people. Yet by definition worship cannot be comprehended; on the contrary, it must be apprehended and apprehending, and able to take hold of the whole person and to take us where we would neither necessarily choose to go, nor by our own devices or enthusiasms be able to go.

It is all right to have the order of service printed out; indeed, in many ways, with a prayer book that is really a lengthy resource book and most certainly not a handbook or a pew book, you could argue that printed weekly orders of service are essential. Furthermore, anything that releases the congregation from the incessant invasion by the clergy giving out hymn numbers or page numbers is to be strongly supported and applauded. Yet at the same time let us try increasingly to release the congregation (and, indeed, also the clergy) from worshipping God with a piece of paper or a book in their hands. Both alike put an over-emphasis upon the brain and the mind to the exclusion of other senses and aspects of our total selves. So the words of worship, like the words of a drama, are perhaps best apprehended, not so much by following them on the printed page (at least not at the performance, hopefully), but rather by allowing the sheer power of the words to take hold of us and to 'speak' to us in all kinds of ways and at all sorts of different levels. In other words, you can participate in a service without necessarily following the service, and perhaps you could go even further by saying that a slavish addiction to 'following' everything in the book might even detract from our wholesale participation in the action and drama of worship. In any case, we do far better to come before God empty-handed, literally as well as metaphorically. Furthermore, if we have nothing in our hands there might be a chance that as both catholics and charismatics we might use our hands along with the rest of our bodies (get them in the air, perhaps!) in just the sort of worship which can rescue us from those inevitable wandering thoughts.

Of course, in saying all of this we must realize that any casual visitors at services may well feel rather lost and that there is certainly something to be said, therefore, for having a simple outline of the service available (possibly on a card) on request as you enter the church or, when appropriate, at the back of the church at hand for those attending one of the occasional offices such as baptisms, weddings, funerals or confirmations. In reality, of course, casual visitors are largely the exception these days and must not therefore be allowed to dictate the best ways for ordering the worship of the local church for the faithful core of regular worshippers.

Yet in all this discussion we should not underestimate the sheer power of good worship to reach people, to touch and to move them, precisely because, like some beers claim to do, it most certainly can reach the parts that so many other messages cannot reach – those very parts of our make-up that are starved and neglected in a world of more and more information and less and less communication. In this sense it is possible for good worship to commend the gospel experience (and not just the idea) and to reach and refresh not only regular worshippers but also the uninitiated and the enquirer. We often speak today of 'seeker services' when we really mean 'seeker sermons' wrapped up somewhat indifferently in a hymn sandwich. As we shall see in a later chapter, enquirer services or seeker services need to be very carefully tailored and ordered to create the proper setting in which the Word can not only be spoken but also received, in worship which has shape and direction and which moves to a climax, possibly issuing an invitation to the whole congregation to respond either in repentance, or a new-found faith or a deeper commitment.

All those responsible for leading worship or presiding at the Eucharist in today's Church must, however, take one reality very seriously to heart. The whole relationship between the worshipping Church and the rest of society has radically changed and is vastly different, to the point of being almost unrecognizable, from the situation which existed in the days when the English Prayer Book of 1662 was first published. Public worship at the close of the twentieth century is (and is likely to remain for a long time to come) primarily aimed at a very small minority of the population. From the perspective of Richard Hooker, one of the principle architects of all the political, religious and social implications of the Elizabethan religious settlement, the very fact alone of being an Englishman was exactly the same thing as being a member of the Church of England. The worshipping congregation in any of the thousands of churches up and down the land was exactly the same as the local parochial community, to a man, woman and child. So the various Prayer Books of the sixteenth- and seventeenth-century reformers were public property in one sense, in a not dissimilar way to that in which the Highway Code is public property in Britain today and not just a handbook for people who might like to drive according to the rules of the Highway Code. Today's situation in respect of the relationship between the gathered community in worship and the rest of the population of any one parish could never have been envisaged by those responsible for drawing up worship in the various books of common prayer that we have inherited.

The consequences of all this should lead us to see very clearly that almost all of Cranmer's original working presuppositions no longer apply in pastoralia, in liturgy or in the life of the Church in general in our day. They all need to be reconsidered in the light of the relationship between the active Church and its members and the rest of society at the close of the twentieth century.

This should not mean, nor should it be allowed to be interpreted in terms of the Church with its few worshipping members retreating into a ghetto mentality and pulling up the drawbridge. On the contrary, it should mean that, as active and regularly worshipping Christians, we have been set free and should remain free to see our worship in terms of the life-style of small, fragile communities of faith being built up by deeply spiritual worship to live the life of the Kingdom and to pray and work earnestly for the coming of that Kingdom. And in that sense we would do well to recall again Archbishop Temple's very quotable quote, when he reminds us that the Church is the only society which exists for the sake of those who are not members of it.

All this means that today people seldom, if ever, just drift to church. If people are in church nowadays they are probably there for better motives than they have ever been there since the peace of Constantine, when Christianity first became established and respectable. In consequence of all this, it is increasingly important that the worship and the preaching should give a substantial diet of daily bread for those who are seeking to live the life of Christ out in the world in their daily work and life. Worship today needs to build up the faithful in order that they might be faithful in their daily discipleship. In other words, the worship must be substantial and must go deep.

Of course, there will be, and indeed there should be, those times when worship is more informal – informal, yes, but never trivial. There most certainly is a place for the right kind of informality, an informality arising naturally out of the kind of occasion in which the worship is taking place. As we have already seen, on such occasions the preaching and the praying will tend to be in rather different styles in a large building where several hundred people are present, in contrast to the styling of a house communion or a small prayer group consisting of only a handful of people, gathered together in someone's home. Nevertheless, there must be about all our worship, whether in cathedral, church or cell, that ultimate sense of God's presence, the *mysterium tremendum,* for when all is said and done (and good liturgy employs both), worship is an encounter with God who is not only our friend and brother but also our Creator and Judge. Against that perspective, worship will stand or fall. As we have already said, worship will necessarily include the ingredients that speak to our minds, to our hearts and to our wills, and all these become vehicles carrying the worshipper along the way that leads to the larger and fuller realization of transcendence and coherence. It is in that transcendence and coherence that we find our healing and our peace.

So informal, then, depending upon the occasion, but never trivial; supernatural, but never unnatural; tailored for the immediate and the local, yet never trapped in the relevant and the banal as mere entertainment or, even worse, as therapy, seeking to bring about the 'feel-good factor' for its own sake. And finally, in order to be all these things, worship must be both structured and spontaneous. Like a skilful dancer it balances these two qualities in interdependence; like a bird in the heavens, it is lifted on the wings of the Spirit and ultimately brought to its place of rest and restoration in the environment of the worship of our heavenly home.

5

Signs, symbols and ceremonies

Signs and symbols in everyday life

Living worship and true liturgy are essentially the gospel in action – an action that, like all actions, has the unnerving potential of being able to speak far more loudly than words. In ordinary everyday life, we rightly regard actions and facial expressions as having great significance in what we often refer to as 'body language'. Much of our lives are conditioned and fashioned by signs, symbols and strange little ceremonies heavy with meaning, as well as powerful in evoking nostalgia. From the ceremony of inauguration of a new President of the USA to the lighting of the Olympic flame; from the breaking of a bottle of champagne when launching a ship to the passing of a loving-cup at a ceremonial dinner – in these, and in so many other ways, our everyday life, and especially our corporate and national life, is littered with outward and visible signs and ceremonies intended to convey inner meaning and deeper significance. In some ways they are a kind of shorthand, quickly conveying what would not necessarily be easily put into words. Or – and perhaps this is more important – the apt sign, symbol or ceremony is eloquent when and where words might fail or seem trite, banal or just totally inadequate or even, possibly, insensitive. Interflora thrives on that very human need of preferring to 'say it with flowers'. The ring or rings given at weddings or on the occasion of an engagement likewise bring financial returns to jewellers. In these as in so many other everyday events, the human race employs outward signs and symbols to express inner feelings and motivations. Canon Michael Perham writes that in liturgical practice we are learning that actions often speak louder than words. We need to re-educate people to think symbolically, to let the action or the gesture or the movement convey its meaning to them. In the same way that I do not (usually) before kissing my wife tell her that I am going to, and what it will mean, so with symbolic actions in liturgy, over-explanation is probably over-kill.[1]

In the liturgy and worship of the Church, the signs, symbols and ceremonies of worship are intended to convey in outward form the interior meaning and experience of the gospel. Furthermore, this gospel in its turn addresses itself to all the senses in humanity in its challenge to bring out a total and all-embracing response.

In our worship, we should become more fully human and more fully alive, more and not less alert to the signs and symbols around us at each turn in the road. So *Wachet auf* ('wake up') is not only the cry of the season of Advent in the Church's year, but it is also in a real sense the central challenge of the whole gospel. 'The glory of God is a human being fully alive,' said Irenaeus. In the words of Isaiah, it is 'the opening of the eyes to see' and the 'opening of the ears to hear'; 'the loosening of the tongue; the leaping of the lame and the speaking of the dumb'. These are all significant signs which herald the gospel and point to the coming Kingdom (Isa. 29:18–19; 35:5–6; 61:1).

In that context, it is not insignificant that when John the Baptist sent from prison to enquire whether Jesus was the Messiah, Jesus told John's enquirers to observe the signs of the Kingdom and to report back to John what they had seen, in fulfilment of that messianic text of Isaiah (Luke 7:18–23). For the Bible contends that fallen humanity is only half awake and half alive. Most of us, most of the time, are at least half deaf, dumb and blind to the ever-present glory of God right there in our midst. Little wonder, therefore, that God requires the 'sign language' of the sacraments (analogous to the sign language employed for the deaf) to convey to us his love, quite literally in flesh and blood.

In recent years, especially in the more evangelical tradition, visual aids have come to have a place of prominence in worship. That is good as far as it goes, but the trouble is that it does not go far enough, for, as Michael Perham comments, there is a difference between a visual aid devised for an occasion and a liturgical action of sacramental quality. One makes its impact by its very novelty, the other by being experienced over and over again and going deep into the soul. It is as Ash Wednesday or Maundy Thursday or Easter Day come round each year with their distinctive liturgies, that I am able to get a little closer to Christ, and become a little more deeply conformed to his pattern. But not, if the liturgy keeps changing and we never do what we did last year.[2]

In other words, there is a sense in which novelty at the level of symbols and sacramental signs can become counter-productive. The language of symbolism relies more upon nostalgia for its effect than upon novelty.

So, then, it is in the language of symbolism that the good news addresses our humanity at all kinds of levels and in the language of the senses – touch, sight, smell, sound and taste – if God's message of love and redemption is to invade and to take hold of us in the deepest recesses of our imagination. A two-dimensional message which merely goes 'in one ear and out the other' will never change lives. Thomas Carlyle wrote:

> It is in and through symbols that man, consciously or unconsciously, lives, works and has his being; those ages, moreover, are accounted the noblest which can the best recognize symbolic worth and prize it the highest. For is not a symbol ever, to him who has eyes for it, some dimmer or clearer revelation of the godlike? Of this thing, however, be certain. Wouldst thou plant for eternity, then plant into the deep infinite faculties of man, his fantasy and his heart.[3]

Worship must surely carry this capacity to plant in the fantasy and in the heart, if it is to draw mankind Godward and to tease men and women away from self-obsession and self-centredness.

Signs and symbols in Scripture

It is therefore in the nature of things that all worship must be catholic – able to speak to the whole man, all mankind, and at all times. Words are simply not sufficient for this elusive and all-encompassing means of communication. The Bible, from cover to cover, is rich in images, signs and symbols, for it addressed itself in the first instance to a people who were, happily, less sophisticated than we are today, and yet a people who were nevertheless more sensitive and open to the power and influence of the symbolic. As Christopher Bryant comments, 'The unseen creator makes himself known through things which can be seen and heard, touched and smelt, tasted and eaten.'[3]

If any or all of this rings any bells, then it is surely not surprising that we find prophets in the Old Testament acting out symbolic signs or gestures. The prophet's message was not only conveyed by words, but more dramatically by accompanying actions – actions calculated to arrest attention and to challenge at every level (Ezek. 3:1–3; Jer. 18). For the prophet had the dangerous but important task of getting under the skin of people, where it irritated and challenged most. Our worship cannot afford to be any less powerful. Good worship is not just superficial; neither is it merely cerebral and educational. It must have about it that dangerous potential to get under the skin, to irritate, to displease, but also to move and to challenge.

It is true, of course, that sometimes ceremonial signs and symbols are counter-productive, because they draw attention away from God by focusing upon themselves. Symbolism can become obscured – even obscurantist – and tamed by aesthetic considerations until it actually distracts from the very message it purports to convey. So it was that by the fifteenth century the ceremonies of the Church in the West had become so decadent that it was scarcely possible to see through them: the icon had become an idol; the means had become an end. It was against that background that the Puritans, understandably so iconoclastic, sought to tear down all that hindered plain speaking and a forthright communication of the gospel message. They wanted their worship to be clearly understood, putting all their gospel eggs in the basket of the spoken word of the gospel – pure and simple truth. (However, they were in danger of forgetting, as Oscar Wilde aptly said, that 'truth, like love, is seldom pure and never simple!')

The truth about all of us is that we are complex beyond measure in our make-up, but catholic by nature, using all our senses to explore the world around us. Just stop and watch a baby playing on the floor. Every visible object receives fascinated and wide-eyed attention. Everything has to be touched, shaken, even smelled. And, as if this were not sufficient, the object under examination is always in danger of being put into the mouth to be tasted, bitten, or even swallowed! Frequently all this is to the annoyance or bewilderment of those who would make the questionable claim of being grown-ups, who have outgrown all that sort of thing, in the name of good manners. Yet could it be that we all begin life as little 'catholics' and only later, when we have been tamed and trimmed, groomed and inhibited by manners, etiquette and the rational claims of a sensible society, are we then reduced to becoming 'puritans', restraining our senses – only half alive, partly blind, dumb, deaf and lame? If so, then the challenge of Jesus to be born again may need to be heeded more literally than perhaps we had first imagined. A born-again Christian may well need to be more aware of his senses, as he or she becomes more alive in the Spirit. So with our worship. It needs to recover in some places, and in other places to uncover, the powerful, basic biblical signs, symbols and ceremonies that are part of our tradition, so that our worship can invade every aspect of our personalities, turning our attention and our total selves towards God with a fascination and preoccupation possibly only equalled by a child in its early months, in a new world of light and sound, colour and smell, touch and taste.

This process will always have two principal enemies bent upon restraint and reduction: they are the enemy of the intellect and the enemy of the well-ordered sacristy and the tidy sacristan! The intellect will always be in danger of playing the role of the spoil-sport! It will continually be checking, in an analytical way, whether or not this or that experience 'makes sense'. Of course, in one way there is nothing wrong in that, because it is the responsibility of the intellect to act as a check and balance on the other senses. But that is its proper task, neither more nor less. And it should not claim to be the ultimate and necessarily overriding criterion or to play the judge and jury in every case. The intellect is simply an important instrument in a larger orchestra, while the overriding balance or harmony belongs to that more subtle and intangible presence within all of us – the *anima* rather than the *animus*. Our spirit should permeate and transcend all our senses and sensitivities if we are to be whole and wholesome in our response to the deepest experiences in our lives.

The second enemy of living and authentic symbols, signs and ceremonies in worship is, of course, the altar guild or sacristan. Perhaps, together with the organist and professional church musician as close rivals, it is those good ladies of the altar guilds (second only to the parson) who over the years have been most responsible for the emasculation of worship. Probably the reason for this is that scriptural symbols are somewhat messy and inconvenient. Fire, water, oil, ashes – to name but a few – can soon make an awful mess. It is not surprising, therefore, that before long, well-intentioned sacristans began to look around for tame, nice, clean, ecclesiastical varieties of these rather improper and inconvenient symbols. Hard on the heels of the altar guild (for the one breeds and encourages the other) you will find ecclesiastical shops springing up that purport to sell an ecclesiastical variety of everything from bread (which does not even remotely look, taste or feel like bread) to wine bottled under the label of 'sanctuary' or 'church' wine. So the list grows, from candles that do not burn too much, fonts that are the size of a teacup, palms neatly folded into little crosses so that they no longer even remotely resemble a palm, all the way to the church furnishings – clean, expensive, but no longer 'in touch' with the roots of the original symbol and therefore absurdly emptied of all significance and powerless to speak. Such manufactured symbols are trivial, emasculated and possibly, therefore, impotent to convey the inner message of the gospel towards which they should be drawing the attention of the worshippers.

Renewal demands that in this area of preparing and styling our worship we be genuinely radical. We must go back to the Scriptures and traditions of the Church to find out the inner meaning of each symbol, sign and ceremony and then look around (and, if needs be, shop around) for the most powerful and authentic contemporary equivalents for use in our worship of God, who is beyond common sense or plain, straightforward communication.

Water

It is not surprising that there are over 700 references in the Scriptures to water or waters, for water is the most basic ingredient in all life. It is the very environment in which we were conceived and a fundamental necessity for all new life. In hot, desert countries water is carefully guarded and its use is even legally restricted. Among the aborigines in Australia, the watering holes are the holy places and the shrines, so that for a long time to misuse these places or to violate them was punishable with death. It is significant, perhaps, that in the Bible water appears in the opening verses of Genesis as well as in the closing verses of Revelation. The presence of water is there at the beginning and at the end. In the book of Ezekiel, the vision of the prophet portrays water – and especially flowing water – as the dynamic of new life and mission.

In the New Testament the largest number of references to water appears in St John's Gospel and in the book of Revelation. For as in the rest of Scripture, in the imagery of St John, water and new life go together. Where there is water there is life; where there is no water, life will not last for long. This fact of life is especially striking as you fly low over the desert: wherever there is water, the unbroken arid brown is suddenly relieved by a belt of green on the edge of a river or by a wadi.

Roughly speaking, the long list of biblical references to water can be divided into three main categories. There is water for washing and cleansing; there is water for drinking, refreshment and sustenance; and there is the more subtle image of water as a sea, flood or river through which we pass, in which we can be drowned or overwhelmed, and from which we are delivered and raised up. It is appropriate that in the order for baptism in the *New American Prayer Book* there is an eloquent prayer which expresses this:

> We thank you, Almighty God, for the gift of water. Over it the Holy Spirit moved in the beginning of creation. Through it you led the children of Israel out of their bondage in Egypt into the land of promise. In it your Son Jesus received the baptism of John and was anointed by the Holy Spirit as the Messiah, the Christ, to lead us through his death and resurrection, from the bondage of sin into everlasting life.[5]

Water also marks an overwhelming experience of going under and undergoing – a drowning – the experience of being out of our depth and all which that suggests.

The theological implications of the waters of baptism are simply massive, spelled out in an extended vocabulary of imagery. It is not too much to see baptism as the fountain of all renewal in the life of the Church, and yet it is this symbol which the established churches have tended to trivialize almost out of all recognition. The font has become the play-toy of every church architect, seeking to speak only to our aesthetic sensitivities, to the point where the deliberately inconvenient and dynamic symbolism of water – and flowing water at that – has almost been completely obscured. This is apparent in the practice of indiscriminate child baptism and the place that it still so often holds in the timetable of church services, where it is tamed and relegated to the proportions of cosy tea parties on Sunday afternoons. It is also demonstrated by the way in which the fundamental sacrament is so frequently and wrongly administered.

Ideally, the font should be housed and located in a proper baptistry that either adjoins the entrance to the church or is a separate building altogether. We should physically, literally and architecturally enter the church through the baptistry. Furthermore, the concept of 'undergoing' and drowning is central to the imagery of baptism in the New Testament, and that is certainly a long way from the pious reductionism of the average 'sprinkling' that so often masquerades as immersion. Even worse is the practice (so often seen at services of baptism and confirmation) of placing a plinth at the front of the church with a small flower bowl on top of it, containing a glass bowl full of water and naively expecting that this reduced and tamed symbol can 'speak' to the imagination in the name of washing, cleansing and renewing, let alone in the more profound symbolism and imagery of drowning and death.

It is refreshing to see in many new churches an architectural commitment to the many-faceted symbolism of baptism. Sometimes the baptistry is built in the floor of the church, making possible the image of moving or living water, and even permitting baptism in a fashion akin to that of immersion. There is now available special commercial lighting which, if allowed to flood the font, brings the water in the font 'to life' in appearance, in a quite dramatic and significant way. These, together with the ceremonial of a solemn procession to the font for adult baptism, can recall the whole people of God to the central reality of the new life in Christ which baptism is intended to stimulate and symbolize. In churches where incense is used to highlight other significant moments and places in the liturgy, it is no bad thing to cense the font after it is blessed and before people are baptized in it.

The ceremony at the font at the Easter Day Eucharist, if conducted by the bishop at dawn, with new Christians for baptism as well as confirmation, fresh from lengthy catechesis and preparation culminating in a devout observance of Lent, can bring annual renewal to the whole congregation. The font is then genuinely seen as the womb of the new life of the church, made fertile by the invoking of the Holy Spirit, through solemn prayer, fasting and vigil. In this liturgy, the procession to the font – in which the new Christians are led by their bishop to the waters of initiation – is traditionally accompanied by the singing of the age-old 'litany of the saints'. Such revitalized liturgy sets this great sacrament and sign of baptism in the context of eternity and within the framework of the fellowship of all God's people, living and departed. 'Our citizenship is in heaven,' while on earth, our status is ambivalent – at best, perhaps something more akin to that of resident aliens!. For baptism in Christ is the watershed of the evolution of the human race, and living liturgy will always seek to do all it can to identify and locate this reality on the map of human experience. It should be recognized, as it is in the prophecy of Ezekiel (Ezek. 47), as the huge river of new life, flowing northwards, southwards, eastwards and westwards from the temple of the presence of God through the historical Christ, irrigating and watering the desert of human history, retrospectively to the dawn of mankind as well as pointing forwards to the end of time.

Bread and wine

Whatever other layers of significance may have rightly been accrued to the eucharistic act since New Testament times, it is still essentially a meal or a banquet at which bread is broken and wine is drunk. 'Man is what he eats,' wrote Feuerbach in what he intended to be a very reductionist and materialistic statement. Paradoxically, however, he could not have made a more Christian and sacramental statement. For we are indeed what we eat, and that is why Christians are invited to eat Christ's Body: in order to become his Body (precisely as St Augustine so insistently taught). Furthermore, as eating and drinking are so very basic to the whole of human life, they have become part of the natural ritual of civilization, with all the appropriate conventions, ceremonial and habits that have become attached to this daily and (generally) corporate activity in the common life of all nations and cultures. We become 'companions' (Latin, *cum pane*) with those with whom we eat or share our bread. Places where people have met to eat and drink have frequently become centres of new life, new thought and civilization, whether it be the coffee houses of Parisian life or the English public house.

It is not surprising, therefore, that liturgy becomes more powerfully expressive wherever this basic and central imagery of the meal is made explicit in eucharistic worship. Jesus, during his earthly ministry in Palestine, was nothing less than notorious for his habit of eating and drinking with sinners. For example, on the occasion when Jesus went into the house of Zaccheus for a meal, his Jewish critics were swift to observe that once again he was keeping company with publicans and sinners, and eating with them in just those places where the formal rules and rituals of good Jewish practice were probably not observed. Similarly, Christ's enemies were all too ready to comment on his presence at a great feast given by Matthew on the day of his call and conversion. Most of the recorded resurrection appearances were in the context of a meal together with the disciples, and it is surely not insignificant that Jesus' apostolic commissioning to Peter in St John's Gospel is recorded in terms of feeding, and not just as an abstract call to a ministry of preaching or to the spreading of his gospel idea: 'Feed my lambs: feed my sheep,' said Jesus. Some New Testament critics even wish to build up a whole concept of the teaching literature of the Gospels around the table talk of Jesus, so basic was the concept of the corporate meal to the identity of Jesus and his disciples – the Body of Christ. Everything, therefore, that helps to express this basic and central imagery of a meal at the Eucharist leads to an enhancement in eucharistic worship. Clifford Howell writes:

We begin from a fundamental meaning: to share food and drink with others is to have a meal together. Bread and wine are food and drink. Our Lord took bread and said 'Eat', he took wine and said

'Drink'. The memorial of himself which he then instituted has therefore the form of a meal. In the beginning it looked like a meal, had the character of a meal and was experienced as a meal by those who took part in it. Why? Because they did in fact *eat* by putting food (bread) into their mouths, and then masticating and swallowing it. Also they *drank* by imbibing and swallowing liquid (wine). These are the actions usual at a meal. They knew indeed that what they ate was not ordinary bread (though it continued to look like bread). It had become the Body of Christ given for them. And they knew that what they drank was not ordinary wine (though it continued to look and taste like wine). It had become the Blood of Christ shed for them. But this knowledge derogated in no way from their consciousness that they were sharing a meal together. They realized that it was a very special meal, a sacred meal, an act of religion and not merely the taking of nourishment. But it was nevertheless a genuine meal. It was, moreover, a unifying meal. The bread brought to the altar was in the form of flat loaves, half an inch or more thick, several inches across. To be eaten, such loaves had to be broken into pieces of manageable size after the consecration. These were distributed. Thus each loaf was shared among several people – ten, a dozen or more. And the wine was in one or more cups according to how many people were present. From each cup a number of people drank the consecrated wine. The meaning of all this as expounded by St Paul (I Corinthians 10, 16 and 17) was quite clear. They 'got the message' that those who shared in one loaf or drank from one cup became one in Christ.[6]

Sadly, eucharistic symbolism has degenerated, as has so much other symbolism in the Church. The symbolism has become an end in itself, and the grit of the symbol – which is intended to fascinate and stimulate the imagination – has been worked over to such an extent that it has been largely lost inside a liturgical pearl – albeit a beautiful and aesthetically pleasing one. In that sense, the eucharistic species are in serious danger of becoming a defective sign. It is true, of course, that if a chemical analysis were to be made of genuine bread and then of the eucharistic wafers made in convents or by some ecclesiastical manufacturer, the results would be sufficiently alike to enable us to be fulfilling the Lord's command of taking bread. Yet, if we are honest, we must surely admit that the eucharistic wafers used in many churches simply do not *look* like bread. So often the 'bread' used in our churches for the Eucharist defies all the basic necessities of the original eucharistic imagery and symbolism. The bread is not substantial enough for us even to feel that we are really eating it. It just melts! Jesus told us to take it and to eat it. Furthermore the basic imagery of taking and eating a loaf of bread divided among many is further lost when the priest – as so often happens – retains a so-called 'priest's host' (a large host); and although he eats it, it is not for the purpose of sharing – on the contrary, it is peculiarly *his* host! Hence much important further symbolism is lost.

However, neither are things significantly improved in those churches where white sliced bread is used. On the contrary, the whole image of the fraction, the breaking, is completely lost in a soggy mess of crumbs. There are even churches where only the small white wafers are used for the Communion, without even the benefit of a larger priest's wafer, and in such cases any concept of breaking the bread is totally absent and utterly obscured. In such ways as these, a classic and basic symbol is lost and rapidly degenerates, whenever the secondary (and generally aesthetic) considerations leave other, more primary, considerations far behind. When something symbolic has become simply symbolic, it is no longer a pure symbol. Rather, it becomes contaminated out of all recognition. For whatever else the Eucharist in the New Testament was intended to portray, this basic action of taking bread, giving thanks for it, and then breaking it, is surely fundamental to the whole eucharistic liturgy.

It is clear from the very manner in which Jesus took bread, handled and broke it that his actions so riveted the attention and imagination of his disciples that it was supremely those same actions that disclosed the risen Lord in the post-Resurrection appearances – most significantly of all on the road to Emmaus.

Having criticized the trivializing of the basic image of bread so common in many churches, it is a good deal less easy to come up with an answer which is both practical and effective in recovering bread as a sacramental sign. In the case of a small eucharistic gathering in a house group, it is perhaps easy to take a round wholemeal bun and use this as eucharistic bread, easily broken (for it should never be cut), preserving the symbol of sharing one bread –

and all without too many crumbs. But it is quite another matter to use such breads on an occasion when there is a large congregation. In some places, there is the practice of using priest's wafers and breaking these into four or six parts. There are also recipes for making large, flat, round crisp-breads. These can be broken conveniently and they taste, look and feel like bread.

Although we must not make an issue out of all this, we must recognize the absolute necessity of recovering authenticity in the basic symbol of the central and characteristic act of Christian worship. So, equally, with the wine, and with the manner in which it is used, at eucharistic celebrations. It should be good wine (mixed with water, as in the East) and not ecclesiastical wine, which is generally inferior in quality and unnecessarily expensive for what it is. Whatever wine is used, it should, however, be offered in a cup or chalice that clearly resembles a common cup. There are some lovely ceramic eucharistic cups available today and also some simple pottery cups that are most effective in an appropriate situation, and all of these are certainly more suitable than the ecclesiastically marketed silver-plated ones frequently made in bad imitation of medieval chalices. Indeed, at large eucharistic gatherings few things look more unedifying than rows and rows of silver chalices of all different shapes and sizes on a large altar. (Frankly, they can sometimes resemble Grandmother's display of silver on the sideboard on high days and holidays!) Simple, identical pottery chalices are far more telling and are probably best held by the assisting ministers during the eucharistic prayer of consecration rather than stacked in rows upon the altar.

In these and in so many other ways the image of the Eucharist as a meal needs to be uncovered in our generation, and we need sensitivity as well as imagination to get it right on differing occasions where numbers and locations vary so enormously.

One further eucharistic image is worthy of mention at this point. For eucharistic food is traditionally also perceived as food for a journey – whether it be the journey and pilgrimage in this world or that further journey through death to the fuller life beyond. In the old Israel, the Passover meal was eaten in haste with shoes on the feet and staff in hand, ready for the journey. Food for the journey is perhaps best received standing, walking to a Communion station in the church, singing together with all

God's people as men and women on pilgrimage and on the journey of life. Pious, individualistic attitudes and postures in the Eucharist are in this sense alien to the corporate nature of eucharistic celebration.

We shall probably not get this right, however, until we redress the balance between corporate worship and personal spirituality. Each has its place. At the moment, 'going to church' represents so often the sum total of the Christian's life of prayer and worship. Naturally, therefore, there is a danger that we try to use the liturgy for all aspects of spirituality, with the constant danger of falling between all alternatives. Of course, there must be a place and time for the personal prayer of the heart, with silence and stillness, in which various individual postures, such as kneeling or sitting upright with hands extended, can rightly be adopted. This should be balanced, however, by the corporate expression of worship in the liturgy of the whole people of God. Both are needed and they are complementary to each other, yet they should not be confused. In particular, the corporate activity of eucharistic worship should not degenerate into individual piety. Kneeling, as in the Middle Ages, and sitting, as in the Reformation reaction, are both distortions of corporate worship. Happily, there is a return in our own day to a more primitive and basic understanding of the Eucharist as food for pilgrims on the move together, singing as they go, and any practical arrangements (even down to church furnishing and layout) which by implication emphasize this dimension of the eucharistic journey should be strongly encouraged – though these will doubtless be strongly resisted in the name of 'interfering with *my* Communion'. Alexander Schmemann carries this symbolism even further when he writes, 'The liturgy of the Eucharist is best understood as a journey or procession. It is the journey of the Church into the dimension of the Kingdom ... The journey begins when Christians leave their home and beds.'[7]

Lights of the world

There can be few more basic images and signs in religious language in general, as well as in Christian symbolism in particular, than light and (by implication) its contrasting opposite, darkness.

It is well worth scrutinizing a Bible concordance and looking up all the references to light, especially in St John's Gospel, where it is an important and recurring motif throughout all the chapters.

Christ is the light of the world, and Christians in their turn are challenged also to be lights of the world, and to 'Let your light so shine before men, that they may see your good works and give glory to your Father who is in heaven' (Matt 5:16). It is significant that in the Early Church the great liturgy of the dawn of Easter morning, celebrated wherever possible by the bishop, centred on the liturgy of Christian initiation – baptism and confirmation. The great vows of the new Christians would be taken as the dawn was breaking and as the light of Easter broke through the darkness of sin and death. So when those about to be baptized were asked to turn to Christ they would literally turn from facing the darkness of the night to facing the light of the day, from west to east. Further-more, among the many ceremonies and symbols accompanying baptism from early times, there was the practice of handing to the baptismal candidate a lighted candle as a token and sign that he or she had 'passed from darkness to light' and must therefore hence-forth 'shine as a light in the world to the glory of God the Father'.

Liturgically, light is used at its most powerful as a symbol in the first part of the paschal liturgy, the Easter vigil. Increasingly, the whole Church is beginning to recover the centrality of the Holy Week liturgy in general, but especially the liturgy of the Three Great Days (the Triduum) – Maundy Thursday, Good Fri-day and Easter Day. These liturgies employ every device of Scrip-ture and symbolism to demonstrate the reality of Christ's death and resurrection – the central mystery of our faith, the pattern of our redemption, and the shape and profile of our Christian identi-ty. In one sense, the more arresting and extreme the timing of the Easter liturgy can be, the better. Ideally, it should be at dawn on Easter morning, forming the climax of a whole night of vigil.

Vigil is central to Christian spirituality, and this should increasingly be expressed liturgically. Many young people today have responded to the challenge and opportunity of vigil. The ideal shape and substance of vigil is to tell the story of redemption by readings, songs, and reflection throughout the whole night. The much-reduced seven readings allotted for the Easter vigil nowadays, followed by chants and prayers, constitute a skeleton outline and a framework for what can be a remarkably powerful experience. Rather a whole night should be spent watching and reflecting upon the story of our redemption (perhaps, for the sake of the weaker brethren, punctuated with flasks of coffee!), culminating in the kindling of fire, lighting of candles, and the renewal of baptismal vows. Neither should the use of a vigil necessarily be restricted to Easter, for it can well form the focus of renewal festivals and celebrations in parishes and dioceses at all times of the year. All great feasts should be preceded by a vigil: not so much a silent or individualistic one, nor indeed a vigil only for the pious, but rather a corporate and boisterous activity of all God's people – children of the light and lights of the world.

The first part of the Easter vigil is essentially the service of light, when we pray that we may share in the light of God's glory, through Jesus, the light of the world. So it is, that from newly kindled fire, the large Easter (paschal) candle is lit and carried into the darkened church in front of the congregation. It is held high and is splendidly accompanied by the threefold proclamation: 'The Light of Christ'. From this candle, all individual candles in the church take their light, until the darkened church is aglow with the Easter light of Christ's resurrection.

But the paschal candle (if it is really large and held high in procession by the deacon, as is the tradition) carries with it also the further symbolism of the deliverance of God's chosen people from the bondage of Egypt through the Red Sea of baptism, into the desert, and on to the promised land. Ahead of the Israelites journeying through the desert by night was a pillar of fire, and so the paschal candle should always be a large tall candle, realistically capable of carrying this further symbolism so obviously evoked from our story as God's people delivered from the bondage of sin and journeying to the land of promise. Since all this symbolism belongs essentially in the context of deliverance and redemption, the most appropriate resting place for the paschal candle throughout the year should be in a conspicuous position beside the font. The candles given to the candidates at baptism should be lit from the flame of the paschal candle. In every way this central symbolism of the Easter candle must have about it a shape, size and significance that enables God's people to pray and sing with credibility the glorious words of the *Exultet:*

Rejoice heavenly powers, sing choirs of angels,
exult all creation around God's throne.
Jesus Christ the Lord is risen, sound the trumpet of salvation now.

The singing of the *Exultet* (if it is sung) must be done very well
indeed by a soloist, traditionally a deacon, but it may be sung by
the congregation in unison from a modern version. It should be
sung so boisterously that it could well resemble a dance around
the paschal fire. If it is not well sung, it is probably best recited and
proclaimed boldly instead. It must not become just an ecclesiastical and tamed (even tiresome and tedious) plainsong rendering! It
is essentially a proclamation with all the fire of the gospel about it.
Indeed, the paschal liturgy well done is perhaps one of the greatest
gospel experiences of the Church's liturgy and is worthy of the
greatest possible care in its preparation and presentation.

Although the paschal candle is central in our use of fire and
light as powerful scriptural symbols in worship, the extensions of
this symbol are many and varied. In the twentieth century, the use
of candles or illumination in a church building presupposes the
proper use of electric light. With the help of dimmers and framing
spotlights, referred to elsewhere in this book, together with many
other contemporary lighting devices, the lighting of the church
building has today very remarkable possibilities indeed for good
drama and theatre – which also have their part to play in good
worship and liturgy. Properly used, it should highlight the important and significant parts of the church building, probably leaving
whole areas of the building in softer light or even deliberately in
the shadow. Against such a background, candles have an important place and can be used to great effect – for example, to highlight and flank the Gospel book or Scriptures, or the cross,
whether stationary or carried in procession. A light near icons or
religious pictures or statues is also very effective. Thank goodness
these things can be discussed today without raising questions about
the brands of churchmanship or party slogans. Many places which
are experiencing renewal in common prayer from both the Protestant and Catholic traditions effectively use small votive night-
lights and candles, creating as they do so a gentle and comforting
atmosphere and a heightened awareness conducive to prayer.

In the newly published office book, *Celebrating Common Prayer* (extensively examined in Chapter 8), there is provision for a simple service of the blessing of lights. If the church is in some darkness at the beginning of worship, then special anthems of light (*Lucernaria*) can be said or preferably sung while the lights are lit. There is provision for incense to be used as an accompanying symbol to the words 'Let my prayer rise before you as incense' (Ps. 141), and the use of the ancient and well-known canticle from the Eastern Church, the *phos hilaron*:

O gladsome light, O grace
of God the Father's face.
The eternal splendour wearing;
Celestial, holy, blest,
Our Saviour Jesus Christ,
Joyful in your appearing.

As day fades into night,
we see the evening light.
Our hymns of praise outpouring:
Father of might unknown,
Christ, his incarnate Son,
and Holy Spirit adoring.

Such an evening ceremony can then continue with evening prayer, or Compline, or the Eucharist, or a simple fellowship meal. It is a wonderful use of a basic and simple image, partially functional in origin, certainly scriptural in significance, and incidentally powerful and aesthetically persuasive in creating an environment for prayer and worship.

In the Christian understanding of time, as in the tradition of the old Israel, the evening has a very special place, belonging as it does to the following day. So Alexander Schmemann writes:

Contrary to our secular experience of time, the liturgical day begins with Vespers, and this means in the evening. This is, of course, the reminiscence of the biblical 'and the evening and the morning were the first day' (Genesis 1:5). Yet it is more than a reminiscence. For it is, indeed, the end of each 'unit' of time that reveals its pattern and meaning, that gives to time its reality. Time is always growth, but only at the end can we decide the direction of that growth and see its fruits.

So for a Christian, the evening service

> does not begin as a religious 'epilogue' of the day, as a prayer *added* to all other experience. It begins at the *beginning,* and this means in the 'rediscovery', in adoration and thanksgiving, for the world and God's creation. The church takes us, as it were, to that first evening on which man, called by God to life, opened his eyes and saw what God in his love was giving to him, saw all the beauty, all the glory of the temple in which he was standing, and rendered thanks to God.[8]

It is in that context that our evening worship makes scriptural sense, and it is in that context that we light the evening lights in anticipation of the dawn, not only of the next day, but of the new age for which Christians are called to be in constant vigil.

A final word concerning lights and their place in outdoor processions and services. By and large the established churches in Britain, at least, are not very good at this sort of worship. They have never been compelled to learn to deal with the hazards of worship outside the cosy and constrained limits of a church building. So very often, such church processions as we undertake appear dreary and timid, because we insist upon carrying our indoor church furniture out into the street, where it is dwarfed into insignificance by competition with a larger environment, in every sense. A cross in an outdoor procession, for example, probably needs to be specially made (almost to life-size proportions) if it is to *register* in the imagination and make a statement about Christ's cross on the larger stage of an outdoor service.

Furthermore, it is no use having ecclesiastical candles purchased from ecclesiastical manufacturers if you are intent upon effective worship in the market place or the town square. In fact, experience would teach us that nothing less than flaming torches will stand up to the challenge of a more robust environment. Burning torches to represent candles are probably best obtained from hardware stores, or it may be necessary to go to firms where it is possible to buy well-engineered lights and fires and flames that burn butane gas or other fuels. All this demands imagination, thought and very careful planning.

Oil

The return throughout all the churches to the primitive use of anointing with oil should be welcomed on the grounds of its scriptural authority. Oil in the Bible generally refers to olive oil, which formed a part of the threefold essential economy in the ancient world: corn, wine and oil. Oil was used medicinally on an open wound (Isa. 1:6; Luke 10:4) and therefore it is not surprising that the Scriptures should speak of anointing with oil in miraculous healings (Mark 6:13; James 5:14).

Oil also had a cosmetic use, so that in Luke 7:46 it was expected that the host would anoint his guest at a banquet. It was the Pharisee's neglect of this apparently expected courtesy that is so devastatingly contrasted with the sinful woman's lavish use of the much more expensive myron (oil of myrrh) to anoint the feet of Jesus. Add to all of this the use of oil by athletes in the ancient world (as indeed, in our own day), and it can be seen that oil is a sacramental substance, an outward form with a distinctive use that easily points to an interior and deeper significance. For St Augustine, confirmation was the oil of chrism, an enriching in Christ, so it is good that in some churches today oil is restored for use in baptism and confirmation as well as for anointing the sick and anointing (for further chrismating) on occasions of renewal and rededication.

It is appropriate that the oil used in the diocese for all of these ministries should be blessed by the bishop, especially on the occasion of the reaffirmation of priestly vows on Maundy Thursday. In the whole extension of our understanding of ministry, diversified yet unified under the oversight of the bishop, the healing ministry has happily been placed high on the agenda. To be anointed nowadays is not regarded as necessarily the same thing as receiving the last rites in preparation for death, but rather as a further strengthening and refreshing for the pilgrimage of faith. Seen in this wider context of ministry, anointing with oil can be used at the end of a parish mission and indeed at all times when there is a real reaching out to a further and deeper commitment to Christ and to a further chrismating of God's people.

Anointing with oil, however, should never be allowed to deteriorate or degenerate into a fancy or fussy 'high church' ceremonial. Rather, it should always have about it something of its robust Old Testament character. In the Old Testament, the anointing of God's people is intended to renew the vocation of the old Israel to be a truly priestly people, a royal priesthood and a dedicated people, which in turn was a prophetic sign of God's desire to set his people apart for their royal and priestly responsibilities and vocation in and for all the nations of the world. Paul extends this symbolism when he reminds Christians that they have embarked upon a race and a rugged combat.

We can see how oil can be used in conjunction with the laying on of hands, but it should be reserved for its primary sense of the further chrismating of God's people. Laying-on-of-hands is for a specific purpose (usually named in the accompanying prayer) and is sometimes administered to people on the fringe of the Church to bring healing, comfort and solace. Anointing with oil is a specific encounter related to our life in Christ and our distinctive vocation in baptism, as branches of the One True Vine, recalling us ever more closely to our basic identity in relationship to Christ, to our mystical life in him.

Stillness and movement: silence and space

In just the same way as light presupposes shadow and darkness, so all church furnishings and ceremonials are set within the context of space. It is so sad to see a church cluttered with pews. There are few things more telling in church architecture than the nave of a vast cathedral where the pews have been removed. We see the pillars then as they were intended to be seen, rising out of the ground like vast trees, uncluttered and majestic in their isolated splendour, irresistibly drawing our eyes heavenwards towards the larger and more generous environment in which all our earthly activities find their proper context and proportions. The clutter of church furniture so often contradicts or even obliterates the basic lines of a building and all that the building is trying to say in its architectural eloquence. How often a church building has come alive for worship when, for some practical reason or other, it has been compelled to be stripped of all its furnishings. In fact it is not a bad exercise from time to time – for cleaning or other purposes – to strip the church building in order to disclose the hidden potential of the whole space which the building demarcates. In this way it is possible as well as desirable to leave plenty of space for movement. Teach people to come into church and sit or stand in all parts of the building, viewing from different aspects and using the lines and lights of the building as aids to worship.

Space leaves the opportunity for movement and dance, which are increasingly employed in worship and liturgy today. For, ideally, the liturgy in itself is a kind of dance with a rhythm of stillness and movement. If worship is to have something of the dance about it, then each part of the liturgy should naturally flow into the next part without a hiccup of self-consciousness and without any stumbling. In fact nothing in a well-ordered service needs to be 'given out'. Readings should flow into silence and then from there into a vocal response either with an anthem or in the singing of a hymn. All 'prompting' should be kept to a minimum. When dance is used, it should heighten and elaborate a movement already integral to the liturgy, like the Gospel or the offertory procession, rather than being an isolated event in itself intruding into the liturgy. The Gospel narratives cry out for some form of dramatic reading (as in the passion narratives) and also for some accompanying dance or drama, and always the more simple it is, the more effective it is likely to be. It should never deteriorate into a sophisticated and eclectic activity, for nothing could be further from the hallmark of good liturgy. The stillness and the movement belong to each other and lead us – as in a great symphony or in a ballet – to the natural climax. We should not be ashamed to see good liturgy as an art form, requiring all the discipline and skills of other art forms, as it creates an interdependence between stillness and movement, silence and speech, symbols and space.

And so to the place of silence in the worship of God. Why is it that we find silence in liturgy so difficult? Of course, we all find silence difficult today. Bishop John Baker writes:

Silence can be a terrifying thing. Silence, you see, is quite different from peace and quiet. You can have peace and quiet over a drink with friends in a pub, or listening to records with your girlfriend, or using up your energy resources driving out on Sunday. If you are feeling dreadfully ill, say, with a severe virus infection, but not delirious, to be left alone in bed, warm and undisturbed, that is peace and quiet. But suppose you feel all right: suppose you are in hospital, or in isolation, waiting for the results of crucial tests, perhaps in a darkened room wanting to know whether your life can be saved, or immobilized after an eye operation: that is not peace and quiet, that is silence. And silence is not necessarily peace.

Silence is loneliness, perhaps the most acute form of loneliness there is. If you shut someone in total darkness for long enough, the brain will invent hallucinations because the absence of visual stimuli would otherwise drive them mad. In much the same way, if there is nothing to hear, babel breaks out in our head. Our own mind starts talking to us, frantically, in a panic. Of course, it says the first thing that comes into our head, so to speak; but that may be the very last thing we want to hear.[9]

And there is the clue to the right kind of silence. For silence in liturgy is not the absence of words or any audible activity: it is the culmination of words. It heralds the presence of the Word in a way that no words could ever do. Silence is the other side of speech and the natural fulfilment of it, as well as the climax of all that has gone before it. It is this understanding of silence that will guide those responsible for leading worship. There will be nothing awkward or self-conscious in silence, if clergy and congregation alike have learned to be at home in silence and to respond to it with expectation and attention. Lessons will not abruptly end with a verbal guillotine: 'The Word of the Lord' or 'Here ends the reading.' The words of the lesson will end, but they will point us to the presence of the Word in our midst and will lead us therefore to penitence, thanksgiving and adoration.

There have been recent experiments with a silent liturgy of the Word. After the entrance of the priest, the introductory prayers and an act of penitence, there is then a period of up to ten or fifteen minutes of silence in the place where Scripture is usually read. After this the liturgy continues with the eucharistic prayer.

Such a practice does not arise from any downgrading of the importance of Scripture in worship, but rather from a realization that the power and authority of the written or spoken words of Scripture are derived from the presence and Spirit of the silent Word. The words of Scripture are but a 'sacrament' of the presence of the hidden and silent Word. All sacraments as well as the Scriptures are but vehicles, helping us to receive into our hearts the presence of the Word, so that he may be enfleshed in his people. In this way the Incarnation becomes a continuous and contemporary event. 'When all things were in quiet silence, and night was in the midst of her swift course, thine all powerful Word leapt down from heaven, out of thy royal throne' (Wisd. 18:14–15). Although this is especially the experience of Christians at Christmas, it should also be the joyful experience of all Christians at all times, and not least when we are gathered together for worship.

Worship should afford us all kinds of opportunities for silence. What about the silence before the service begins? Why do we necessarily have a prelude or voluntary right up to the beginning of the service? It is a pity to think of music being used as a kind of acoustical polyfiller! Perhaps after some music, at about two minutes to time, the simple welcome from the local priest with the announcements and even perhaps a few page numbers as 'stage directions' could then be followed by a bidding to silence and expectation. Then at a given (silent) signal, the organ bursts out with a play-over of the first hymn, and people rise unbidden to their feet for worship and praise. The silence during the service, especially after the solemn reading of God's Word, is very important. No one moves – not even the reader – as the last words of the scriptural passage are allowed to ring out with their clarion call to obedience and discipleship. (There is something to be said, sometimes, for no concluding sentence of any kind at this point in the service, as this suggests the termination of the Word, which, as we have already said, is not what is intended at all.) There is a particularly appropriate place for silence after the sermon, and certainly at some point during the intercessions in what was sometimes termed 'the Prayer of the Church'.

Properly understood, stillness and silence belong together as the context for attention and listening. The place of bodily stillness cannot be too strongly emphasized for those responsible for leading worship or for presiding at the liturgy. Mannerisms and fidgeting detract from worship and attention. So for goodness' sake 'Stand still! Don't fidget!' There should be no pieces of paper or books in your hand, and there should certainly be no cleaning of spectacles or fidgeting with handkerchiefs! For God's sake and the sake of his people – quite literally – be still, so that you may be a still centre for the whole proceedings. (For some clergy this discipline will require a whole course of learning and even a total reordering of their lives; clergy are, as a race, such inveterate fidgets.)

The hands in worship should be empty: extended, preferably raised in prayer before God our Father. The collect (or prayer for the day) should be said strongly and slowly after a bidding and silence, with hands extended and raised (and the book from which it is read should be either held by an attendant or placed on a reading desk). The hands are so important in all worship, and the whole people of God should be taught how to use them expressively in their prayer and worship, both privately and publicly.

And finally, the voice. The voice is such an expressive and sensitive instrument of the body. So seldom do clergy know how to use it. Most clergy need to be retrained to discover a good, strong, natural, sensitive voice, pitched neither too high nor too low, too loud nor too soft for the particular occasion. There must be no affectation of any kind. (It is so sad that it is frequently possible to tell from which seminary a priest has come the very moment he opens his mouth in public, and in every case it represents a hideous distortion of the good voice that God originally gave him!) The parsonical voice is perhaps only a close second to that most hideous of all distortions – the hearty voice – with its studied 'friendly' and informal note. Worship may be informal, but it is never trivial. There is nothing of the cosy chat about Christian worship; it is an encounter with God, who is both our judge and our king, as well as our Father and our friend. The tone set must be that of taking God seriously, just as we have to take our friends seriously and those whom we love.

So in every way, from the moment of entering the church to the moment of leaving it, everything must conspire to the one end: to bring men and women personally and corporately into the presence of God for service, worship, praise and adoration. The whole enterprise is nothing less than a massive and skilful undertaking, while at the same time it ultimately depends totally upon the free and unsolicited gift of God's grace and his presence, without which it would degenerate into a meaningless charade. In worship, as in every other area of Christian life, the balance between what we do and what God does for us and in us is not so easy to find. It is perhaps best summed up in the aphorism of St Augustine: 'Without God we cannot; without us he will not.'

Nothing less than all of this is the agenda next Sunday morning in every church all across the country, as well as in a thousand different cells of Christian worship in homes and in ordinary places where men and women, boys and girls, gather to worship God in Christ. The task for next Sunday morning is powerfully summarized and expressed in the lovely words of William Cowper:

> Here may be prove the power of prayer,
> To strengthen faith and sweeten care;
> To teach our faint desires to rise
> And bring all heaven before our eyes.[10]

Or in the words of T. S. Eliot:

> You are here to kneel
> Where prayer has been validated.[11]

6

Music and worship

Music as the bicycle of the liturgy

Music and worship have always belonged together, and at its best this has been a partnership of complementary roles rather than a competitive struggle. For music is essentially the bicycle of the liturgy. C. Henry Phillips writes: 'From experience, men have found that music not only kindles the imagination but serves as the most practical vehicle of corporate utterance.'[1] Winifred Douglas expresses the close affinity between music and the surge of the inner life of man:

> Music is thus not only closely related to life by its power of personal utterance, but still more by its essential character as rhythmic flow; for our life is a continuous movement, of which we are conscious through periodic recurrences of experience. Life is never a state, but always a process; never a being, but always a becoming. Of music alone among the arts is this wholly true. The dream and the dance possess rhythmic flow in varying degrees, but they remain external to all but the participants. Other arts are static in their relation to the life of man. Architecture permanently shelters and expresses the various manifestations of his social activity; painting records his interpretation of the world which he sees; jewellery and clothing adorn his body; sculpture perpetuates the forms of that body in its more perfect or passionate state; poetry delineates the particular aspects of his thought and feeling. Only music moves and changes as his whole being moves and changes, lives parallel with his life, agonizes with his struggle, mourns with his grief, exults with his joy, prays with his adoration. From the far dim dawn in barbarism of that 'light which lighteneth every man that cometh into the

world', the sense of divine vision has evoked the mysterious power of music to express man's reaction to the numinous to vitalize speech in the utterance of worship.[2]

Indeed, the essential relationship between music and worship is so keenly felt by at least half the Christian world – the Orthodox Churches of the East – that what we in the West like to think of as a 'low mass' or a 'said service' is unthinkable for the Eastern Churches, however small the congregation may be. And so alien is the idea of worship without music, that ordination to the priesthood in the Orthodox Churches presupposes at least a reasonable ability to sing. This is no mere preference of one part of the Christian world. It reflects a deep conviction about the very nature of worship and the essential condition of those who worship. For worship brings release; it is the expression of those who have been set free from the bondage of self-consciousness – they are 'free to worship'. In that release, song and music are as inevitable as laughter at a comedy and as closely related to each other as tears are to tragedy, sorrow and sadness.

In fact this has been the basic attitude and outlook of all the churches at all times of renewal. It might not be too much of an exaggeration to say that there has never been a renewal in the history of all the churches which has been unaccompanied (literally) by a musical expression.

The evolution of music in Christian worship

From the moment when Paul and Silas in Macedonia sang hymns together in prison at midnight (Acts 16:25) and were dramatically 'released', there has been a long and continuing story of release and renewal in worship through 'hymns and psalms and spiritual songs' – to adopt Paul's threefold classification (Eph. 5:19, Col. 3:16). We find a similar scene in Milan in the fourth century. Bishop Ambrose of Milan, besieged with his people in his basilica during Eastertide, began to sing and compose beautiful hymns, some of which are still sung to this day. By the beginning of the seventh century the Church possessed the fruits of the Gregorian reforms in the chant of the *Antiphonale Missarum*, which some consider the most perfect of our inheritances from antiquity in any art.

It represents a drawing together of the best of three traditions of music: the Greek, the Latin and the Hebrew; the three languages that headed the cross of Christ in the accusation of Pilate. The Hebrew element picked up the psalmody from worship in the Jewish temple. It reflects the continuity that we see in Acts between Old Testament, Jewish and early Christian worship. The liturgical psalms were sung in three parts in the temple, and at the end of each section the great trumpets were blown while the congregation prostrated themselves before God.

Christian psalmody today has very little in common with this gorgeous and elaborate ceremony except insofar as some Christians stand to sing the 'Gloria' at the end of each section of the psalms and in some traditions bow their heads as they directly address the Blessed Trinity. But there are distinctive elements in the singing of Hebrew psalmody which are worth noting. The congregation, for example, repeated the first verse of the psalm after each verse was chanted as a kind of antiphon, and, according to the book of instructions, the Mishnah, on special festival days when the Hallel or praise psalms were sung, the people broke in with 'hallelujah!' after each clause. So there was established in the Hebrew tradition of worship the important principle of a congregational refrain punctuating the elaborate singing of the choir. Furthermore, there is strong evidence in the Hebrew tradition of the use of themes and tunes borrowed from local folk songs and incorporated into the worship in the temple at Jerusalem. In Isaiah there is a direct quotation from an ancient vintage song: 'As the wine is found in the cluster, and they say, "Do not destroy it, for there is blessing in it."' The melody for this folk song, 'Do not destroy it' (*Altashhith*) is prescribed as the tune and setting for the singing of Psalms 57, 58, 59 and 75.

The second of these influences, the input of Greek music upon the Christian musical tradition, is admittedly rather slight. Bishop Athanasius (AD 296–373) gave certain directions to the church in Alexandria concerning principles of church music, because the Greek insights supplied what we have come to call the diatonic scale, a form of alphabetic notation later used in the West. Probably we have also inherited some of these Greek melodies.

The Latin influence upon church music in general has, however, probably been the most dominant and more lasting by its emphasis upon accent and rhythm. So St Augustine, the great bishop and doctor of the Western Church in the fourth and fifth centuries, in his unfinished work *De Musica* defines the nature of accent and rhythm and later even writes his *Psalm against the Donatists* in a rhythmical style. The *cursus*, not named as such until the early Middle Ages, regulated the word-rhythm at the end of sentences and gave to music that congregational element that comes from an easily grasped sense of rhythm, accent and shape. Music requires the three ingredients of rhythm, melody and harmony, as Yehudi Menuhin puts it: 'Music creates order out of chaos; for rhythm imposes unanimity upon the divergent; melody imposes continuity upon the disjointed, and harmony imposes compatibility upon the incongruous.'[3]

Choir and congregational singing

By the seventh century the three elements – Latin, Greek and Hebrew – created the Gregorian repertoire of music which was suitable for use in Christian worship. By that stage music had become an integral part of liturgy and worship and not a decorative addition, an intrusion or just a performance. Furthermore, in that sense it was never individualistic, but rather represented the voice of the whole church. Each member of the congregation could join in the active praise of the whole church in accordance with his or her own degree of musical skill. The congregation would be supplied with refrains and simple melodies (frequently folk melodies) suitable to most people's ability, while the choir or solo cantors were free to exercise more elaborate tones according to their particular skills. Congregation and choir were not in competition! The music was always subordinate to the sacred text and was the servant of the worship. No phrase or word was repeated for the sake of musical expedient. The practice of melisma (dwelling on a word or syllable by the use of several notes) enforced the principle that the music must serve the sacred text and not the other way about. In all these ways, certain principles and checks and balances emerged, and for a while held sway amongst all those who were concerned with worship and the place of music within that worship. So, as Winifred Douglas says,

> The corpus of the strictly Gregorian music at the beginning of the
> seventh century is the most complete artistic treasure bequeathed to
> us by antiquity . . . It is the world's primary treasure of wholly artis-
> tic melody . . . The perfect, the unmarred choral song of the seventh
> century after Christ, uplifts the mind into a perennially vital expres-
> sion of worship directed to the one true God, as revealed through his
> eternal Son in words inspired by the Holy Spirit.[4]

Nevertheless, it is easy to see how from time to time in the history
of music in worship this balance has been lost and these principles
distorted. From time to time throughout history, the music all too
easily became an end in itself and the words were lost in musical
elaboration for its own sake. The choir tended from time to time
to dominate all else, while the people in the pews were left to their
own devices, unable to open their mouths in the music of the
worship.

It was against this kind of distortion that the Reformers in the
sixteenth century set their faces. Merbecke rigorously adhered to
the principle of one note to one syllable; and the Lutheran
Reformers returned to the chorale, with a place both for congregation and choir, according to the ancient principle of the
antiphon. Other Reformers took the principles of rhythm as an
important and practical method for including the congregation in
the singing of the Psalms, and adapted the words to the metre and
rhythm that made congregational participation easy and strong.

In the growth and development of Wesleyan spirituality, we
find that music in the shape of popular hymns was central to the
whole evangelical revival of the eighteenth century. Charles Wesley, the brother of John, was the most gifted and indefatigable
hymn-writer in the world, writing over 5,500 hymns in all.
Hymns also had a vital part to play in the catholic revival of the
Oxford Movement in the nineteenth century, through the pens of
such writers as Keble, Newman and Faber. During that same
period of revival and renewal the place of the robed choir came
into prominence, starting at Leeds Parish Church, while the Victorian choral traditional flourished in the cathedrals and large
parish churches, with the singing of thousands of new anthems

together with the Anglican chants for the Psalms. Samuel Wesley (1810–76), the grandson of Charles Wesley (music really is conveyed through the genes!) was brought up as a boy soprano at the Chapel Royal, and subsequently became organist and choirmaster of no less than four cathedrals as well as at some point being organist of Leeds Parish Church. He composed many fine Victorian anthems which became the backbone of the English cathedral musical tradition. These revivals continued to have an influence on music in worship through to the present day, from the revivalistic movements of Moody and Sankey to the charismatic and other contemporary movements of renewal.

In such a brief survey of the story of music in Christian worship, we can perhaps see how some musical elements in contemporary renewal belong to a long and well-tried tradition. First, there is the balance between those with particular musical skills (the choir) and the rest of the congregation. The Psalms set to the lovely melodies of Père Gelineau in the 1950s reaffirm the principle of the popular congregational antiphon, punctuating the more elaborate and more sophisticated singing of the Psalms by the choir. The chorus or refrain is a well-tried principle that maintains a proper balance between the choir and the congregation in worship. There is room for further application of this principle in other prose sections of the liturgy, and not least in musical settings for the Eucharist.

Then again there is the principle of rewriting biblical passages in a rhythmic form, such as we find in the excellent rewriting of the Psalms in the well-known and well-tried *Psalm Praise*.[5] The singing of passages of prose Scripture is also part of the tradition, quite wonderfully rediscovered in much charismatic worship and especially well in publications such as *The Sound of Living Waters*.[6] In this example, however, we are not so much dealing with hymns or psalms as a third category – that of spiritual songs, sung quietly and reflectively in the release of the Spirit.

The singing of scriptural passages has always been a strong element in the tradition of Christian worship – for example, the singing of the Gospel or the dramatizing of the Passion Gospel on Palm Sunday and Good Friday. It is a wonderful way for the Christian to interiorize the Word of God and to take phrases and sentences from the Bible and use them as a really effective prayer of the heart. For music helps us to worship God with both sides of the brain. As has already been pointed out, we are told on good scientific authority that we use different sides of the brain for (literally) different sides of our personality; this is known as 'hemispheric specialization'. The well-known psychiatrist Anthony Storr writes:

> The language used both by philosophers and scientists is neutral and objective. It eschews the personal, the particular, the emotional, the subjective. No wonder it is principally housed in a separate part of the brain from that concerned with the expressive aspects of music. Whilst it is perfectly possible to study music from a purely objective, intellectual point of view, this approach alone is insufficient.[7]

Worship in Spirit and in truth needs to occupy both sides of the brain, and music is the unique tool and vehicle for that full-blooded worship that can and does speak to both sides, and to all sides of our personalities. It was not for nothing that Augustine of Hippo so long ago said those famous words: 'To sing, is to pray twice.' Perhaps if he had lived in the twentieth century and had had the privilege of reading Anthony Storr, he might have written something more like, 'To sing is to pray with both sides of the brain'!

It is indeed to this other side of the brain – inspiration and not just information – that the 'spiritual song' can speak so very powerfully. Perhaps it is not pressing it too far if we draw a distinction, however tentatively, between the singing of hymns and the singing of spiritual songs. Hymns are frequently rather boisterous, even sometimes somewhat militant (if not positively militaristic) and not unnaturally, it often seems right to stand up to sing the good strong hymn – lungs fully expanded and with a straight back! But the spiritual song is something much more sensitive and subtle, even more intuitive, and is often best sung kneeling or just sitting, sharing in a quiet melody of the heart, with hands extended open, repeating a simple phrase or sentence from Scripture. In such worship it does not matter if the words are in a different language, such as Latin. Indeed, the use of another language (like speaking in tongues) can release worship from the bondage of only speaking to the informative side of the brain and can open up the other side – the inspiration and intuition (viz the popularity of the *Adoramus te, Domine* of Taizé). Such a song is less strident than a hymn and can form a powerfully reflective and prayerful part of the liturgy. It is essentially a song of the heart, and when sung by a large congregation forms an especially tender and beautiful environment for prayer, worship and sheer adoration.

Singing in tongues is equally beautiful and is a thousand light years away from the hysteria of a revivalist meeting. The genuine article of this phenomenon defies any form of notation according to any of the principles known to the author – at least in Western music. However, there are frequently somewhat bogus and self-induced manifestations of this phenomenon, which do most definitely border on the edge of hysteria as thirds, fifths and octaves are struck up somewhat arbitrarily.

The genuine article, however, when offered in worship, is most beautiful and authentic, building and mounting slowly to a crescendo and then resolving and dying away, giving place to prayer-filled silence and awe. Yes, singing in tongues is most certainly appropriate music for the worship of God. Indeed, it is possible to go further and to claim that it is music not quite like any other music on earth. Such music must have its place in living liturgy, though it must belong within a structure and also in the wider context of formal and structured music, whether for choir or congregation or both.

In any one service it is important to get the balance right between these various musical ingredients. There must be room for a well-sung anthem or motet 'in choirs and places where they sing', as well as for the singing of rhythmically structured and well-known hymns, firmly accompanied. In a church building with a fair-sized congregation, the worship needs to begin with a rousing, well-known hymn and most certainly not with a reflective spiritual song. Yet equally there is also room within the same service for those more reflective spiritual songs, and even for singing in tongues, when and where this is given by the Spirit, and where it is appropriate. There is no reason why there should be rivalry between the professional musicians and other members of the congregation. In a well-ordered service there is plenty of room for varying musical ingredients, giving plenty of scope for those with greater musical talents and gifts, all of which need to be employed for the worship and service of God.

Organs and organists

We must now tackle what has proved to be a very difficult and thorny question in the life of the Church. I refer to the place of the choir, the organ and the organist. If we are honest, the choirs and the organists of our day constitute a real problem and sometimes even a positive hindrance to the whole of renewal in Christian worship. Those are strong and, perhaps some people would say, unfair words, and they are clearly not universally true. Nevertheless, they are sufficiently true to be of real concern among those who are committed to the renewal of the worship of the Church and to the place of music in that renewal movement.

The root of this difficulty lies in the insistence by many organists and choirs on trying to be what they clearly are not. Of course, in a cathedral or large parish church, the organist and a robed choir still have their part to play, and it is an important and vital part. It is equally important to say, however, that in other places of worship, such as in a small inner-city church, a mission church, a church hall, or even a small worship group, choirs and musicians destroy appropriate and authentic worship. C. Henry Phillips comments: 'From the strictly practical point of view music becomes more of a necessity, the larger the building and congregation, as it alone can ensure unanimity.'[8] (The more frequent use of loud-speakers and sophisticated amplification systems may, however, nullify this statement.) The place of organs and music is largely related to the size of the occasion. And wrongly used, they are totally out of place and a great hindrance to Christian worship.

The organ has had a notoriously checkered history in church music. It is such a magnificent instrument that it easily becomes a dominating tyrant – literally a one-man band. The musicians' gallery was, for part of our history, a far more locally representative way of making music to the glory of God, less individualistic as well as less domineering in its accompaniment of congregational singing, sometimes providing a musical interlude during the giving of Communion or at times of reflection during a service. Little wonder that the Puritans, for a host of reasons (some good and some bad), were strongly opposed to organs in churches, and for a while they banished them altogether from church buildings to the more secular atmosphere of pubs and taverns. Here they soon became very popular for musical occasions that were the forerunner of the music hall! Yet – again 'in choirs and places where they sing' – the organ is the right and appropriate instrument for the liturgy of the Church. In all these matters we need to be flexible, able to tailor the music to the occasion, building, environment and congregation. In certain situations a good and sensitive pianist accompanying from a piano provides a far more authentic and appropriate form of music than any accompaniment by an organist. Equally, the guitar or the flute certainly have their place in church music, depending on the occasion.

A further word needs saying at this point about the new and remarkably sophisticated technology of keyboards and electronic organs. Until very recently, any self-respecting organist – or pianist, for that matter – would have probably disdained to use an electronic keyboard. In the first place, in the early days of electronic keyboards, the touch was likely to ruin technique, and secondly, and perhaps more important, the sound produced was obviously synthetic and most unsatisfactory. Neither of these two objections can any longer be sustained. In recent years the structuring of the keys on the keyboard is such that, especially in the case of pianos, the touch of the keys is for all practical purposes as good as is to be found on first-class pianos. Furthermore, the sounds of both pianos and organs are so well simulated by the technology of computerization that very high-quality results are produced. It has to be said, therefore, that for new churches a good keyboard for perhaps as little as £2,000 will provide a very flexible and appropriate accompaniment for the whole range of music that is likely to be required.

If this is true of the organ and the organist, perhaps we need also to raise some question-marks over robed choirs. The Royal School of Church Music, the Guild of Church Musicians, the Hymnal Society, and the Association of Church Organists have done great and valuable work in raising the expectations and standards of ordinary church choirs in town and country. The Guild of Church Musicians currently offers an ecumenical certificate in church music under the joint patronage of the Archbishops of Canterbury and Westminster. All this has done much to raise the standards of church music in every way. Yet it must also be said that the success of these various initiatives at the same time constitutes a potential danger. The robed choir, with head choristers and medals, well drilled and well turned out in cassocks and surplices, has its place, but I suspect it is less of a place now than in our recent past history. Small congregations and living cells of Christians meeting for worship – and these constitute the growing edge of the Church in many places – will become an increasingly important ingredient in the whole life of the renewed Church. In such places it would be inappropriate to have a robed choir. In fact, few things can hinder a small occasion of worship more than a fixation with robed choirs, organists, and all that goes with that kind of liturgical mixture.

It is pathetic to see an otherwise perfectly edifying service in, say, perhaps, a church hall with about twenty or thirty people present, at which there is an organist seated at the piano (possibly insisting upon wearing a hood and gown) plus a choir of four girls, two boys and three women clad in cassocks too long or too short, minus several buttons, together with surplices of varying styles and displaying differing degrees of cleanliness. For everything then becomes a misfit. Frequently the arrival of the local bishop on such a scene will goad the choirmaster and choir to attempt an anthem! It might be well known from some recent royal occasion. Everything rapidly deteriorates into a kind of 'Monty Python' version of worship at St Paul's Cathedral, Westminster Abbey, or the National Cathedral in Washington!

The renewal of the music ministry

One serious word about choirs and professional church musicians. They are a very important part indeed of the life of the whole Church. Music well done is a very powerful ministry, and these people share in the priesthood of all believers in a very special and creative way. It is so important that all church musicians are convinced that they belong to the whole Body, while having a particular and vital part to play in worship and liturgy and, indeed, in the evangelistic ministry of the whole Church. They must not be allowed to become separated into an alien unit. Much will depend upon a good relationship between the pastor and the musicians. If there is a breakdown of trust here it will soon show up on Sunday mornings.

So the good pastor will pray with the choir and take good pastoral care of them, encouraging them to see their offering as a ministry and even in terms of an appropriate stewardship of their gifts. He will take trouble to explain the shape and direction of a service and the place the music has in that overall strategy. He will spend time with the organist or director of music, making sure that they share the same vision about worship, its structure, and the place music should have in that worship. The organist or director of music will take his or her place in the whole ministry team of the parish, attending their meetings and planning alongside the preacher, the readers and all others involved in the worship of God's people. For whenever the musicians are allowed to become an alien group, cut off from the rest of the Body, then there will arise an unhealthy rivalry between the congregation and the musicians, and the pastor must bear most of the blame for this.

Frankly, it is sometimes far better to start preparing a service without any musical ingredients whatever. Start from scratch. It is bad to construct a service with the maxim, 'When in doubt, sing a hymn.' It is worse, when something of doubtful significance is happening in the liturgy, to cover it up with a hymn – and it is even more fatal to use a procession as 'polyfiller' in order to make a grand occasion.

An appropriate occasion, appropriately expressed

An act of worship has integrity when it is an appropriate occasion appropriately expressed. Everything is all of a piece and in total keeping with the overall occasion – its size, its make-up, the available resources, the environment and the nature of the building in which it is all happening.

Picture the scene. A small mission church hall in the inner city. The total congregation of between thirty and forty people are arriving for worship. There is no organ or organist, but a concealed tape recorder is playing Albinoni's *Adagio* through good loudspeakers. The people are sitting rather quietly on arrival, for there is no way of kneeling in such a setting. The priest enters from the side and the people stand for worship. There is no entrance hymn. After all, there is no nave and no entrance worth making a song and dance about, literally! After a moment of silence and stillness, the priest says the opening sentence of the liturgy for the day, and so the worship begins in an atmosphere of stillness and reflection. After the epistle, a single voice starts a well-known spiritual song and the people, still sitting, join in quietly and reflectively. A well-known hymn accompanied on the piano is sung by everyone during the offering of the elements of bread and wine. After Communion there is a time of stillness during which the small congregation and the priest remain sitting while a spiritual song begins, again without any accompaniment. The service concludes as it began in stillness, and after the dismissal the people sit on for a moment in silence before moving to the back of the church hall, where there is coffee or tea and an opportunity for that other apostolic ingredient in the life of the Church – fellowship .

Such a service in such a setting requires neither organ, organist, choir, cassocks, surplices, servers, pulpits, kneelers, ornate vestments, nor any other such encumbrances. Of course, it could be argued that such a diet, if unrelieved by larger occasions of worship, would be deficient, and a congregation in such a situation and location should perhaps make a point from time to time of 'going up' to the local cathedral for the bigger occasions. Nevertheless, such a service in the local community is perfectly edifying and well able to build up the people of God in the life of the Spirit through prayerful worship. Furthermore, worship in such a setting carries with it an integrity of presentation. It is not trying to be what it evidently is not: it is not a cathedral, but it is no less authentic because of that. It is a living cell of Christian life without pretensions or apologies for its existence.

Of course, there are many other situations where the organ with a well-robed choir has its rightful place. Here again, if renewal is to be the order of the day, all the presuppositions about music need to be reconsidered. Start by stripping the structure of the service down to the bare bones. Only after that rather austere process are you ready to see what is appropriate. The most important ingredient will be the choice of hymns: the right hymns with the right tunes.

In a church which shall be nameless, the bishop was visiting for a confirmation service. He entered the large and impressive church from the west door to a nave full of people, and processed behind a large and impressive choir up to the sanctuary, where he was due to be seated at the beginning of the service. The opening hymn was a fine one: 'Let all the world in every corner sing'. What better start to a service, you might ask? Unfortunately, however, the hymn – fine though it is and even finer with a descant in the second verse – only has two verses. The hymn ended while the bishop, at the rear of the procession, was still only a third of the way down the centre of the nave. So for a further minute or so – in awkward and self-conscious silence – the choristers shuffled rather noisily into their stalls and the bishop made his way to the sanctuary. What a start!

When the incumbent was asked why such a short hymn had been chosen for the opening procession, he retorted rather indifferently that he had not chosen the hymn at all. The organist had chosen the hymn for the sole purpose, as the rector himself later admitted, of getting the choir off to a good and impressive start with the 'glorious descant of the second verse'. Such is a case of the tail wagging the dog and, worse still, of there being no connection between the tail and the dog. The work of tailoring the liturgy in a large church or cathedral requires the joint disciplines and skills of priest and musician, each working to a common end – the glorifying of God and the building up of the congregation in worship, prayer and praise.

All this is a skill and a lifetime's work. Sensitive ministers of religion will acquaint themselves with the many dozens of hymnbooks that are now available. They will probably have a whole shelf in the study given over to nothing other than hymns, psalms and spiritual songs in various settings and with various tunes. From their detailed knowledge of a rich supermarket of varying musical opportunities they will, in consultation with the readers, the musicians and the leaders of worship, with great care style the liturgy for a particular Sunday or a particular event in a particular place. This, together with sermon preparation and background reading, will form a large part of any priest's working week. After all, a priest is primarily a minister of God's Word and sacraments, and that work, properly undertaken, will easily take care of a large proportion of a working life. To tailor the worship of God's people in this sensitive and imaginative way is an awesome and yet joyful responsibility that we treat lightly at our peril.[9]

The place of the cathedral

So we must conclude, as we began, with the picture of music as the bicycle of the liturgy: a handmaid but never a tyrant or an end in itself. Winifred Douglas asserts: 'No valid church music was ever made merely to be listened to as a sensuous pleasure.'[10] That is true, and yet great music, well performed and dedicated to the glory of God, will always have its place in Christian worship. There can be little doubt that our cathedrals, renewed and rightly used, will be in the vanguard of Christian renewal in our age. 'Small is beautiful,' but small must also be balanced by large centres of excellence. Cathedrals have a great future in the mission of the whole Church. The cathedral is the mother church of the diocese and brings a larger perspective to congregationalism, that particularly prevalent disease especially rampant in the Episcopal Church of the United States. As a recent report says, 'Cathedrals are shop windows of the Church of England,' and as such will play a role of ever-increasing importance in mission and evangelism.[11]

Deans have more potential as leaders for renewal than bishops. Like Taizé, cathedrals could increasingly be shrines and centres of renewal that people will travel far to see and to experience. The small occasion of worship in the inner city or rural areas, when it is authentic, will create an appetite for this larger statement of the cathedral or large parish church, for there will always be in the heart of humanity this deep desire and quest for the *mysterium tremendum*, the holy place, the centre of pilgrimage. In such places, although there will be rounds and choruses (as there are at Taizé) and many other dimensions of music, there will always be a need for the agency of professional and well-trained choirs and highly skilled church musicians. All this is, of course, very costly today, but it will be a necessary cost in a diocese in order that God's people may have the larger and richer experience of worship through membership of the world-wide Church.

The cathedral as the seat of the bishop should also ideally be the centre of Christian catechesis, training for ministry, lay and ordained, and many of the other aspects of renewal in the life of the contemporary Church. An Anglican Commission has said recently:

> At the centre of the life of the cathedral is the daily offering of worship and praise – Eucharist, Morning Prayer, and on most days choral evensong. The offering of daily choral worship in cathedrals is one of the most significant contributions made by this country to European culture.[12]

Yet while music clearly holds a central place in the cathedral, it should not be seen as a model to be imitated badly in every other church, congregation and cell throughout the diocese. What is on offer in the cathedral is different from that which is available, possible or practical in smaller buildings with fewer and different resources.

In many and differing dimensions, music is once again making its mark in authentic worship. The good news of the Christian gospel was heralded by a chorus of angels singing. The handmaid of the Lord herself broke into words that have subsequently and significantly become the gospel song of the redeemed, who, like Mary, acknowledge 'the greatness of the Lord'. From vast choirs with major orchestral accompaniment to simple folk-tunes as settings for scriptural texts, music has formed the texture of Christian witness and worship throughout the ages. Doubtless it will continue to do so until all our earthly worship is finally subsumed into the worship of heaven, where surely music in some form or another – a form appropriate to its resources and environment – will have its eternal place.[13]

7

Receiving the Word of God

The authority of the Scriptures

At the heart of all renewal movements at the present time is an ever-increasing reverence for the word of God in Scripture. Across the whole spectrum of all the churches, and conspicuously – some might say surprisingly – even in the Roman Catholic Church since Vatican II, the people of God are finding within the Scriptures an authority, power and presence and are deriving from the reading and study of the Bible a deep and enriching scriptural spirituality. *Laus Deo!*

It must also be said, however, that in some areas of renewal, this quite proper reverence for Scripture has unfortunately toppled over into a neo-fundamentalistic approach, which is as sad as it is dangerous. For throughout the history of the human race, never very far below the surface there has been a persistent quest for and an obsession with infallibility in one form or another. It is, of course, motivated by that most ancient of all diseases – idolatry – and is based upon the misguided conviction that authority and infallibility are necessarily the same thing. In reality there is no need for anyone to be infallible in order to speak with authority. My doctor is far from infallible, yet he truly speaks with authority when it comes to matters of health. Authority is rooted in experience and is a word that is strongly personal. Infallibility, on the other hand, is more related to data and facts. We need from the outset, therefore, to establish the nature of the authority that is rightly (and indeed uniquely) attributed by Christians to the Holy Bible before we go on to discuss its use in liturgical worship and its presentation from the pulpit in preaching and proclamation.

In St Luke's Gospel, in that remarkable story of the resurrection encounter on the road to Emmaus, Jesus demonstrates for the benefit of those two disciples, and therefore for the whole Church, the correct way of reading the Scriptures. Jesus, God's last Word, tells the two disciples how, 'beginning with Moses and all the prophets', the events of the Old Testament are to be 'interpreted' to the extent to which they relate to Jesus, the Word of God made flesh in our midst (Luke 24:13–35). For the Scriptures derive their authority from the extent to which they bring us into a relationship with Jesus the Word of God, and to the extent to which they point to Jesus *and* beyond themselves to the *living* Word of God. Therefore the authority of Scripture is not to be found *in* the words of Scripture themselves, but rather *through* and *between* the words: we have to learn to read, as we often say, '*between* the lines'. Put another way, the Bible is an icon: we must look through it and not at it.

So in John's Gospel, Jesus actually upbraids his listeners for placing a wrong trust in the words of Scripture: 'You search the scriptures, because you think that in them you have eternal life; and it is they that bear witness to me; yet you refuse to come to me that you may have life' (John 5:39).

Furthermore, the relationship between the Scriptures and the Word of God is a living link through the Holy Spirit. When we recognize this, it enables followers in every generation to witness together with those two disciples on the Emmaus Road and to exclaim with them, 'Did not our hearts burn within us?' For we also experience this opening up of the Scriptures, the Word of God, by Jesus, the Word of God made flesh. In that way the Scriptures are no longer a dead letter but a living Word.

So anterior to our understanding of the Bible as the Word of God must be our love of Jesus as the Word of God. All authority in Scripture is bound up with the relationship which Scripture has to the living Word of God – the Logos – through the action of the Holy Spirit and by the relationship with that Word through the 'ears' of our hearts, as St Benedict would say. Cyprian Smith comments:

Reading Scripture is not exactly like reading Tarot cards or consulting I-Ching. In those non-Christian forms of divination all we are looking for is an answer to the problem perplexing us; the question of who it is who is speaking or providing the answer matters very little, provided we believe what we are told and act upon it.

A proper reading of the Scriptures, however,

> puts us in touch with God, it establishes a relationship with him, just as prayer does and also as the sacraments of the Church do in a slightly different way. It is a meeting point, a place of encounter.[1]

The epistle to the Hebrews says: 'For the word of God is living and active, sharper than any two-edged sword, piercing to the division of soul and spirit, of joints and marrow, and discerning the thoughts and intentions of the heart. And before him no creature is hidden, but all are open and laid bare to the eyes of him with whom we have to do' (Heb. 4:12–13). It is noteworthy that the writer of the epistle suddenly changes from the Word of God as 'it' to the Word of God as 'he'. This is because the two are essentially related and the one derives its authority from the other. Yet if we go back to the very opening verses of Scripture in the book of Genesis, we find that same Word of God in action in creating and forming the universe: 'In the beginning God . . . said, let there be light: and there was light.' We see God's Word enfleshing his will in creation. His Word is his deed, his Word is not simply some spoken utterance or some written formula: it is his creating power. Isaiah, in the eighth century before Christ, wrote of the same Word:

> For as the rain and the snow come down from heaven, and return not thither but water the earth, making it bring forth and sprout, giving seed to the sower and bread to the eater, so shall my word be that goes forth from my mouth; it shall not return empty, but it shall accomplish that which I propose and prosper in the thing for which I sent it (Isa. 55:11).

So we should not be surprised that for those with eyes to see and ears to hear, the face of this same Jesus is hidden and veiled, we might say, in practically every page of the scriptural record. Somewhat similar to the *leitmotif* in a Wagnerian opera, the great themes are present, however dimly and tentatively formed, from the earliest records of the Scriptures, becoming increasingly clear, until they are openly orchestrated in the historical events of the life, death and resurrection of Jesus Christ. This process continues in the New Testament, where, by the work of the Holy Spirit of God, we see the Word of God, Jesus, formed in the events and lives of the new Israel. 'And we also thank God constantly for this, that when you received the word of God which you heard from us, you accepted it not as the words of men but as what it really is, the word of God, which is at work in you believers' (1 Thess. 2:13).

Reading the Scriptures

So when the Word of God is preached or read aloud it must not be viewed as a mere reminiscence but rather recognized as a presence. In Word and sacrament alike, Christians know the presence of Jesus – what we often speak of as 'the real presence' of Jesus – making us far more conscious of that contemporary presence than of any memory from the past.

In Old Testament prophecy, the Holy Spirit forms the Word of God and points forward to Jesus the Word of God made flesh. In the New Testament and the subsequent history of the Church, that same Spirit *re-presents* the Word of God by taking the things of Jesus and re-presenting them to us (John 14:26; 16:15). Therefore, the history of revelation is not so much to be seen chronologically – before and after Christ – as existentially, as a point of convergence when our 'hearts burn within us', when our 'eyes are opened', and when we 'recognize' him, active and present in us. He in turn re-presents us to the Father (Matt. 10:32) who 'recognizes' again his first created Word, taking delight in this further creation, as he did at the outset in Genesis when he first created us in his image and looked upon us with pleasure.

So in many ways we should expect the Bible to be at its most eloquent when it is read formally and unequivocally in the presence of God's people in the course of the liturgy. This is the context in which the words of Scripture take on their fullest meaning, forming and informing God's people week by week with the story of God's revelation and of his purposes made evident in the face of Jesus Christ. This being so, it is a grave and onerous responsibility to read the words of Scripture in public worship. For the prime purpose of Scripture is not to stimulate only the intellect or to hand on some ideas or information about God, but rather to become truly a part of the Christian's daily discipleship.[2] A proper reading of Scripture does not give us answers to questions – that is little better than pagan divination – and sadly, that is the way many Christians read the Scriptures in the fundamentalist churches. The Scriptures are not there to give us answers but rather to engage us in an encounter with the living Word, with the Truth made flesh – Jesus – the One who Himself is the answer.

A proper reading of Scripture establishes an encounter with that Living Word of God – Jesus. This union is profound, of a sort that inevitably calls for the metaphor of nothing less than eating:

> And he said to me, 'Son of Man, eat what is offered to you; eat this scroll, and go, speak to the house of Israel.' So I opened my mouth, and he gave me the scroll to eat. And he said to me, 'Son of Man eat, eat this scroll that I give you and fill your stomach with it.' Then I ate it and it was in my mouth as sweet as honey (Ezek. 3:1).

So, this metaphor of 'eating' is continued in the words of the ancient collect, instructing us that we are intended to 'read, mark, learn and *inwardly digest*' the Word of God.[3] Here is the living link between the Word of God in the sacrament of the Eucharist and the Word of God in preaching. Both are in a real sense for the diet and sustenance of the Christian. Both alike need to be a banquet (as Augustine would say of Word and sacrament), and not fast or trash food!

Few things are more important when rehearsing and preparing for worship than the careful choice of the right scriptural passages to be read with reverence and expectation – expectation as in that old prophetic question, 'Is there a word from the Lord for us?' This should be the expectation, and nothing less, that heralds the reading of Scripture in public worship and its subsequent proclamation in the expounding of that Word of God in preaching.

To read the Scriptures, therefore, is a skill, requiring patience, ability and a particular charism. In the ancient liturgy of the Church, a special blessing was bestowed before the reader stood up to read. It is still traditional to this day to bless the deacon before the Gospel is read. It will simply not do to let just any member of the laity, on a democratic basis, read the lessons in church. As much care and consideration should be given to this activity in the liturgy as is given to authorizing the laity to give the cup at Communion. Furthermore, it should be undertaken in such a way that it shows from the outset the important place which the Scriptures have in living worship. There must be no informal walking to the lectern, carrying a scrappy copy of the service on which the passage from Scripture is printed. Rather, the Bible should be carried into the church formally and solemnly (preferably by the deacon) at the outset of the service and held high in the opening procession. Placed on the holy table, it is then taken to the place in the building from which it is to be read. It is the Holy Bible, and we must make this clear and explicit in the way in which we handle it, as we do so rightly in the way we 'handle' the Blessed Sacrament.

In passing, it may not be inappropriate to comment upon a new habit that has been introduced in many churches of reading a short passage of explanation before the passage of Scripture is read. May it be suggested that this really overlaps with another valid – but rather different – exercise and that this exercise is not appropriate to Christian worship? Of course there is a place for commentaries and of course there is a place for some kind of summary of a passage of Scripture. But the Word of God in formal worship must be allowed to speak for itself or to be formally expounded in the sermon or homily. It is not right to superimpose upon it from the outset just one, partially valid expression of its power and force.

Spoken clearly and read well, the words of Scripture have the power to convert as powerfully as they had when St Anthony of Egypt first heard the call of Jesus through the solemn reading of the Gospel at the Eucharist.[4] Can you imagine anything more calculated to rob Jesus' challenging demands of their power and authority than some well-intentioned and soft-edged 'explanation'? The Scriptures do not primarily call to be explained. They demand first, and before all else, to be obeyed.

'Read, mark, learn and inwardly digest.' We need, as God's people, to know whole passages of Scripture by heart, just as Jesus himself knew the words of Scripture. Three of the seven words from the cross are words of Scripture, regurgitated as 'comfortable words' when ordinary words and articulation were no longer possible. At the outset of his ministry and again in crisis and stress, Jesus confronts the devil in the wilderness with three words of Scripture: 'It is written . . . It is written . . . it is written . . .'

So then, we must ask seriously about the multiplicity of translations used in worship today. Perfectly good though these may be on the study shelves for reference, in Bible study groups or in private study of the Scriptures, they cannot provide the staple diet of God's people. Sooner rather than later, we need to settle on one basic translation that can be the agreed text of the people of God and become increasingly known by heart by a churchgoing generation that is (strangely enough in an age of reading) almost scripturally illiterate. *Embarras de choix* is all right in a supermarket, but it has robbed a whole generation of churchgoing Christians of a basic part of their diet: that inward digestion of well-read, well-marked, and well-learned Scripture.

Such must be the priority given to the reading of Scriptures in the liturgy of the Church that, when the passage of Scripture is finished, if there is to be silence for a while (and probably in most cases there should be), then there is no need for a concluding sentence, whether it be 'The Word of the Lord' or 'Here ends the reading.' Such phrases have the effect of cutting off that section of the service. Much better if, as the last sentence of the lesson dies away, the reader remains standing for a period of silence – a silence only broken by the playing over of an unannounced anthem or motet from the choir reflecting upon the previous words of Scripture. (Incidentally, it is especially important at this point not to lapse suddenly into giving out hymn numbers or stage directions.) The reading should lead naturally into recollection, and the recollection should lead naturally into a response in song, prayer or praise.

Opening the Scriptures

Then he opened their minds to understand the scriptures, and said to them, 'Thus it is written, that the Christ should suffer and on the third day rise from the dead, and that repentance and forgiveness of sins should be preached in his name to all nations, beginning from Jerusalem. You are witnesses to these things.' (Luke 24:46–48).

Encapsulated in that text is the basis of all Christian teaching and preaching, for it has the authority of the risen Christ and shows us the model of apostolic preaching, commissioned directly by the risen Lord.

There are two aspects to preaching: 'the opening of the minds' to the record of Scripture and the validating of what is heard in the insight and experience of those who are listening, who are intended to be 'witnesses'. So once again, at every moment and at every turn, we see the Word being made flesh – enfleshed – in the lives of those who hear and receive this Word of God. The Word of God forms the people of God, so when Karl Barth was asked how he prepared his Sunday sermon, he replied: 'I take the Bible in one hand and the newspaper in the other.' The Incarnation is therefore a continuing process: Jesus, the Word, is received by and enfleshed in his people, by Word and sacrament, so that the people of God in their turn enflesh that same Word of God. Just as Mary did by the power of the same Holy Spirit. All this is through the work and overshadowing of the Holy Spirit, as it was at the outset when the Word was made flesh at the Annunciation. And the end product is always the same: to form the Word of God, who dwells richly in the hearts of those who receive him. We are all in that sense intended to be *theotokoi* (God-bearers), as was Mary, the mother of the Lord.

It is the unique character and activity of the Holy Spirit to re-present Jesus and to make him present at all times and in all places for his people, by the breaking open of the Word and by the breaking of bread. For the preacher is not commissioned or called to preach about Christianity, but rather to preach Christ, and so to represent and re-present him. When Christian preaching takes place, as St Augustine is at pains to point out, God himself is present in it.

The doctrine of preaching

When God's Word is 'preached and in as much as the preacher speaks the truth, Christ speaks through him'.[5] With such a high doctrine, you might well ask, 'Who is equal to these things?' The answer must reside primarily in our doctrine of preaching rather than in the skills and technique of the preacher. For no one achieves the gift of preaching, since, like all gifts in the New Testament, it is not achieved but rather received. It is a mighty and awesome commission. The most important thing will be that we know what we are doing before we seek to know how to do it. It is perhaps in the realm of the doctrine of preaching that the Church in recent decades has most conspicuously lost its nerve. There can be no doubt that we need to recover our doctrine in this field if we are to recover our confidence as preachers. For supremely, preaching is the activity of God. It is an event and not simply an essay or an exercise. Perhaps that is the reason why a sermon which moved us and was so formative in our Christian discipleship is frequently rather a disappointment and even a let-down when we subsequently read it some time later. A large part of its power belonged to the event and is not contained in a visual representation of the words in the script. For something *happens* when the Word of God is preached among the people of God, under the Spirit of God. But does it?

What happens does not have to be spectacular – though it frequently has been in the history of the Church, changing people's lives dramatically. Nor does it have to be memorable – though it frequently has been in the lives of those who often recall it until the end of their days. But it does have to be substantial and authentic and part of a regular and balanced diet, so that God's people may be regularly fed and built up and sustained. Sermonettes make Christianettes! There can be no doubt that there will be no lasting renewal in worship unless there is a real renewal in our expectations about preaching, both by the preacher and by those who receive God's Word through that ministry. St Augustine saw preaching essentially as feeding the Lord's people and the pulpit as 'the Lord's table, at which the minister ought not to defraud his guests'.[6] He sees the Christian congregation assembled for nothing less than a banquet in which the preacher has the responsibility of feeding the guests until they are satisfied. It is not true that sermons are necessarily boring or that the spoken word is no longer effective. Bad preaching will always be boring and certainly will not be effective, but there will never be a church in which there is not a place for preaching. Furthermore, there is no doctrine in the New Testament that demands that sermons have to last only twenty minutes! It does, of course, have to be admitted that preachers must have skill as well as sincerity if they are to arrest our attention. Where there is a living preacher there is a living church, and that fact alone lays upon both the ordained ministry as well as upon other ministries in the Church a heavy and costly responsibility. Donald Coggan writes:

> Here is the miracle of the divine economy, that between the forgiveness of God and the sin of man stands – *the preacher*! That between the provision of God and the need of man stands – *the preacher*! It is his task to link human sin to forgiveness, human need to divine omnipotence, human search to divine revelation.[7]

For preaching is not quite like anything else on earth. It is not the same as teaching, or a straight lecture, an essay, or an oration; yet it clearly overlaps with all these categories of communication. In many ways, it is most like an old-fashioned music hall. Preacher and congregation are both participating and both get caught up in this great event. The congregation should participate to such an extent that the preacher will see people's faces changing before his very eyes, maybe with anger, puzzlement, or indifference, or they may nod (hopefully not just because they are falling asleep!) as the 'penny is dropping' and the preacher is making a telling point that rings true in the experience, the hearts and lives of those who are listening.

In St Augustine's day, the congregation would frequently applaud in the basilica and sometimes would show other responses, either of appreciation or the opposite. All of this we see in Book 4 of his *De Doctrina Christiana,* where the Bishop of Hippo describes his daily experience of expounding the Word of God, generally seated on his *cathedra* (chair) in his basilica at Hippo. Augustine was a preaching man from start to finish, who had given his life over to the study of Scripture and to the expounding of it. Like St Paul before him, Augustine spoke of preaching as the paying of a debt.[8] 'Preach wherever you can, to whom you can and as often as you can.'[9] It is indeed a lifetime's craft and a daily burden and responsibility, but above all else it is a wonderful privilege.

What is increasingly clear in the renewal of the contemporary Church is that a written sermon in a detached style, which is distinctive and reminiscent of an art-form of an earlier age, will simply no longer fit the bill. There was a time when worship was institutionalized and, likewise, when the sermon in its turn became an institutionalized art-form. Read and study the great nineteenth-century preachers, value them and applaud them, but do not seek to copy them. Today, preaching is best learned on the small occasion, a house Eucharist, or even a low mass when the lectionary of the day provides the 'bread' which demands to be taken by the preacher and broken open in the presence of the people of God.

Preparation for preaching

Preaching today demands a much more spontaneous style. Yet make no mistake about it, all preaching (great or small) requires preparation. The question is, where and how and what sort of preparation? The answer is that it requires more and more remote preparation, and less and less immediate preparation. For true and authentic preachers should carry around with them day in and day out, the burden of their message. This requires daily and detailed study of the Scriptures and an alert and sensitive mind tuned to the casual remark during visiting, a line from a poster, an advertisement or a song, a newspaper article, a television series, or just 'the words of the prophets . . . written on the subway walls'.[10] John Stott in his excellent book on preaching tells how he studies four chapters every day to enable him to read the whole of the Scriptures in the course of one year – the Old Testament once and the New Testament twice.[11] That is the preparation for which there is no substitute. Of course, the secret of preaching is not just in the words (however appropriate). St Augustine is swift to remind us that

> the sound of our words strikes the ear, but the master is within. You must not think that anyone learns from the man. The noise of our voice can be no more than a prompting; if there is no teacher within, that noise of ours is useless . . . Outward teachings are but a kind of help and prompting: the teacher of hearts has his chair in heaven.[12]

Nevertheless, there is no substitute for the daily study of the Scriptures as the background to all our preaching. This is the raw material of a lifetime's desire to expound the Word of God.

The purpose of preaching

The trigger point of the sermon is the Word of Scripture. The Word becomes flesh again by the activity of the Holy Spirit; we find Christ truly in our midst in the contemporary applications of the Scriptures just as surely as he is present when bread is broken and wine is outpoured. What thus appears spontaneous is part of a well-chartered process with a thorough-going theological explanation. The preacher is free to stand or sit, to look at his hearers, to be flexible to the needs of the moment, to relate to his congregation and to change his tactics at any point if someone is looking bored, if anyone has to leave because they are suddenly not well or if a child starts to cry. Augustine counsels us to look out for the signs of weariness in the congregation (there really is nothing new under the sun anywhere!) and challenges the preacher to respond to this

> by saying something seasoned with discreet cheerfulness, and suited
> to the matter in hand, or something very wonderful and amusing, or
> it may be, something painful and mournful; and such as may affect
> himself rather than another, in order that being pinched by concern
> for self he may continue to be watchful.[13]

In all this, a living relationship strikes up between the preacher and those who are listening: 'One loving heart sets another on fire.' (It is not insignificant that the symbol of St Augustine – intellectual though he was – is nevertheless a heart with a flame coming from it.) Yet such preaching cannot be done in a stylized setting with a well-turned and stylized script. Augustine, who was the professional orator and rhetorician of his day, trained in the art of speaking in the ancient world, nevertheless cautions the preacher that all these models must be thrown to the winds for the sake of this one sacred and unique vocation of preaching God's Word. So he could remind himself, as well as others, 'What matters it to us what the grammarians please to rule? It were better for us to be guilty of a "barbarism" so that you understand, than that in propriety of speech you are left unprovided.'[14]

Of course, there is always a place in preaching for the illustration, but the illustrations must always be pertinent, realistic, vivid and easily at hand. They must not be forced, calculated or self-conscious. Augustine's preaching is brimful of basic stories and illustrations that have about them an authenticity. These homely illustrations stand, as parables do, as good stories in themselves, proclaiming the truth without too much help from the preacher's purple pencil. For although preachers are in the persuasion business, that is not the same as the propaganda business. There must be an integrity running through all the illustrations which must stand up by their appeal to truth rather than whether they make a point powerfully or persuasively.

In his handbook on Christian preaching, Augustine is not ashamed to admit he was in the persuading business: 'A preacher is not a salesman. It is his duty to persuade, but not necessarily to please.'[15] Augustine writes, 'To teach is a necessity, to please is a sweetness, but to persuade is a victory.'[16] It has to be admitted that such a victory is frequently lacking in much preaching today. We are frequently informed and given information but seldom transformed through inspiration.

For men and women should not leave worship the same as they entered it. The task as well as the glorious responsibility of the preacher, is to convince and to convert. He slowly moves God's pilgrim people along the king's highway, making sure (by loving persuasion, by skill, by word and by power of speech, but above all by the anointing of the Holy Spirit) that they have not settled down at some 'tavern' on the roadside, moved in, put up the drapes, pulled down the shutters, and put up their feet! Each year, for God's pilgrim people, is intended to be a year of grace, marking movement and growth, and much of this can only be achieved by regular feeding through God's Word, ministered faithfully and skilfully, week by week, under the power and direction of God's Holy Spirit. In this way the Word of God forms and transforms the people of God.

Content and structure

We might well ask what the right subject matter is for preaching. Robert E. Terwilliger says, 'It [the sermon] need not be eloquent, but it must be about God and have within it the awareness of his presence.'[17] It is still a useful discipline for most preachers most of the time to take a text and to expound it. For preaching must be biblical, but that is not the same as saying that the preacher will only preach about the Bible. As Terwilliger remarks, 'A sermon needs to be expressed in the great thought forms of the Scriptures as well as using their content. It is the interpretation of the scriptural point of view, not simply, as it were, quotations from the book.'[18] We might also go on today to ask whether there is a place for politics from the pulpit. Like so many things, it all depends on what you mean by politics. It is party politics which must be avoided at all costs. Bishop Terwilliger, himself conspicuous as a distinguished preacher in the Anglican Communion during the seventies, puts it most succinctly: 'The preacher has no right to use his apostolic authority outside the apostolic realm. That is to say, he is not ordained to preach economics or politics, but he is ordained to declare the relationship between the word of God and the ways of man.'[19] St Paul puts it perhaps even more succinctly with the caution: 'Woe to me if I do not preach the gospel!'

The outworkings of the sermon are of course very important through Bible study groups, house groups and prayer groups. No one would pretend that all the teaching ministry in a parish can or should be done through sermons, but it is a huge misconception that groups can be a total substitute for the spoken proclamation of the Word through a sermon or homily in the context of worship. In many ways the only suitable culmination of a sermon is worship itself.

Education (as we see in the story of the wise men) is a pilgrimage or journey of exploration culminating in worship. When men and women have been persuaded by the power of the spoken Word they need to move into repentance, worship, or adoration: saying, 'My Lord and my God.' This is especially true in mission services. There must be such a shape to mission services so that the sermon points beyond itself to further worship, deeper praise and adoration, or a new commitment of heart and will. Indeed, there should be in all preaching, as there is in the Eucharist, a real *anaphora* – a lifting-up of the hearts of the hearers into the environment and experience of the Kingdom. The culmination of a sermon is the realization that the Word is present. Then there is only one thing to do – shut up! Let heart speak to heart.

Silence is perhaps the most appropriate response and worship the proper posture when a sermon has reached its point, as surely as worship and the release of gifts marked the goal of all the journeyings of those wise men in search of their king. Augustine used to say that there were only two responses to the preaching of the Word: either we should rise to our feet to confess our renewed faith, or fall to our knees to confess our sins!

Edward King, Bishop of Lincoln, used to say that the shape of a sermon was more or less the shape of a traditional church building: entrance and introduction (narthex); a central theme (the nave) with illustrations on the side as you went along (the aisles). Yet all this must lead men and women into the sanctuary and into the presence and awareness of the holy. That is the point of it all – to be brought into the presence of God. It is not enough to inform, entertain, or even educate – though all that is part of the task of the preacher. In the end, true apostolic preaching must really and truly move people into a closer and deeper awareness of the presence of the Word made flesh, Jesus Christ, their Lord and Saviour. So in the Eucharist, a sermon or homily can inform and direct the time of prayer that generally follows it or, equally, lead straight into a Christian affirmation of faith, as in reciting the words of the Creed. In other services, it is good to lead from preaching into silence or a hymn, sung kneeling (perhaps before the Blessed Sacrament) or just into the reflective singing of choruses of Scripture, seated still and open to the sweet and blessed influence of God's presence in his Word. Above all, the sermon should not be just another thing put into the service: 'Is there to be a sermon today?' The sermon flows inevitably out of the reading of Scripture and flows freely into prayer, affirmation, confession and adoration. It is an integral part of the movement of all worship.

The renewal of the Church today will draw much of its power from the Word of God in Scripture and in preaching as surely as it did in earlier chapters of renewal throughout history. Speaking of the reformation movement, E. C. Dargan comments:

The great events and achievements of that mighty revolution were largely the work of preachers and preaching; for it was by the word of God, through the ministry of earnest men who believed, loved and taught it, that the best and most enduring work of the Reformation was done. And, conversely, the events and principles of the movement powerfully reacted on preaching itself, giving it new spirit, new power, new forms, so that the relation between the Reformation and preaching may be succinctly described as one of mutual dependence, aid and guidance.[20]

This could be said of all movements of renewal in the history of the Church and equally so of the contemporary movements of renewal in the Church today. We need to conclude with the realization that the first victory is the basic doctrinal conviction about the primacy and priority of God's Word in the life of God's people. It was perhaps precisely that conviction that had slipped so far from what it should be in the conventional church at the beginning of this century; and it is the recovery of that conviction, accompanied by great and vigorous expectations, that is uppermost in the work of renewal today. Dr Martyn Lloyd-Jones wrote:

To me the work of preaching is the highest and the greatest and the most glorious calling to which anyone can ever be called. If you want something in addition to that, I would say without any hesitation that the most urgent need in the Christian Church today is true preaching.[21]

Or, from a different source – the Second Vatican Council – the preacher and the priest are exhorted with the words:

Since no one can be saved who had not first believed, priests, as co-workers with their bishops, have as their primary duty the proclamation of the gospel of God to all . . . The task of priests is not to teach their own wisdom but God's word, and to summon all men urgently to conversion and to holiness . . . Such preaching does not present God's word in a general abstract fashion only, but it must apply the perennial truth of the gospel to the concrete circumstances of life.[22]

8

The Daily Office

In recent years there has been a refreshing development in the corporate prayer life of the people of God throughout many of the traditions. The Daily Offices of morning and evening prayer are once again returning to pride of place in the daily, corporate worship not only of the clergy but also for the laity. Of course, this is no new phenomenon both because, as we shall see, it dates back to the very earliest days of the Christian Church and also because the daily offices were given a very special place of prominence at the reformation by Cranmer. From the earliest drafts of his prayer books continuing through into the prayer book of the Elizabethan Settlement and up until 1662, the daily offices were retained with equal prominence.

Patterns of daily corporate prayer in the Early Church

In the early days of the Christian Church, immediately after the events of Pentecost, the Jewish Christians in Jerusalem, according to the book of the Acts of the Apostles, continued to meet daily in the temple at the appointed hours for prayer and worship. We read that the first crop of Christians (some 3,000) baptized in the aftermath of the events of the day of Pentecost 'devoted themselves to the apostles' teaching and fellowship, to the breaking of bread and the prayers' (Acts 2:42). Furthermore, we are told a few verses later, that they continued 'day by day, attending the temple together and breaking bread in their homes'(Acts 2:46).

Although the picture is far from clear in every detail it is sufficiently distinct to give us an outline of the life of worship of the early Christians in Jerusalem. In the first place, we notice that these Jewish Christians continued to go to the temple for the daily times of prayer. We read in the Old Testament about the practice of Daniel who, as a devout Jew, insisted upon praying three times a day at set times. Daniel 'went to his house where he had windows in his upper chamber open towards Jerusalem; and he got down upon his knees three times a day and prayed and gave thanks before his God, as he had done previously' (Dan. 6:10).

In the book of Psalms we are told that the practice of devout Jews constituted a daily sevenfold pattern of prayer: 'Seven times a day I praise thee' (Ps. 119:164). The early Christians saw no reason whatever to discontinue this practice of daily corporate prayer, since after all they were praying to the same God and Father as they had done before their baptism. So the *Didache,* a document from the late first or early second century, prescribes the use of the Lord's Prayer three times daily ('thrice in the day, pray ye this'),[1] presumably at the third, sixth and ninth hours which are referred to as hours of prayer in the Acts of the Apostles – 'Peter and John,' we are told, 'were going up to the temple at the hour of prayer, the ninth hour (Acts 3:1; see also 10:3, 9, 30). Furthermore, there is a whole string of references in the Fathers of the Church speaking of daily corporate prayer at set times. These references go back as early as Clement of Alexandria (c. AD 95) and Tertullian (c. 200).

From this and other material we have a glimpse of the shape of daily worship – common prayer and corporate worship – from the earliest times of our Christian story, and we can be certain that a very similar pattern continued from the time when the Church broke out of the enclaves of Jerusalem into the Gentile world and into the culture of the whole Mediterranean world. *Celebrating Common Prayer* notes that

> Daily prayer, offered by the whole Christian community, was an important feature of the early life of the Church. Such prayer consisted of only a relatively small number of psalms and canticles. Certain psalms and canticles were chosen for their appropriateness to the time of day and repeated regularly. Praise, and the offering of intercession, formed the core of these daily prayers rather than the reading of the whole psalter and the entire scriptures in course.[2]

So we see that in order to live the life of the coming Kingdom, the whole people of God gathered daily in the Early Church to pray the prayer of the Kingdom, to recite the Psalter and to read, to reflect upon and to interiorize the Scriptures – the Old Testament as well as the New, for the Old Testament is also part of our Christian story. All this was in addition to the unique Christian worship in the liturgy of the Eucharist, which while being the distinctively Christian act of worship is by no means the only act of worship for Christians from the earliest days.

The Daily Office and the monastic movement

With the Peace of Constantine (AD 313), Christianity became respectable throughout the whole of the Roman Empire, and not surprisingly many people became Christians as a matter of form and to conform to the acceptable norms of the day. Furthermore, the note of urgency and expectation of the Second Coming had rather gone from the forefront of the Christian mind. Christians tended to throw their energies into building the empires of this world with all the compromises that such a radically different world-view implied. The concept of the Kingdom of God and the need to pray continually for its coming receded somewhat in the Christian imagination as the Church increased in worldly power and took its place at first alongside and subsequently in the vanguard of world powers. In its turn the Church became worldly, both firmly planted in this world and most definitely of this world in many aspects.

Beginning in the East with St Anthony and later taken up in the West, both men and women alike felt the call of God to come out into the desert to recapture that first love and so no longer to be either in the world or of it. At first these were largely lay men and women, not priests, and their corporate life of prayer and worship was built upon the daily recitation of the Psalter in its entirety, together with the systematic reading of Scripture in the round of the Church's year.

In the East, especially in Egypt, in the early days of monasticism, the monks tended to settle for the primitive services of lamp-lighting at sunset and sunrise, while the monks in the West set themselves to carry out the more literal meaning of those words of the psalmist: 'Seven times a day will I praise thee.' Under St Benedict, the Father of Western monasticism, and according to his rule, the Eucharist was significantly kept as a special service for Sundays and other festivals only, not least because most of the monks in the growing monasteries throughout Europe were lay-men and not priests. As the medieval monastic movement devel-oped in the great monasteries of Cluny and Citeaux, the Daily Offices became more and more complicated and ornate, drawing on more and more books, while the number of services increased to eight within each 24-hour period: Matins, Lauds, Prime, Terce, Sext, None, Vespers and Compline .

Anglican practice

It has frequently been noted how Anglicanism has been so very strongly influenced by the whole spirit of St Benedict. Certainly the spirit and ethos of the various Anglican prayer books of the Reformation were strongly Benedictine in flavour, and especially so in the renewed emphasis given to the Daily Offices of morning and evening prayer. So it was that Cranmer, in drawing up the essential framework of the Book of Common Prayer in 1549 and 1552, based the whole of the emerging Anglican spirituality upon the daily recitation of the Offices.

Writing about these, he begins with a classic sentence which should not be forgotten: 'There was never any thing by the wit of man so well devised, or so sure established, which in continuance of time hath not been corrupted.' From Cranmer's point of view, as he reviewed the corruptions of the Medieval Church, and not least in its liturgical practices, he found that matters liturgical were certainly no exception to this general rule. With the passage of time the Daily Offices, especially in the monasteries but also in the medieval breviary, had become over-ornate and had lost their original purpose dating back to the Early Church – namely, pray-ing the Scriptures.

Originally, Cranmer rightly claimed that the Daily Offices were so ordered that all the whole Bible (or the greatest part thereof) should be read over once a year; intending thereby, that the clergy, and especially such as were ministers in the congregation, should (by often reading, and meditation in God's word) be stirred up to godliness themselves, and be more able to exhort others by wholesome doctrine, and to confute them that were adversaries to the truth; and further, that the people (by daily hearing of holy scripture read in the church) might continually profit more and more in the knowledge of God, and be the more inflamed with the love of his true religion.

A fine and contemporary sentiment, as important today as in the sixteenth century or at any other time. Sadly, Cranmer reflects that

these many years passed, this godly and decent order of the ancient fathers hath been so altered, broken and neglected, by planting in uncertain Stories, and Legends, with multitude of responds, verses, vain Repetitions, Commemorations and synodals; that commonly when any book of the Bible was begun, after three or four chapters were read out, all the rest were unread.

In the light of all this, Cranmer went to work with alacrity, tearing away all the accretions to the medieval offices of the Church so that their main content, and indeed the main reason for their practice, should be recovered and made evident and obvious.

He simplified the very ornate and highly complicated order of prayer as it had developed in the monasticism of Western Europe through the Middle Ages, with its many books and multiplicity of options, putting everything in the one book and with a minimum of seasonal options and variations. And, most significantly, he conflated the sevenfold monastic office, producing simply two Daily Offices of Morning and Evening Prayer.

His explicit intention in doing this was to encourage not simply the clergy but also the laity to attend church daily and to pray the common prayer of the whole people of God. So he instructs that the church bell shall be tolled to call people from the surrounding neighbourhood to prayer:

All priests and deacons are to say daily the morning and evening prayer either privately or openly, not being let by sickness, or some other urgent cause. And the curate . . . shall say the same in the parish church or chapel where he ministereth, and shall cause a bell to be tolled thereunto a convenient time before he begin, that the people may come to hear God's word, and to pray with him.

The Office was not to be muttered in Latin, as in the monasteries, but rather was to be said reflectively in English, thus opening up the Scriptures and especially the Psalms for devotional recitation. So it was at the Reformation that at least the Church of England recovered the vision and practice of the Early Church in reading and praying the Scriptures daily. The Archbishop of Canterbury writes:

> This was always Cranmer's intention in *The Book of Common Prayer*. Although his version of Morning and Evening Prayer has long provided a non-eucharistic form of public worship on Sundays and has done much to characterize Anglican public worship, it has only rather patchily achieved his other purpose of being the regular worship attended by the whole congregation and offered day by day in parish churches throughout the land.[3]

However, we find in the seventeenth century both George Herbert (1593–1633) in his parish of Fugglestone with Bemerton, near Salisbury, as well as Nicholas Ferrar (1592–1637) and his lay community at Little Gidding, encouraging people to live out this life of daily prayer – 'Seven whole days, not one in seven,' as Herbert says in one of his more famous poems and hymns. In 1632 (the year before his early death), Herbert wrote his classic work on the life of the country pastor entitled *A Priest to the Temple; or the Country Parson*. In that work he influenced the course of the pastoral ideal for Anglican clergy and laity for many years with his picture of the well-read parson, temperate in all things, a man of duty and prayer and devoted to his flock. Daily prayer and reading the Daily Office and the Scriptures were for Herbert the mainspring of parish life.

Sadly, the witness of Herbert is conspicuous by its singularity, although the reciting of the Daily Office has always been an Anglican ideal which in practice many clergy have maintained, but largely as a personal discipline rather than being shared with the laity.

Our own day is witnessing a return to the Daily Offices as being the bedrock of the daily corporate prayer and worship of God's people. At St Gervaise in Paris, both Morning and Evening Prayer are celebrated by large congregations of Parisian workers daily throughout the week. For many years now the Protestant community at Taizé has popularized (if that is not too strong a word) the Daily Office as a basis for a scriptural spirituality. They have linked this with a quite remarkable musical tradition which is distinctive, almost popular in the best sense, yet with echoes of the more reflective plainsong of the medieval monastic life and worship.

All this is both arising out of as well as in turn feeding a lay spirituality which has great attractions to men and women (and most certainly to the young) whose life and work are rooted in the world and yet who look for the coming Kingdom. As Bishop John Robinson used to say, they are men and women seeking to live 'the end in the middle' – that Kingdom life-style to which the New Testament and the teaching of Jesus point so powerfully.

With the acute shortage of priests, the practice of a daily mass in many French churches has been replaced with the kind of spirituality and worship that arise out of the Daily Office. In this way God's people are still fed with the Word and receive their daily bread, by interiorizing the Scriptures, by intercession and reflective, meditative prayer and worship. The present situation may well prove not to be loss but rather gain. Indeed we might say, 'Come back, Cranmer, all is forgiven!'

The calendar and the lectionary

It is not unusual today to find committed Christians who follow a daily Bible study of one sort or another. There are many schemes and plans which are available. All these schemes are helpful, but they can fall short of the ideal in one very important way.

Broadly speaking, since the Enlightenment, the Church – especially in the West – has pursued knowledge mainly and sometimes exclusively through the intellect and reason, seeking to attain a detached and objective knowledge of the truth. There are two words for knowledge in French – *savoir* and *connaître*. *Savoir* knowledge refers to the way in which we know things, facts and the inanimate universe. *Connaître* is reserved for the way in which we know people – relational knowledge. The former concentrates more on the mind while the latter also brings in the intuitive and reflective aspects. Middle English and Medieval English retained this distinction, so that to know a person carries the meaning of intimate knowing, perhaps as clear as sexual intercourse. So Mary asks the angel of the Annunciation, when told that she is to expect a child, 'How can this be, since I know not a man?' (King James version) – meaning, 'I have not had intercourse with a man.'

After the Age of Reason people generally drove a wedge between subjective feeling and objective knowledge. 'In the course of life,' wrote Schopenhauer, 'head and heart grow more and more apart; men are always separating more and more their subjective feeling from their objective knowledge.'[4] Both theologians and theology, especially in the West, have fallen prey to this distortion and fragmentation (one might almost say schizoid mentality), for they have ceased to make the proper distinction between the way we know facts and the way we know people, both in our language as well as in our mind-set. So when the evangelicals of the eighteenth century spoke of knowing God and knowing the Scriptures, they put all their eggs in the *savoir* basket, so to speak, seeking the same kind of knowledge, and indeed certainty, in relation to the Scriptures and God as the scientists of the age were propagating in the realm of facts and objects. Hence the claims to inerrancy in Scripture, together with the fairly recent phenomenon of infallibility and the fundamentalism arising out of that, which crept into the vocabulary of the Church. Surely the words of Jesus, 'I am the Way, the Truth and the Life' demand much more than mere intellectual assent, but rather a relationship of trust and discipleship in which we discover the truth about God only by living the life of God – 'Christ in you, the hope of glory.'

If we follow this argument through we shall see how Bible study is so much more than mere intellectual study, for Christianity, unlike the faith of Muslims, is not the religion of a book, but of a Person who has revealed himself through the books of Scripture and in other ways as well. Only if we live the life shall we know the doctrine. In other words, the proper environment for Bible study, as we see on the road to Emmaus, is in the presence of the

Word whom we can come to know through the words of Scripture. The proper context for Bible study is neither primarily the lecture room, the library or the study, but rather on our knees in worship in the presence of the One who delights to reveal himself to us in the depths of our heart and in the course of a growing love and trust. Bible study snatched out of its proper context of worship is lopsided, leading us to ask the wrong questions and to seek the wrong answers.

As the Christian tradition encompasses a rich variety of doctrine and because of the comprehensiveness of the Scriptures, there is more to take in than is possible for a daily diet, unless it is part of a whole cycle of prayer, based not on ideas about God so much as upon the celebration of the mighty acts of God. So at Christmas we celebrate the theological doctrine of the Incarnation; at Easter we celebrate the theological reality of the Resurrection; at Pentecost we celebrate the theological truth of the Holy Spirit, and so on throughout the whole of the Church's year. Furthermore, by celebration we mean so much more than cerebral appreciation: we celebrate in a highly personal way the mystery of these great truths which only make sense in relationship with the One who is the source of Truth.

The Church's lectionary naturally divides our reading of Scripture into appropriate passages according to the various seasons of the Church's year. That enables us to come to Scripture with all our antennae alert to the message of the season. Our minds are enlightened, but our hearts are also warmed and above all else our wills are fired for the conversion of life (*conversatio morum*, as St Benedict calls it), as we become what we worship and adore with our hearts, our souls, our minds and with all our passions.

'The Bible is like a telescope,' said Phillips Brooks, the celebrated preacher of the American Episcopal Church, and also, incidentally, the writer of the famous carol, 'O little town of Bethlehem'. 'Look at it and you will see nothing except the telescope; look through it and you will see the glory of worlds beyond.' Yes, the Bible must be seen as an icon – not primarily something you look at, but rather something that you look through. The Eastern Churches still come to the Scriptures with this iconographic approach, which has rescued them from both

the fundamentalism and extreme liberalism of biblical interpretation so endemic in the West. The Bible is not there primarily to be
understood and to address the reason: rather, it is there to resonate
with our life experiences, to be recalled in all kinds of situations as
a living Word, and above all to address the imagination, that
much-neglected part of our human make-up in the post-Enlightenment world. This whole process of interiorizing the Scriptures,
therefore, is best explored through celebration, reflection, meditation and worship.

The place of the Psalms

At the heart of the Daily Office is the recitation of the Psalter – the
prayer book of Jesus, which the record of Scripture would suggest
was known to our Lord by heart. Under stress and temptation in
the wilderness, three powerful words of Scripture are recalled (literally) by Christ as he confronts evil: 'It is written . . . It is written
. . . it is written . . .' Again, on the cross in his dying moments, two
of his last seven words are taken straight from the Psalter.

It is interesting to note that when the Emperor Charlemagne
had asked Alcuin (c. 735–804) to draw up for him a scheme of
daily prayer, the good royal tutor provided a book of extracts from
the Psalms interspersed with brief prayers. King Alfred also was
well known for carrying with him at all times in his pocket a similar book of Psalms and prayers for use in his daily life. Alcuin told
Charlemagne that:

> In the psalms, if you look carefully, you will find an intimacy of
> prayer, such as you could never have discovered without their help:
> you will find words for an intimate confession of sins, and for a per-
> fect supplication of the divine mercy. In the psalms, too, you will find
> thanksgiving for all that befalls you. In the psalms you confess your
> weakness and misery, and thereby call down God's mercy upon you.
> You will find every virtue in the psalms, if God in his mercy will
> deign to reveal to you their secrets.[5]

So 'an intimacy of prayer' is what this whole business of common
prayer is all about, in which the Scriptures are interiorized and, as

in the case of Mary, the mother of the Lord, they are pondered and reflected upon in the hearts and not simply in the minds of the worshippers. Music and simple chants should frequently be used, therefore, throughout the office to aid this opening up of the heart to receive God's Word and to make it our own. In the singing of plainsong chant in the old medieval offices, there were special places in the plainsong which encouraged the monks to 'dwell' upon the word or phrase. Thomas Moore writes:

> Sometimes in their chanting, monks will land upon a note and sing it in a florid fashion, one syllable of text for fifty notes of chant. 'Melisma', they call it. Living a melismatic life in imitation of plainchant, we may stop on an experience, a place, a person, or a memory and rhapsodize in our imaginations. Some like to meditate or contemplate melismatically, while others prefer to draw, build, paint or dance whatever their eye has fallen upon.

But he concludes, 'living one point after another is one form of experience, and it can be emphatically productive. But stopping for melisma gives the soul its reason for being.'[6] Sadly, in the West we have only been taught to read the Scriptures as though they were addressed to one side of the brain, reading one verse immediately after the other. In the Daily Offices we are introduced to another way of reading Scripture – melismatically – dwelling upon it and making it our own or, as in the great Anglican collect, praying that we should read, mark, learn and inwardly digest the Scriptures so that they become our daily bread, feeding the imagination and the heart and getting into the subconscious which is really at the root of all our motivations.

There will be an important place for times of silence – and extended silence at that – in the course of reciting the Daily Office. Certainly, after each passage of Scripture has been read, there should be a time of silence, melismatically speaking! It is often best not to terminate the reading of Scripture with the 'guillotine' phrase – 'This is the Word of the Lord' – as though that part of the service has now been cut off and finished. Much better to leave the last words of the scriptural passage floating in the air, inviting melisma, so to speak.

The formal prayers (the collects) should be said slowly so that they 'stand up' in the course of many words, and such spontaneous prayers and intercessions as are invited should be made with short sentences (few, if any, relative clauses): they should be pithy and addressed to God the Father directly, and not little sermonettes directed to the congregation, emphasizing the favourite hobby-horse of the person leading the prayers!

Structured prayer and spontaneous prayer

Happily, there can be little doubt that the growing edge of the corporate prayer life of the Church today is to be found at that point where structured prayer and spontaneous prayer converge. For too long these two different ways of praying have been separated in somewhat opposing traditions: the Catholic witness tending to go for the more structured forms of prayer, while the more evangelical and Protestant traditions have tended to regard structured prayers read from a book as being necessarily insincere and have therefore opted for somewhat wordy forms of spontaneous prayer.

There is a very natural place in the structure of the Daily Offices which encourages times of extended spontaneous prayers and biddings from the congregation. It is sometimes helpful if the person leading the Daily Office will give a minimum guidance for those wishing to offer personal intercessions from the whole congregation, with such words as 'I ask your prayers and intercessions for the Church' and then 'for God's world', 'for the local community', 'for the sick and those in need', 'for the dying and the departed'. And then in conclusion the leader should pick up all the prayers and intercessions into an invocation, asking God that 'these and all our prayers may be united with the prayers of the saints, as together we pray the great prayer of the Kingdom, which Jesus himself taught us to pray . . .'

The shape of the prayers in the 'prayer for the Church', as it used to be known in the old prayer book, which takes its structure from the prayers in the Good Friday liturgy, has become fairly well known by most people who attend church regularly and seems to flow quite naturally.

Finally, it goes without saying that, as St Paul exhorts the Corinthian Christians in their practice of corporate worship, times of common prayer are not the place for people to speak aloud in tongues. In informal prayer groups, where there is an interpreter present, the prayer of tongues can be a wonderful gift to the whole group, but in church buildings during more formal worship it is doubtful whether such prayer normally has a place at all.

The Daily Office and the spirituality of God's people

Alasdair Macintyre writes:

> What matters at this stage is the construction of local forms of community within which civility and the intellectual and moral life can be sustained through the new dark ages which are already upon us. And if the tradition of the virtues was able to survive the horrors of the last dark ages, we are not entirely without grounds for hope. This time however the barbarians are not waiting beyond the frontiers; they have already been governing us for quite some time. And it is our lack of consciousness of this that constitutes part of our predicament. We are waiting not for a Godot, but for another – doubtless very different – St Benedict.[7]

To that prophetic statement of Alasdair Macintyre we would perhaps wish to add St Hilda of Whitby, St Hildegaard of Bingen – indeed, all men and women of community. For that is what the local church must become in the next century as we wait for the return of the Lord and look and pray for the coming of the Kingdom: the local, little, fragile communities of faith, witnessing to resurrection in their stories and life-style – a counter-culture of subversive, undercover men and women.

A warning! These little cells of resurrection must not be permitted to degenerate into ghettos with a drawbridge mentality. Rather, they must see themselves as salt, light and leaven for the world; distinctive from the wider surrounding community in which they live and work, and yet deeply engaged with the world, working as well as praying for the coming Kingdom.

It is a totally false picture of the Early Church to suppose that it was a ghetto cut off from the rest of the world, just waiting passively for the *parousia*. On the contrary, according to Bruce Winter's substantial thesis, *Seek the Welfare of the City*, Christians from the very earliest days 'were deeply involved in the culture of their time'. And the 'early church taught a civic consciousness among its members', developing 'new perspectives on social ethics'.[8] For the spirituality of the New Testament Christian was essentially corporate. So I see a picture of small congregations, engaged with local life, meeting daily for prayer and worship to reflect upon the Scriptures and to watch, wait and work for that Kingdom to which their daily life-style is a living testimony – 'the end in the middle'! For ultimately, as Lesslie Newbigin so rightly says, the only hermeneutic of the gospel which can speak to our post-modern culture 'is a congregation of men and women who believe it and live by it'.[9] In the words of Jesus, 'When the Son of Man comes, will he find faith on the earth?' (Luke 18:8).

By God's grace he will, in the form of these fragile local communities of faith, the remnant living and praying for the many. As William Temple fondly reminds us, 'The church is the only society that exists for the sake of those who are not members of it.' The right people in the right place at the right time, doing and saying the right things, are the fulcrum on which history turns.

So intercession is not so much a form of prayer as the new way of life in the Kingdom. All Christians, by their baptism, share in the priestly vocation of Jesus, our one true and great High Priest, who ever lives to make intercession for us. In the empires and kingdoms of this world it is, as we say, 'every man for himself', the survival of the fittest and the law of the jungle. But not so in the coming Kingdom. There it will be every man for others in every aspect of our lives – the way we spend our time, money and energies as well as the way in which we pray.

So Christian spirituality today will resemble very much the spirituality of the book of Acts and of the New Testament in general: community based, a sharing group of men and women, interdependent, with a story of resurrection to tell both corporately and personally. Leadership in this community will be expressed essentially through service. This life-style will be priestly in the sense already explained, but it will be very much expressed by a willingness to lay down life sacrificially for the sake of others. It will be essentially a lay spirituality to equip men and women to work and witness in the world of the market-place and the family. Perhaps we can now begin to see how those Daily Offices of Morning and Evening Prayer, which go right back to the very earliest days of the corporate worship and significantly of the Church, are an ideal whose time has come full circle once again.

Celebrating Common Prayer

The fundamental purpose of *Celebrating Common Prayer – The Daily Office SSF*, wrote Archbishop Carey in the Foreword to that book in 1992, was to help 'the Church as a whole to pray together daily in a reflective and structured way'. He continued:

> For many regular Sunday worshippers, personal prayer during the week is unstructured and haphazard . . . A pattern of daily prayer which complements eucharistic worship, such as this book, offers a major resource to the Church.

You might be tempted to ask why the Church of England or indeed the Church generally needed yet another prayer book after all the revisions for worship in recent years. Dr Carey addresses that issue when he writes:

> Since the publication of *The Alternative Service Book 1980*, our knowledge of the origin and purpose of daily common prayer in the early Church has grown enormously. As a result, many people long for a return to a simple and more celebratory form of common prayer for our time. In this book . . . there is a simple structure for Morning and Evening Prayer, when desired. The services can be led by lay people as effectively as the clergy. There is an emphasis on celebrating together rather than 'saying the office' as a private and exclusively clerical obligation.[10]

Yes, the note of celebration is strong in this new office book. Suggestions are given for simple ceremonial, for the use of simple symbols. So Dr Carey goes on to say,

> As well as the texts, suggestions are made as to how the services might be celebrated in a wide range of circumstances. The use of

music of different styles and of a visual focus – the Bible, a lighted candle, a large cross, for example – will enrich the worship for many.

In addition to endorsing very strongly the need for this worship to be corporate where and whenever possible, it is important to give a structured form of daily prayer to lay men and women whose lives in the world of work do not permit them the luxury of joining with others daily for the celebration of common prayer. Like King Alfred, there are many who would welcome, in the words of the archbishop, 'a structured form of prayer when they are on their own, whether it is in hospital or on a commuter train, those peculiar forms of isolation when there are many people around'. For the Church especially in our own day needs 'to recognize and cater for the many Christians who are not part of a family which shares their faith'.

So may God bless this particular vehicle of worship and corporate prayer for our age, and in turn may we as God's people, looking for the coming Kingdom, be faithful and joyful in our daily life of personal and corporate prayer, daily praying the prayer of the Kingdom while seeking to live the life-style of that Kingdom as it has been revealed to us in that King who came in the form of a servant two thousand years ago and who will one day return to claim that Kingdom as his own.

'When the Son of Man comes, will he find faith in the earth?' is the question of Jesus, today as at the first. The answer is most assuredly 'Yes.' He will find small, fragile communities of faith and resurrection, living the life-style of the coming Kingdom, heralding that Kingdom by deed as well as by word, engaging with the wider community, yet remaining distinctive from the rest of the world, as salt, light and leaven.

9

Alternative patterns of worship for a Church in mission

The growing need for alternative patterns of worship

Much of this chapter is written necessarily and quite deliberately from a specifically Anglican perspective. However, to write such a chapter most certainly does not imply that other churches are not also presently engaging in more freely expressed patterns of worship – both eucharistic and non-eucharistic – nor that the Anglican Church is alone or in the forefront of developing alternative styles and patterns of worship. On the contrary, both the Roman Catholic Church, as well as the Free Churches and the churches of the Reformation on the Continent, are re-forming and re-shaping their worship under the gentle yet powerful influence of the Holy Spirit, who is clearly at work in our day, refashioning as well as refreshing the worship of God's people in many and differing patterns and liturgical expressions. For in the Western world at large, along with our Christian brothers and sisters in the Third World and in developing countries, we also are now beginning to see ourselves, along with them, as churches ministering the gospel in an essentially missionary context.

It is the same Holy Spirit who is leading the churches to place a new emphasis upon evangelization, as the Spirit who is at work in and through new expressions of worship. For worship at its richest can scarcely avoid being a carrier for the gospel experience both for those who regularly attend church as well as for those on the fringe or completely outside the institutional Church.

In a post-Christian world – a world which is even termed 'post-modern', whatever that may mean – the Church itself is necessarily and increasingly the primary agent for mission. As Lesslie Newbigin remarks, 'The only hermeneutic of the gospel is a congregation of men and women who believe it and live by it.'[1] If, as John Westerhoff claims, 'The purpose of the church is to manifest an alternative way of seeing and living life,'[2] then it follows that much Christian witness and commending of the gospel reality will be expressed through worship and liturgy, in so far as worship is formative of the core life-style of God's people.

Perhaps it should be said at this point that the Liturgical Commission of the Church of England has risen to the challenge of the Decade of Evangelism as well as to the challenge issued from the quite radical report *Faith in the City* (1985), both of which, implicitly or explicitly, required more and differing forms of services than those already provided in *The Alternative Service Book* of 1980. The publication of the *ASB* certainly marked a new stage in the development of Anglican worship. Although it was put together in the light of all the current experiments in liturgical reform, especially in the sixties, and had placed all the new texts in one book, following the pattern established by Cranmer in the sixteenth century, it was also a very forward-looking book in that it opened up possibilities for greater flexibility in the ways in which the services could be celebrated through the use of extensive *optional* material and rubrics. Yet the *ASB* most certainly did not mark the end of liturgical reform (much as many more cautious and traditionalist spirits would have wished), but rather it signalled the beginning of a new chapter which demanded even more and not less flexibility in corporate worship.

For example, if the Liturgical Commission were to respond faithfully to the challenges of *Faith in the City*, then all patterns of worship would need to 'reflect local cultures', allowing 'a greater involvement of the congregation'. Furthermore, patterns of worship would need to be 'more concrete and tangible than abstract and theoretical'. In 1986 the House of Bishops agreed that the Liturgical Commission should proceed to prepare supplementary books, the primary purpose of which should be:

- to provide some indication of different ways of doing liturgy, taking into account sociological, architectural and churchmanship differences;
- to indicate where advantage might be taken of notes and rubrics

in the *ASB* to develop and enrich the liturgy;
• to provide outline structures and mandatory sections for some main services, which, if authorized alongside the *ASB*, would provide greater freedom for those who wish either to enrich or shorten the services (including family services and worship in urban priority areas).[3]

If the Liturgical Commission had not taken all this on board over the years since 1980, we could have expected revolt at the local level, where the ordering of worship would be in the hands of many people who were almost certainly neither qualified nor trained for such a ministry.

Therefore, since 1984, the Liturgical Commission has produced a whole series of supplementary books. It is an impressive output (*Lent, Holy Week, Easter; The Promise of His Glory; Enriching the Christian Year; Celebrating Common Prayer* and *Patterns of Worship*) which deserves our gratitude as well as our commitment to become partners in an on-going period of experiment and further exploration. *Patterns of Worship* arose out of a request from the General Synod Standing Committee for the Liturgical Commission to compile

> a 'directory' with a wealth of resource material including supplementary material for each of the many points in the service where there is room for the individual's own words. The directory would need to set boundaries to the proposed freedom, and points which might be theologically divisive would have to be watched.[4]

Local and seasonal colourings and variations

In many ways the *Alternative Service Book* of 1980 had left many doors open, inviting future exploration and experiment. There are many parts of the services in that book where rubrics positively invite variations according to the season of the Church's year as well as according to the locality in which the worship is being offered. The very phrase from the traditional liturgy – 'at all times and in all places' – might well suggest that there would be variations and colourings which reflected both the nature of the occasion (i.e. time), as well as something about the local community or the specific location of the worship (i.e. place).

Repeatedly in the *ASB*, the rubric enjoins that the following paragraph or sentence 'may be used' or 'some other suitable words' in places such as the introduction to the confession of the people; the greeting of peace; the preparation of the gifts. At the invitation to come forward to receive the sacrament, we read that 'additional words of invitation may be used', and again, 'alternative words of distribution may be found', referring the reader to another section in the book, or indeed, to other official publications.

So in this and in several other ways, it had become established policy to leave plenty of room for spontaneity and variation, so that the old 'Prayer for the Church' according to the rubrics of the *ASB* permits of many and varied permutations: 'not all paragraphs need be used on every occasion. Individual names may be added at places indicated.'

And so it was that the subsequent supplementary volumes were in demand when the *ASB* was scarcely off the printing press. For, as experience has shown, these options, when taken up either by clergy or by lay readers, tended to become stereotyped and so convoluted that the final state of spontaneity is often far worse than the former condition of rigidity and formalism.

Furthermore, although a wild generalization, it is nevertheless painfully true that few clergy or laity have the gift for leading corporate prayer in ways which move the congregation along or which incorporate with facility all the little personal prayers and intercessions that are rightly in and around the place on a Sunday morning.

Enriching the Christian Year is most helpful in supplying succinct and brief variable introductions to confession and to the greeting of peace, as well as some seasonal variations for the refrain, 'the mystery of faith', with its accompanying congregational response. All this is done on the understanding that a clear structure lies at the foundation of the service: 'its main components should stand out so that worshippers can see the shape, development and climax of the service – so that they "know where they are going."' 'It is helpful,' concludes the introduction to *Patterns for Worship*, 'if this is reflected in the way the service is laid out for printing.'[5]

In the second part of *Patterns for Worship* there is a long section offering sample services with suggested layout for printed orders of service. Snappy and tasteful little drawings accompany the text, which is well laid out with the various sections of the service clearly marked, together with helpful rubrics about sitting, standing or kneeling. All this is to be commended very highly.

All the outlines, together with the resource sections and the commentaries in all of these supplementary books, should be seen, according to their authors, as

> skeletons, or the bare bones and outlines of services, flesh to clothe them with, in terms of the resource material, and the working instructions or hints on how to make it all work. But like Ezekiel's army in the valley of dry bones, the skeletons need not only flesh and instructions, but the breath of the Lord himself, to bring them to life.[6]

Special non-eucharistic services

It is becoming increasingly clear that one 'main' service on a Sunday morning cannot possibly serve all categories of people who might wish to attend church, ranging from the totally committed Sunday communicant or even week-day communicant, all the way across the spectrum to the enquirer, the first-timer or the occasional visitor to church. In many places, the one Sunday morning 'main' service is falling between sets of stools: it's too *in* for the outsider, but not sufficiently deep for the regular; it's too early for the outsider but probably not early enough for those who are committed to church attendance on Sunday, and who, possibly as part of a lifetime's habit, have built their Sunday life around morning worship and the Sunday lunch, and who naturally both wish as well as need to get on with all kinds of other duties or hobbies later in the day. Often such people, not unnaturally, opt for the 'early service' – the said eight o'clock Communion – not only for its earlier and more convenient timing, but also because it uses the corporate worship slot to feed a much neglected daily and personal devotional life.

The whole Church at the present time needs to learn that corporate liturgical worship is not a replacement for a personal life of devotion and contemplation, but rather that it is intended to be the focus and centre of Christian discipleship, overflowing in a thousand and one different ways, ranging from ejaculatory prayers, intercession and meditation, to say nothing of work, service and vocation. Our corporate worship is intended to flood every corner of our lives, until the whole of life is worship.

In any event, we are going to need to tailor specific services and specific timings in an age when society is very fragmented, pursuing all sorts of different life-styles, linked to different timetables and various responsibilities. It's very doubtful whether the normal Sunday timetable of services in most parishes could easily accommodate doctors, nurses, entertainers, people whose work is in essential services, such as waiters and those who work in hotels or those engaged in sporting activities. For all such people we need to be offering all kinds of options, not only in relation to times of services, but also in the kind of services that we are offering. For those on the edge of the Church or who have just started to come to church, we need to develop a style of worship which is not ashamed to be known as user-friendly, at user-friendly times and styled in user-friendly ways.

In America, the famous case of the success of this approach was at Willow Creek, a 'yuppy' suburb of Chicago. The response to that well-researched initiative was so overwhelming that the 'regulars' decided to have their time of extended eucharistic worship on Thursday evenings rather than on Sunday mornings, with a fellowship meal and with plenty of space and time for prayer, silence, worship and teaching.

All this might lead us to suppose that there is likely to be a greater, rather than a lesser need for non-eucharistic services, especially for a Church which is at last beginning to see itself as being a Church in mission. Such services will need to be tailored and put together for all kinds of events and for all kinds of different people at different stages of discipleship. The family service and other such non-eucharistic services can provide 'a place where those unfamiliar with formal worship can begin to feel at home', for the simple reason that 'it can be a bridge, in reflecting local culture more easily than the rest of the church's worship'. A further reason for all this, according to *Patterns of Worship*, is that people sometimes welcome the excuse to accompany their children, and then find they understand teaching which is simple and visual, and sometimes at a more 'introductory' level. It is a place where genuine inter-generational activity takes place, with adults and children learning from each other in worship. It can help regular church attenders to discover new dimensions in worship. It provides an opportunity for people to grow and use their gifts by sharing in the planning, leading and contributing to worship.

Last but by no means least, 'it provides a way of introducing new elements into worship [in a congregation likely to be less critical of them?] – drama, dance, audiovisuals, new hymns or methods of teaching.'[7]

If this is at all on target, then surely it is vital that non-eucharistic liturgies should be put together carefully and 'professionally' rather than being limited by the competence or inclination (possibly at the last minute or even spontaneously) of the local priest or lay minister responsible for leading the worship.

The Liturgical Commission has set out reasonable expectations and standards about such DIY worship which we would do well to heed, underlining some principles which 'should be safeguarded for those who wish to stand in any recognizable continuity with historical Anglican tradition'. Taken at face value, that can sound stuffy, pompous or even over-protective in a negative sense. Yet there is much wisdom in this plea, as the events at St Thomas', Sheffield in the mid nineties demonstrated. Just because worship 'turns people on', it does not follow that such worship is either appropriate or worship offered in truth as well as in Spirit. For worship is not a democratically designed affair. The experience of the Church throughout the centuries in what constitutes good or bad worship is surely of some value and should demand our study and careful attention – experience often learned in hard ways, which frankly we ignore or despise at our peril.

According to the guidelines of the Liturgical Commission, such non-eucharistic services require 'a clear structure for worship; an emphasis on reading the word of God and on using psalms; liturgical words repeated by the congregation, some of which, like the creed, would be known by heart.' It is recommended that a collect is used, plus 'the Lord's Prayer, and some responsive forms of prayer', and that throughout all of this valid and important experimentation with alternative forms of worship there is a clear 'recognition of the centrality of the Eucharist' and 'a concern for form, dignity, and economy of words'.

The liturgy of the Word

Of course, in one sense the structure of what we generally refer to as the one, main service – the Eucharist – in reality, if not in practice, falls into two quite distinct parts: the liturgy of the Word, from the beginning until the kiss of peace, followed by the eucharistic liturgy, beginning at the preparation of the bread and wine through until the end of the service. In the Early Church only the faithful, the committed and the baptized were permitted to stay on for the second half of the service – the sacred mysteries. The catechumens and seekers were compelled to leave after the liturgy of the Word.

In the present climate it might be no bad thing to make a similar clear-cut division between the liturgy of the Word, along the lines of the long-established Anglican practice of a service of 'ante-Communion'. Such a service is in fact a concentration on the Word of God: the readings in Scripture, the singing of hymns and psalms and spiritual songs, a full-length sermon, an extended time of prayer, including a confession of sins and absolution, and culminating either in some sort of altar call, inviting people to come forward for the laying on of hands, a personal blessing or anointing. Conclude with an extended greeting of peace, spilling over into coffee hour and fellowship.

In any event, there is no reason why what is technically a liturgy of the Word should not constitute the basic outline for a family service, or a mission service or a guest service. After the reception or at a later time in the day, the eucharistic liturgy could be celebrated either with a truncated liturgy of the Word or omitting the liturgy of the Word altogether, and beginning with a time of confession and prayer and then going straight into eucharistic action.

However, it cannot be too strongly stated that such services should not be allowed to degenerate into mere 'hymn sandwiches' providing little more than a top and tailing of the sermon. There

must be a well-planned structure expressed through action, movement, direction and a climax – and please note, only one climax,
not several climaxes endlessly banging on, looking for an ending!
There is much to be said for the structure of the liturgy of the
Word following fairly closely the structure of the first part of the
Eucharist, if only because it does have a familiar structure and can
serve as initiating people into the fuller service of the Eucharist at
a later stage, by building on what they already know and have
experienced.

In such services there is a great deal to be said for one of the
readings from Scripture being read dramatically by several
people, expressed perhaps also through dance, or for a piece of
reflective music to be played perhaps by a flute or classical guitar,
or some such combination of non-percussive instruments. These
and other aids can help people to interiorize the Word and to
receive it into their hearts and imaginations where, of course,
most of our motivations are rooted.

There is also a place in such services for a short dramatic, even
humorous presentation or sketch, which makes the same point as
will eventually be taken up in the sermon. Of course, it goes without saying that such services most certainly need to be printed out
in full, carrying, as they should, the genuine expectation that there
will be people present for whom the whole environment of a
church building and of church worship is alien and uncomfort-
ably different.

And finally, such hymns as there are must either be very well
known or the service should begin with a music practice for the
whole congregation, terminated by a time of quiet in preparation
for the formal act of worship, which will have a clearly defined
beginning. A congregational hymn practice has much to commend it, not only because it most certainly raises the standard of
congregational singing, but also because, suitably punctuated with
informal humour, it relaxes non-churchgoers and enables the congregation to see the essentially human face of the church.

Sunday evening worship is returning again after a blight of
many years, and it could be that a liturgy of the Word (not called
that, of course) could come into its own again on Sunday evenings
in some places, and take up again the spot that was so splendidly
reserved for 'Evensong' years ago, until the end of the fifties and

the onset of television, when Sunday evening worship practically disappeared.

The important point to make in this section on the place of the liturgy of the Word is that there is plenty of room for experimentation, trial and error within a more or less established framework. We need to be bold in this respect and always keep on the lookout for newly published material that has arisen out of good practice.

Special seasonal services

At various times of the year there is a crying need for 'special' services, for which no provision is made either in the traditional prayer books or in the *Alternative Service Book* of 1980. The three books mentioned above, produced by the Liturgical Commission, are intended to take us through the year from Advent to Pentecost, giving both special seasonal material with which to enflesh the skeleton eucharistic worship of the prayer book, as well as some totally new services or sections which can be slotted into the regular worship or constitute a totally separate occasion.

As early as 1979, the Episcopal Church in the USA produced a most helpful Book of Occasional Services, covering a vast range of occasions, which invited liturgical expression, and all in keeping with the best of Anglican ethos. It is only possible here to mention a few of them in the hope of giving some idea of the range of possibilities which this excellent book covers. The services fall into three categories: the Church's year; pastoral services; and episcopal services. This wide selection includes anthems at the candle lighting (Lucernaria); the Advent wreath; stations at the Christmas crèche; a service for New Year's eve; a blessing in homes for Epiphany; the way of the cross; Tenebrae; all the additional Holy Week services; welcoming new people to a congregation; services marking the various stages in the catechumenate; a celebration for a home; the anniversary of a marriage; the founding of a church (ground-breaking and the laying of a cornerstone); the consecration of chrism; the reaffirmation of ordination vows; and the welcoming and seating of a bishop in the cathedral.

In the preface to the book the contributors make the following comments:

Those services which have ancient roots have been studied in their historic forms. Many of the texts and ceremonies included in this book have a very long history indeed (for example, the rites of the catechumenate). Others have been designed to meet needs which have arisen only in recent years (for example, the festivals of lessons and music).[8]

All this may help to show how churches all over the world in different traditions have felt the need to expand resources for those concerned with preparing and leading worship and services which are not aimed at the run-of-the-mill churchgoing Christians, and services which are not to be held at the normal times on Sundays or in church buildings. There is no reason why we should not all draw on such world-wide resources and join in global Christian fellowship with those who see liturgy as a living stream flowing through the ages, adapting itself to the environment and needs of the day, leading pilgrims and disciples, seekers and enquirers alike, to the ultimate human experience of the worship of heaven.

The occasional offices

Most people would agree, at least in theory, that it is the occasional offices, as they are termed – baptisms, marriages and funerals especially – that afford the best opportunity for many people outside the Church to have some kind of experience of worship and of what goes on inside church buildings. Turning these occasions from being a chore and another burden for the clergy into real opportunities for outreach and for engaging with those who presently do not go to church requires teamwork at every point of the way.

Instead of worrying over-much whether the parents 'qualify' to have their child done and whether we should adopt a strict or more lenient baptismal policy, there are surely some prior questions which need to be addressed. In the first place, how can we, as a Church, convey to all parents that we really care, and want for their child the very best, and furthermore that we are prepared to move heaven and earth to bring this about?

There are several very good videos currently available which only last twenty minutes or so. When the couple or the single parent arrives at the vicarage or the church office to enquire about having their child baptized, it might be helpful to suggest that a young couple who recently had their child baptized, and who are regular members of the church, would like to visit and to take with them a video. On arriving at the house the church couple introduce themselves and ask if they might sit down and watch the video together. Afterwards, hopefully, all concerned can join in discussing the video, which is mainly aimed at telling in the simplest way what baptism involves and what is required of the parents of the newly born child. The committed Christian parents can speak from experience and share in all of this in ways that many clergy would not be able to do. That session could end, perhaps, with a simple prayer for the child, the parents and the home. *The Alternative Service Book, 1980* also provides a form of 'Thanksgiving for the Birth of a Child' and 'Thanksgiving after Adoption' and may be best used in anticipation of baptism.

The church couple have now made personal contact. They can proceed in a thousand and one different ways, now that the ground-work has been laid, perhaps with an invitation to come, along with other couples, to the church office or to another suitable place to view a second video portraying what actually happens at the baptism. (This second video could well be home-produced without too much bother.) On the day of the baptism, precisely because human contact has been established, the event will not seem strange or alien to the non-church couple, whether the baptism takes place at the main service or on some separate occasion.

The committed laity can similarly be involved in preparation, in the actual event and in the follow-up for marriages and funerals. The important principle at work in all these events is twofold: to involve the Church and not just the clergy in these pastoral opportunities from start to finish, and secondly, to show that we really care and want to meet seekers and enquirers more than half-way at their point of need. It is not for nothing that we speak of celebrating the Eucharist. As a church in any parish, we need to be asking ourselves again and again: in what sort of ways can we help the wider community, individually or corporately, to celebrate those events in their lives that already have meaning and significance for them? 'Grace perfects nature and does not annihilate it.' If that is true, then we shall not seek to lay on top of the life of the local community another dimension of life which we call 'church life'. Rather, we will be prepared to go out of our way to discover what are the things that people are really concerned about and to help to make the connection between what we are celebrating when the church gathers and what is being celebrated out in the community at large – marriage, baptism, bereavement, wedding anniversaries, birthdays, harvest festivals, and so on.

Healing services

In recent years there has been an ever-increasing demand for healing services in one form or another and at various times on Sundays and/or during the week. All this is the outcome of a rediscovery of the centrality of the healing ministry which is common to all Christian traditions. It is to be welcomed.

It is making more than a purely academic point to say in this context that in Tyndale's translation of the Scriptures into English at the Reformation, he quite correctly preferred the words 'healing' to 'salvation', 'healed' to 'saved' and 'physician' to 'saviour'. In both Greek and Latin the two English words have a common root. However, by introducing this etymological nicety, there is an important and valid theological point to be made, which needs to be reflected in an appropriate liturgical expression. Michael Perham comments:

> In the New Testament, in St Mark's Gospel, for instance, where the twelve are sent out to preach repentance and to anoint the sick, or in the Epistle of St. James, where the elders of the church are to be called to anoint and pray over the sick, there is a community setting. People are being put into a right relationship with the community and, through the community, with God. Similarly, repentance, and with it sacramental 'confession', are closely linked with ministry to the sick, not because sickness is a punishment for sin, but because sin itself, offence against God and his people, his community, is a form of disease.[9]

It is largely thanks to the charismatic movement that it is much easier nowadays (some might say almost dangerously easy) to offer personal ministry with or without the laying-on-of-hands; to invite people to confess their sins in the presence of another Christian, or preferably a priest; as well as just to offer to pray with someone after counselling or after the sharing of a problem and need.

Inevitably, such a ministry needs to find expression in some more formal and public act of worship. As with many of these special occasions, it is easy to insert a particular section – like the ministry of healing – into the eucharistic liturgy, either after the Gospel or the sermon, in place of or in addition to the intercessions. In all this the ministry of healing needs to be placed in a fuller context of repentance and renewal. Michael Perham remarks:

> In our own day just as the ministry of healing – Holy Unction – has become far more readily used, so the ministry of reconciliation – Penance – has been used less. Here is a danger and a warning. For all its intrinsic goodness, the ministry of healing can be an escape from responsibility. It need not be this, for penitence should nearly always form part of the preparation for the laying on of hands or anointing.[10]

According to the rubric in the Occasional Services Book of the United States, at one or other of the suggested points in the service the 'celebrant then lays hands on each person and, having dipped a thumb in the oil of the sick, makes the sign of the cross on their foreheads' and says one or other of several suggested prayers. For example:

> I lay my hands upon you (and anoint you with oil) in the name of our Lord and Saviour Jesus Christ, beseeching him to uphold you and fill you with grace, that you may know the healing power of his love. Amen.

In recent years there have been some remarkable pastoral applications of this ministry of healing in all kinds of places of human need and pain (e.g. the healing of memories and even the healing of family trees), all offering various services to help to express liturgically what we believe theologically.

We should not see any of this as innovation just for its own sake, for in fact much of it is certainly not new. Rather, we are recovering many of the tools and aids for worship and ministry which were fundamental in the ministry and witness of the Church in mission at those times and places which demanded a robust liturgical expression of a lively pastoral ministry in the fight against sin, the world and the devil, equipping men and women and the whole people of God to continue as Christ's 'soldiers and servants to the end of their days'. In other words, to provide the means of grace to live out our baptismal status as sons and daughters of God and as heralds of the coming Kingdom. For in one sense, as we have claimed repeatedly in this book, all worship represents us to the Father in Christ, in our baptismal status. A theological conviction about this will help to rescue worship from falling into pietism or quietism and will not only help the people of God to celebrate their identity as the community of resurrection, but will also equip them to live out the new life in the workaday world, as well as in the home.

Table prayers

The Victorians have a great deal to teach contemporary Christians on many fronts, but by no means least on the frontier of the consecration of family life, with a family-based spirituality. For a long time the Roman Catholic Church has taught that 'The family that prays together, stays together.' Of course, in an age of fast food, Sunday trading and working flexi-hours, it is not easy for the family to be together, let alone to stay together or pray together. However, where it is possible to sit down for a family meal, there must surely be space – not least when guests are present – for a short (very short) time of prayer and even for a Bible reading as we gather round the table for a meal. Hospitality is at the very heart of Christian spirituality, while table-talk and table-time afford a literally God-given opportunity to be together in prayer in an unself-conscious and natural way. It is not beyond the ability of ordinary Christians to draw up a form of thanksgiving at table that is simple and short; to print it out and to use it whenever two or three are gathered together at table. Some verses from the

Psalms lend themselves particularly well to a form of thanksgiving at table:

> VERSICLE : The Lord gives food to those who fear him:
> RESPONSE : He is ever-mindful of his promises, (Ps. 111:5).

> VERSICLE : The eyes of all wait upon you, O Lord:
> RESPONSE : You give them their food in due season (Ps. 104:28).

> VERSICLE : He gives food to those who fear him;
> RESPONSE : He is mindful of his promises for ever (Ps. 111:5).

All this, together with a short reading from Scripture, might be accompanied by the lighting of a candle and be concluded with the greeting of peace exchanged around the table. If it is not particularly practical to do this before the meal, it might be done between courses or at the end.

The house church and its worship

We saw earlier in this book that the foundation of growing churches is to be found in the cell or house group. Because this is so, we need to develop worship which is appropriate to these small and intimate occasions.

Out on the road in a hectic itinerant ministry, the author has had an opportunity to observe the characteristics that are constant in growing churches. Top of the list of those characteristics and common to all places of growth is the alternative service at an alternative time and in a different style – call it the family service or what you will. A close second common factor, however, would be those parishes where house groups during the week have become the norm, developing their own spirituality as a prayer group or Bible study or general study group. Here again, with the flexibility of a structured liturgy together with many built-in optional prayers and contents, it is possible to tailor the Eucharist to be the context for Bible study or for extended corporate prayer and intercession, or for a time committed to praying for the neighbourhood (often undertaken nowadays in what are called 'prayer-

walks' – or 'beating the bounds of the parish', to use the old formula of rogationtide; there really is nothing new under the sun!).

Yet with a little imagination and with some team-work, it is
possible to turn the formerly entitled 'sick Communion' (an
unfortunate phrase, to say the least) into a miniature of church
planting. Instead of taking the 'sick Communion' over to Mrs
Jones's house on the housing estate during the working week,
what is stopping us from saying to Mrs Jones, 'Next Sunday afternoon at four o'clock we will have "church" in your house. I will
bring with me, if I may, two or three members of the congregation. You might care also to invite a neighbour or a friend to come
along.'

This will be a case of the church constituting the church where
formerly there was no church. A well-tailored, simple eucharistic
occasion, with a small talk arising perhaps out of the Gospel, followed even by some discussion, leading into informal prayer for
Mrs Jones, her home and family and for the neighbourhood; inviting others to mention names of people in need of any kind in that
neighbourhood – all this roots the Church in the world and moves
us from our turf on to theirs.

But there are all kinds of other ways in which we can trans-
plant the Church by taking the Body of Christ (in every sense) out
of the church building.

From our turf to theirs

In many parishes – especially in the country and in small towns –
the local pub is the first and obvious place for transplanting the
Church, and visibly constituting it primarily as a body of people
rather than as a building. There can be little doubt that if Christ
had been incarnate as an Englishman and in our own age, he
would have spent a great deal of time in pubs, and wherever people are gathered together.

With the support and cooperation of the publican, the pub can
be an excellent place for carols at Christmas, for a harvest thanksgiving or for some local celebration in the village or community.
All this is not to say that we should *not* use the church building
for such occasions as well and in addition, but there is nothing

stopping us from taking the church outside the building and going where people are, if people are presently not coming to where we as 'church' meet Sunday by Sunday.

The Sunday Trading Act has prompted several enterprising clergy to hold the occasional Sunday morning service in the shopping mall. However, as in the case of the pub, we must not be seen to be playing at church. The mandate of 'an appropriate occasion appropriately expressed' is very important in all these instances. For example, we need to make sure that if amplification is needed, it is first class. Secondly, in most circumstances there is no need for choirs, servers or clergy to 'dress up' in church clothes, cassocks, surplices and so forth (an exception to that generalization might well be the occasion of carols at Christmas, round the Christmas tree). The lessons need to be short and well read in a non-churchy way. If there is someone who has the skill to move easily and unself-consciously out of the service into a kind of pub routine at the piano for a good old-fashioned sing-song, so much the better! (The author has spent many hours in this ministry, both as priest and bishop, playing the piano in pubs – golden oldies as well as songs 'ancient and modern'!)

Many clergy at ports and in harbour towns are asked to conduct an annual service for the ships and boats. If we have a sacramental view of the universe and of all creation, then we shall never need to be churchy or self-conscious about this extension of the 'west wall' of our church building, to speak metaphorically. From a sacramental perspective, there is no west wall in our church buildings. All church buildings should open outwards, literally turning the church inside out, driving men and women out, fully alive to the features of a sacramental universe, with eyes wide open to the glory of God latent in every atom for those with eyes to see. As David Jones has remarked, 'It is important to know that a beefsteak is neither more nor less "mystical" than a diaphanous cloud. The painter more than any man must know that the green grass on the hill and the fairy ring are both equally real.'[11]

And finally there is the market-place. If you are to go for this, then it is important to secure the natural centre and focus of the town. Furthermore it is important that such an event is well attended and therefore it should normally be an occasion when all the churches in the area combine, closing their own buildings –

perhaps once a year – and going to the town service for a full act of worship.

Recently the author was invited to preach at such a service in Exmouth, Devon. The local church leaders had worked hard to secure the very centre of the town. In order to do this it had been necessary to obtain permission from the town council. This permission was refused on two occasions on the basis that it would disrupt the Sunday trading in the shops surrounding all three sides of that triangle. On the third request, permission was reluctantly given.

At eleven o' clock, and with the sun shining, nearly 2,000 Christians from all the local churches gathered in that triangle and small park, felicitously marked by a large stone cross as the War Memorial in the very centre. The shoppers in their hundreds were about their business, but could be clearly seen to be captivated by the very moving and authentic act of worship that was taking place. So successful was the event, that it was decided by all the churches taking part, to repeat the occasion annually.

The event had been carefully planned from start to finish with a professionally engineered amplification system; a band of good local musicians to accompany the hymns, supported by a very large choir. The occasion certainly made an impact not only on the shoppers passing by, but on all those Christians taking part.

'The church with songs must shout; no door can keep them out' was the mission spirit of that Anglican priest and poet, George Herbert. Of course, occasions when the Church goes to other people's turf require courtesy and sensitivity on our part, but we should by no means always assume that we are unwelcome in the so-called secular world. Of course, we might well have some bad experiences, but by and large, at least in Britain, there is still a generous disposition to Christian witness, not least when it is expressed through good worship. The stories are legion of how congregations have had their churches burned, and during the months when they have had to worship (often by invitation) on someone else's property – a school hall, a leisure centre or the like – they have found that their worship is invigorated by the fresh air of the larger world.

None of this is to say that we should not use our buildings – they are a gift from God, given through the lives of men and women who longed to make a thank-offering in stone for all that God had given them through the gospel of Christ. The Church's place on the landscape – often at the centre of a community – is something to prize and to cherish, even if it requires in our day radical readaptation and reordering along the lines suggested later in this book.

There is also a further reason for worship to be carried out into the community beyond the church walls, namely to witness that as disciples of the risen Lord, we are not 'ashamed to confess the faith of Christ crucified'; to 'fight valiantly under the banner of Christ against sin, the world, and the devil, and to continue his faithful soldiers and servants to the end of our lives.'[12] To that end we need to seek out any and every opportunity that comes our way, as well as to be ready to respond to invitations to glorify God in the high street as well as in the highest!

10

Reordering church buildings for worship

Problems or solutions

'Problems are solutions in disguise' must surely be the universal mandate for all who believe in the God of the Resurrection! Nearly all God's blessings appear to present themselves to us disguised as problems. In the twentieth century, church buildings are frequently perceived as constituting problems and headaches, especially for the clergy, who often seem to have to spend an inordinate amount of time servicing them and equally inordinate amounts of energy raising money for their maintenance and upkeep.

While fully appreciating that if we were starting *de novo* in a mission to Britain, we would certainly not build the number of churches we still have, in the style in which many of them were built, nor in many of the places where they have been built; while fully realizing that our financial resources should be primarily directed towards mission and people, rather than towards the maintenance of buildings – many of them ancient at that; and also while recognizing that the Church (in terms of people) has grown most rapidly in those countries and parts of the world which simply cannot afford large and expensive buildings; when all this, and more is rightly taken literally into our accounting, it is still possible to maintain that the buildings we have inherited need to be viewed as assets and resources, which rightly used can turn problems into solutions and handicaps into opportunities. Canon Richard Giles remarks:

> The fact that the interiors of the vast majority of our church buildings provide people outside with one of the best reasons for not taking the church seriously, means that whenever a Christian

community does begin to treat the building as servant not master, radically re-thinking and re-equipping its base for worship and mission, the effect is nothing less than electrifying. Jesus is alive and well and living in his church after all!

It is neither accidental nor incidental that all the religions of the world have built shrines, temples and places for worship – many of them constituting the most glorious buildings in their time or in their respective culture. Human beings are both sacramental and institutional in make-up. The Christian faith, of all religions, is theologically predisposed by its emphasis upon the Incarnation, to endorse these natural human aspirations which have been expressed architecturally through glorious buildings over the centuries. For we are not angels. Incarnational Christianity straddles the spiritual and the material; earth and heaven; human and divine, as we are called by God to re-landscape his universe and so to redirect all its lines and profiles, its energies and forces Godward.

Communities do not exist in thin air as ideas and ideals. They are located and housed in brick and stone with an address, a telephone number and nowadays with the inevitable fax! So with the Body of Christ and with communities of faith. They need to make an impression on the skyline of the rest of our life, as continual reminders of the reality of the presence of God, keeping the rumour of God alive in a world which is always seeking ways of attracting our attention with competitive signs and symbols.

The men and women who built so many of those church buildings were undertaking a most worthy two-fold enterprise. Viewed from the outside, the church building was intended to make a statement to everyone in the community, whether they ever entered the building or not. The church building was built to be a sacramental statement – an outward and visible sign of an inward reality and truth. A glorious church building keeps the rumour of God alive in a community whether most people in that community believe in God or not. 'What mean ye by these stones?' children will ask their parents in future generations, according to the book of Joshua (Josh. 4:6). In our secular cities the church buildings constitute signs of contradiction, standing out like a sore thumb, refusing to allow God and all that he might stand for, to be marginalized – stubborn reminders in stone of the persistence of the sacred even in a secular age.

Professor Joad, who was a famous agnostic broadcaster in the forties and fifties and who, throughout his life, had consistently attacked the Christian faith, tells in his book, *Recovery of Belief* how he came to a living faith, shortly before his death. In that book he relates some of the incidents and symbolic events which compelled him to stop and think again. On one occasion he was being shown over the interior of Lincoln Cathedral by the dean. At some point the dean took him up into the triforium and said in a somewhat casual throw-away line, something like, 'I'll now show you the finest carving in the whole cathedral. Unfortunately, it's tucked away right up here where no one can normally see it. I can't think why on earth the stonemason should have carved this fine piece of work in such an obscure place: it must have been done purely and simply to the glory of God, I suppose!'

That casual remark opened up for Joad a totally contradictory perspective on the world; the sudden realization that countless men and women over the ages as poets, musicians, artists, sculptors and stonemasons had done their best work to the glory of a God who, from Joad's cramped perspective, was not supposed to exist. Many of our church buildings afford to the passer-by and indeed to the whole resident community, a constant and sometimes even glorious reminder of another perspective – the unapologetic wholly Other who, even as the centuries go by, stubbornly refuses to be expelled from the skylines and contours of our towns, villages and cities, often occupying prime sights and dominant aspects, pointing beyond and inviting downcast men and women to look up.

And furthermore, don't let us be too certain that they (those numerous passers-by) never go into our churches, or never want to go into our churches, just to see and to look. Sadly, most of our church buildings are not open except at those times when they are being used by churchgoers. This is a sad state of affairs, for the second sense in which church buildings are sacramental can only be appreciated if and when we enter them – when and if we go inside what is intended to be sacred space – sacred precisely because it has been set aside to be different (i.e. consecrated). Paul Tillich wrote:

One of the most important expressions of sacred emptiness occurred in Judaism and Islam – and was then forgotten because of the incarnation idea. Christianity was able to have the Divine again in forms of finitude, and Christianity filled the churches with them. Today these forms, most of them, have lost their meaning. Therefore I do not hesitate to say that I am most satisfied by church interiors – if built today – in which holy emptiness is architecturally expressed; that is of course quite different from an empty church.

Sacred space is the key to good interior church design – a point which was lost largely on our busy Victorian industrial forebears. They cluttered our churches and cathedrals with pews and screens and with lighting that was bad lighting precisely because it drew attention to itself rather than drawing attention to the building it was there to illuminate. On this vexed question of lighting, Tillich makes a most interesting and important point about the ways in which we have abused the gift of sacred space. 'The development of light in the churches' through the ages 'is very interesting,' he claims. 'Slowly the daylight replaced the light that is broken through stained-glass windows. The daylight is not the outburst of Divine light, but rational light by which one can read and the congregation can see one another.' Yes, that contemporary tyrant of rationalism, aided and abetted by the electric lighting so dear to our age, has invaded our sacred spaces along with all the other clutter of domesticity. Yet the news is not totally negative, for some good lighting, as we shall see later, is slowly replacing the Victorian horrors of central lighting and enabling the sense of 'sacred space' to return to many of our church buildings.

Yet Tillich does not go far enough in his criticism of functional clutter. For where Christianity in its worship is precisely distinctive and different from all other religions, is that church buildings are designed not primarily to create a mood, but more fundamentally to create space and a setting for the liturgy and corporate worship of God's people. One book on the subject says, 'The empty church, the church outside the time of the celebration of the liturgy, must proclaim the life of the assembly.'¹ It is only when we have this fundamental theological building-block firmly in place, that we can begin to reorder our church buildings for the primary purpose for which a Christian church building is and should be erected – namely for the liturgy and worship of God's people – the community of faith. Not surprisingly, Tillich reflects in his architectural tastes much of the individualism of his Protestant theology, and while he makes some most important contributions on the frontiers of church architecture, he falls short at just this point. He is most certainly right in making some important and valid criticisms of much that lay behind the Victorian obsession with busy and rationalistic functionalism – their obsession with filling every conceivable space – nevertheless it has to be admitted that he does this for quite wrong theological reasons.[2] Ultimately, all reordered liturgical space is not an end in itself, but should be seen rather as an empty board on which the people of God paint the icon of Christ in their liturgical formation and movement.

A multi-purpose building at the centre of the community

The first requisite for turning problem buildings into opportunities, is to keep them open seven days a week and to maximize their use in every way. Vandalism gravitates to buildings that give the appearance of redundancy and which are permanently locked, except for three hours a week when they are open, but apparently only for those who are in the habit of using them for their own special and, some would say, peculiar requirements. What kind of signal does that send out to the community at large about the Church being in business for the sake of those who are not members of it.

With the increase in vandalism, insurance costs and expensive suggestions for safe-guarding property and furnishings, it has become difficult to keep many of our churches open except at times of worship. With sensitivity some buildings can be adapted in such a way that a specific and particular worship area is enhanced while the surrounding space can often be utilized by partitioning of a permanent or moveable kind. This can have the effect of highlighting the sacred space and making the unused areas available for other purposes. Many of our churches are too large to be used solely for worship. With care we could provide opportunities for the local community to have facilities – office, recreational, or otherwise – within an over-large, reordered Victorian building. In this sense the church building could play a significant role in the community, bridging in some way the gap between the sacred and the secular. Such reordered buildings can be made available to all kinds of agencies, working for the good of the wider community and in turn will convert a problem building into a glorious opportunity for service and growth. All this can be done while retaining and considerably enhancing a perfectly adequate and appropriate worship space. Locked doors will then be replaced by open doors and open hearts. Furthermore, the church building will be constantly in use and occupied by people seven days a week, so that it will no longer invite the kind of vandalism that an empty and apparently redundant building, giving the appearance of a besieged fortress, inevitably does – not least in our inner cities.

At the present time the government is making large sums of money available not to causes, but to any groups in a local community who are prepared to provide one or other of the services deemed necessary in a community where unemployment, nursery requirements and many other needs are not being met. In addition to this source, there is the grant aiding coming out of the *Faith in the City* report which set up the Church Urban Fund as a financial resource for the development and reordering of over-large churches in the inner-city areas. All this is in addition to the large number of trusts which exist and which have listed among their concerns the reordering of church buildings.

With these and other financial resources at hand, to say nothing of the goodwill which still exists in many areas for the local church – especially for its buildings (a goodwill shared by many more than those who regularly attend church) – there is no reason why money should be an overriding, inhibiting factor in the redevelopment and reordering of the churches. Indeed one could go further and say that we simply cannot afford not to have a positive strategy about church buildings. With modest reordering the church building can become a real pastoral centre, and under one roof many services for the wider community can be housed and largely funded from resources other than those provided by the committed congregation. Such reordered buildings could be at the heart of many a community, socially and financially as well as ecclesiastically.

In this way the Church will be exercising precisely what the New Testament requires of all apostolic ministry – namely, hospitality as well as a proper stewardship of its existing resources. Open doors have a certain power to open hearts and lives. Locked doors and barricaded buildings are a living contradiction of the very gospel message they are there to proclaim. A parish audit seeking to survey and list the needs and problems as well as the untapped resources of the local community, could well be the first step towards rediscovering those very purposes for which the church building was first erected. The very exercise of undertaking such an audit would alert many people in the local community to the reality of another sort of church – a church that could become distinctive for its service as well as for its services!

But what now of the reordering of that 'sacred space' set aside quite specifically and indeed exclusively for the worship of God, by the people of God, during the week as well as on Sundays?

Reordering the worship space

From the outset it is important to make it quite clear that the author does not claim in any way to be an expert in this matter of the reordering of church buildings. Far from it. The primary purpose of including a chapter outlining some simple principles on this subject in a book on worship, is simply and solely to highlight and to make the point that many of our buildings, as they are presently constructed, are in many cases the biggest single hindrance to the renewal of God's people in worship and mission. The important principle is to recover an architectural integrity which will help and not hinder or frustrate the accompanying theological and liturgical integrity which the building is there to express and to make evident. So for example, the removal of altars and the erection of over-large and dominating pulpits at the Reformation, abhorrent though it may be to many of us, was nevertheless a necessary and logical sequel to much Reformation theology and its outworkings in worship and liturgy. Every building tells a story. For ideally you cannot have the building saying one thing while the theology and practice of worship are attempting to say something very different.

Another example. Take those Victorian screens and high – very high – altars. They make a very clear and obvious theological statement about the relation between – some would say yawning chasm between – the laity and the clergy, which is totally contradictory to everything we believe and teach today about the nature of the Body of Christ. We need to work towards affirming the relationship that exists between laity and clergy as constituting the whole people of God. In many of our cathedrals and ancient foundations which have their roots and origins in monastic communities, frequently the 'choir' is largely obscured from the main body of the cathedral church and hidden behind a large screen. In a dual-purpose building of that kind – the mother church of the diocese with its seat for the bishop, but also the abbey church of the monastic foundation – it was necessary to set apart the body of the 'choir' for the use of monks in their daily recitation of the Daily Offices. Later, after the dissolution of the monasteries in the early sixteenth century, that same choir and those same choir stalls remained conveniently in place for use by the residentiary canons who then took on the responsibility for saying or singing the much-simplified Daily Offices. Singing or saying the offices necessitates eye contact, hence the choir stalls are usually turned inwards to facilitate the antiphonal singing or reciting of the psalms. Here again is another case of where the architecture needed to be bent and reordered in order to serve the worship needs of the worshippers.

Theologically and liturgically, of course, we are light-years apart from our Victorian forebears and it is not surprising, therefore, that many of us, far from being helped to worship by the hang-overs in stone and brick of earlier generations, actually find the buildings as they presently stand an inhibition to the kind of worship we believe is right and appropriate for our day. They were constructed for a very different Church and a very different age.

Now in an ideal world, it would be possible to reconstruct our buildings to serve the very end for which they primarily exist, namely the worship of God by the people of God. But stone and brick are much less malleable and far more difficult to adapt. Therefore we need to realize, at the outset, that all our efforts will necessarily be something of a compromise between what is desirable and what is possible. If we do not grasp this nettle at the outset, it will not be long before we shall be stung either by the English Heritage or the Diocesan Advisory Committee or some other such body who are primarily (and some would argue justifiably) concerned about the church building as architecture. It is important, therefore, at the outset to befriend all such bodies and to see them as colleagues in the enterprise rather than adversaries. After all, many of these bodies carry much expertise and it cannot be said too often – and especially when it comes to reordering church buildings – that amateur enthusiasm is no substitute for a proper, sympathetic and professional opinion or consultation.

Maximum flexibility

Perhaps the best way to go about a radical reordering of the worship area in a church building is to image the interior of the building with *everything* – yes, everything – removed! Start as near as you can with an empty space. The second ideal which is probably even more difficult to achieve in practice is so to plan that everything that you are going to put back in the building will be able to be detached and will be moveable – *everything* from the altar to the chairs (not pews); the preaching desk or reading desk; the musicians' chairs and stands (not choir stalls) and ideally the organ console or piano (or preferably, of course, the keyboard, spoken of in an earlier chapter).

Proceeding from that point and most definitely at an early stage of planning, it will be important to decide where the focus of the building should be, and to that end it will be crucial to 'decode', as it were, the statement which the original building was seeking to make when it was first built. For example, a Butterfield building was deliberately built to be tall and with all the lines of the building directing our gaze towards the high (very high) altar where the sacrament would probably be reserved. There is a sense in which the integrity of such fine architecture presents us with exactly the situation spoken of above, namely, where the integrity of the original building should not be violated and therefore where compromise might well need to come into play. In such a situation it might be better to leave the dressed high altar where it is, very firmly implanted, and to make a very different statement with a very different kind of 'table' or 'mensa' (deliberately not dressed) and located where, neither by its size nor location, is it even attempting to be in competition with the original 'high altar'.

On the understanding that everything else is easily moveable, it will be important to put on the drawing board – and again at an early stage in the planning – the different kinds of worship occasions that are envisaged. The principle Eucharist on a Sunday will require a different layout of the furniture to other occasions, such as small groups of people possibly gathering for Morning or Evening Prayer or for Compline during the week. There will also be occasions such as Christmas, Easter, Harvest Festival or Sunday evening seeker services, when considerable numbers will be expected. Rows of chairs in nave-fashion might well be appropriate on such occasions. Perhaps a certain formality is desirable for a funeral or a memorial service.

Provided that most of the furnishings are not fixtures – and especially the chairs – it will be possible to keep the building uncluttered, giving that sense of sacred space referred to earlier. Incidentally, in the early days of planning the reordered building it is important to provide proper and adequate chair-storage space. Since empty chairs at a service are demoralizing, the church leaders need to be adept at estimating the correct number of chairs needed for any service, while also being at the ready to bring more chairs out of storage as unexpected guests arrive. Such a procedure not only gives a good 'message' so to speak, but also retains maximum empty space in the building.

In this highly practical way it becomes increasingly obvious how the building can serve and accommodate various groups for different styles of worship, with differing lay-out and groupings. During the week for the Daily Offices it might be helpful to put some chairs in the form of a 'choir' facing each other and grouped around a reading desk in the body of the church; or for mid-week celebrations of the Eucharist, where only a handful of people will be present, chairs could be grouped in quite another part of the building. In a very large church it might be helpful to set aside a part of the building both to accommodate the Blessed Sacrament and also to offer a warm area for personal prayer and devotion. The golden rule in all of this is not to fill the building with more chairs than are required at any particular point.

Ideally the worship space should now have about it a multi-dimensional feel in which immanence and transcendence both play a part. And this effect will be further enhanced by appropriate and discreet lighting. All this, of course, presupposes that *all* previous lighting has first been removed!

Lighting

The test of good lighting is determined by whether or not it draws attention to itself or whether it primarily illuminates neither more nor less than it is there to illuminate and to highlight. Over the past fifty years, lighting in every aspect of our lives, whether domestic, commercial or theatrical has become increasingly sophisticated. Framing spots and focused lighting can be adjusted so that pictures, icons or objects are illuminated right to the edges, but not a fraction over. With such lighting, the illuminated object appears to glow with a light of its own. Similarly, lighting can illuminate a statue, the area on the reading desk or in the pulpit without any over-spill. Local and specific lighting of this kind requires the placing of sockets at many and various points in the building. All the lighting fixtures should be easily removable when not in use. Where permanent lighting fixtures are necessary (for the ceiling, perhaps, in some churches or for ground lighting), it is best if the fixtures can be concealed. Dimmers are nearly always an asset for sensitive lighting, and most buildings benefit visually from being under-lit rather than over-lit.

Probably the best resource for advice about good lighting would be a commercial lighting engineer with experience of stage and theatre-lighting or someone with conference display experience. The basic principle underlying appropriate lighting for worship space is to have available all the possible lighting you might ever require, yet only to employ, at any one time, such lighting as you need for that particular occasion and essentially in those parts of the building where it is required. There should be no superfluous lighting whatever, except to give a carefully calculated effect – such as for the illumination of a large piece of colourful fabric; for the illumination of the space where the holy table is placed in order to heighten the focus of the building and especially in those cases where the architecture is in conflict with the chosen centre of the building as designated by the altar or holy table.

Sound

In most buildings it will be desirable to install some form of sound amplification or, more likely, sound re-enforcement. Expert help and advice should always be sought for this. Some buildings do not need and should not require amplification or even sound-boosting systems, as there is also an acoustical integrity about every building in a similar way to that in which there is an architectural integrity. The advantage of some form of sound re-enforcement system is that for those leading worship the voice will not need to be forced as though one were addressing a crowd of several thousands or giving out the times of departing trains in a huge railway station! Much of the development of the parsonical voice results from the necessity to 'project' in a somewhat unnatural way because of the unrealistic size of many church buildings, especially ancient church buildings. It is impossible to calculate how much the worship at Taizé and in many abbey churches on the Continent has benefited and has been positively enriched by the use of a microphone by the person leading informal prayers and intercessions, evoking a spirit of corporate and even spontaneous intercession from the body of the congregation.

On this point of the tone of voice used for leading worship, it is surely doubtful whether collects or the Gospel reading should be sung in an age of sound amplification. Of course, it was quite different in earlier times and in large medieval buildings, which had no amplification other than the natural enhancement afforded by the architecture itself. In such buildings in former times there was an overriding need to pitch the voice of the reader – and therefore to raise it to a monotone – in order for the voice to carry and be heard. Singing the Gospel is a hangover from such an age, and in most buildings today, with the help of amplification, this is no longer either necessary nor, frankly, desirable. A homily or address to 45 people or so will have its own integrity of deliverance which can also be violated when the voice of the preacher is falsely pitched as though 500 people were assembled in a great cathedral. Each different occasion and each different location will require different delivery and timing, and quite different style and tone of voice. In some cases all this will be helped by the use of some form of amplification or re-enforcement and in others it most definitely will not.

The place of the font and baptistries

It is with regard to the styling and place of the baptistry and font that the need for strong theological foundations for the reordering of church buildings becomes most obvious and self-evident. But-terfield, the nineteenth-century church architect, who had strong theological perceptions, saw to it that his church buildings gave a proper prominence and particular emphasis in the styling of the building to the two sacraments 'essential to salvation' – the Eucharist and baptism – and that this theology was demonstrated by the lines and structure of the building. This is very clearly demonstrated for example at All Saints', Margaret Street in Lon-don, which Butterfield designed and built in 1859. The moment you enter that church, immediately to the left and located at the west end, is the baptistry, with its large and impressive font, mounted prominently on a considerable stone platform. At the same time, the eyes of the visitor are drawn straight across the building to the impressive high altar, which stands splendidly and gloriously up against the east wall, which resembles a huge and colourful iconastasis stretching unbroken by any east window from floor to lofty ceiling.

At a time when even nominal Christian faith is still numerical-ly in decline and when, what we used to refer to as the 'friendly fringe' of the Church has almost disappeared, the place of baptism and its accompanying catechumenate are coming increasingly into prominence and are recovering their earlier place of importance, both theologically and therefore liturgically. For the relationship of the committed community of the faithful to the outside world is increasingly resembling that of the earlier centuries before Chris-tianity became 'established' and respectable – those first four cen-turies of costly faith when discipleship and baptism were far from being a cheap or easy option.

In sixteenth-century Britain, when there was no clear line at all between nominal faith and committed discipleship, and when 99% of the English population would automatically be baptized at birth, the service of confirmation took to itself a greater signifi-cance and prominence, marking such lines of demarcation, so to speak, between the indifferent and the committed. All this has rad-ically changed in Britain in the twentieth century, and generally in the Western world, and even dramatically so in the past fifty years. In the contemporary climate everything is returning to the point where baptism marks a definite point in the life of discipleship, with an increasing number of adult baptisms marking the climax of a quite lengthy period of training and teaching in the catechumenate.

In these and in many other ways we have today a higher doctrine of baptism than we have ever had since the fifth century. This is bound to be reflected in the architectural design and layout of our church buildings, whether they are simply being reordered or where new church buildings are being designed and constructed.

The reduction and trivializing of the symbolism and sign of baptism in the shape of the font is crying out today for a radical reappraisal. A tame bowl of water hidden away in some obscure part of the building will simply no longer do as an appropriate and effective sign of the theology of baptism, as it is now current in all the churches.

In the early centuries of the Church the baptistry was frequently a separate building, generally circular in construction, standing alongside the main church building. Where the baptistry was attached to the main church building, it remained architecturally distinctive from it. In North Africa there are many such baptistries still standing. In the middle of the building there is a pool, circular in shape with three steps leading down into it. In the apse of this circular building is the place where the bishop sat. Round the circular building is a walled ambulatory where men and women – separately – changed into their white baptismal garment before going down into the pool with the deacon, who would actually dip the candidates into the water or probably under the water. In any event, the water had to be flowing, since stagnant water was perceived as being 'diseased' and therefore by definition incapable of carrying the gift of new life, of salvation or health. After the baptism and accompanying confirmation, which were all part of one initiation rite in the Early Church, the new Christians were led into the main church building for the Eucharist.

It should be self-evident from all that is said above that both for theological as well as for liturgical reasons, the one place you should never have the font is up 'at the front' near the holy table.

Misguidedly, when new churches have been built, the clergy have sometimes requested that the font should be brought to the front of the main body of the church or worship space, so that when baptisms are conducted in the main service on Sundays (as they increasingly are for good and sound theological reasons) the congregation can 'see' the baptism from the pews. However, to place the font in such a position is wrong for every conceivable reason. The baptismal liturgy should demand that everyone involved is compelled to move to their 'Galilee' where a new beginning was made on that long pilgrimage from the land of bondage to the Promised Land. To place the font in the sanctuary is to imply that baptism comes at the end of a long journey in which self-striving without grace has finally brought the pilgrim to receive all the promised gifts of the Father. The reverse is of course the case. 'While we were yet sinners Christ died for us' (Rom. 5:8). The gifts of grace are given to us in our 'passage' from the bondage of sin into the life of righteousness. In one sense the Christian life is a continual returning to our 'Galilee' to the place of our first love, reaffirming and celebrating our baptismal status at every step of the road. If the architecture of a church building is to make explicit a proper theology of redemption, then the font or baptistry will be at the entrance to the church, or better still, in a baptistry set to one side at the entrance to the church. Such is both the theological as well as the liturgical place for the font, compelling everyone participating in the liturgy of baptism to be a people on the move.

It cannot be said too often that here as in every aspect of the reordering of our church buildings, there will necessarily be room for compromise between the ideal and what is possible and practical. Most of our church buildings were built at a time when a different theological emphasis was placed upon baptism. Nevertheless, there are many striking examples of where the architectural feature of the font has been restored to its proper theologically eloquent position and status. A visit to Portsmouth Anglican Cathedral is a case in point. There we can see a most imaginative and powerful reordering of the bombed cathedral building with the font sunk in the floor at the crossing between the nave which, in the case of Portsmouth, is more the size of an extended narthex with the 'choir' resembling more the body of most church buildings. There the font is in fact powerfully evocative of a 'coffin', sunk well into the ground. Designed as it is, the font at Portsmouth is making a most powerful theological statement and is also, incidentally, a powerful teaching aid, standing, as it does, at the point of full entrance into the body of the church building in the same way as baptism stands at the entrance to full membership of the mystical Body of Christ, whose members we become at our baptism, when we are 'buried' with Christ and 'raised' to new life in him.

Such an architectural demonstration of the theology of baptism, of course, really comes into its own at the Easter vigil, as it would have done in the Early Church, when the catechumenate who have undergone instruction during the season of Lent are baptized and confirmed, preferably as the sun is rising at dawn on Easter Day. Baptism administered in such a setting and at such an hour on such a day, demonstrates forcefully the significance of our burial with Christ in a likeness of his death as well as signifying the reality of being raised up out of the waters of baptism in the likeness of his resurrection, for anointing with the Holy Spirit and for full incorporation into the eucharistic body of the Church at the first Eucharist of Easter. At the same time, the whole people of God join with the new Christians in the reaffirmation of their baptismal vows, recalling the first love of their own baptism.

Not all church buildings will lend themselves, perforce, to such a radical and liturgical reordering. However, providing we know the statement we are attempting to make in the lay-out of the sacred space of the worship area of a church building, there will always be ways of raising the profile both of the sign and symbol of baptism as well as of its physical and material expression in the architecture, both by the design as well as by the location of the font and baptistry.

Placing the choir

Essentially choirs need to be heard and not seen, rather than the very opposite, which is so often the case after the Victorian revival of choirs, whereby they tend to be seen (very much seen) and not – or scarcely – heard. The origin of choir stalls placed facing one another in the 'choir' area of the old monastic foundations has already been touched upon. The development of choirs and cathedral music is rightly praised as being one of the very special gifts which the Victorian Church gave to our tradition. However, all this took place before the Eucharist and its symbol in the altar had recovered its proper place in the life of the worshipping community. Not unnaturally, when matins was still the principal service in most Anglican churches – before the Parish and People Movement in the twentieth century – the choir was deliberately given great prominence both in practice as well as in the architectural layout of many churches remodelled during the Victorian period.

Today the choir is better relocated at the back of the building, behind the congregation and in many cases in some kind of gallery at the west end, where there is perhaps the console of the organ or in what might have been in earlier times the orchestral gallery. Acoustically as well as practically, this is often a much more satisfactory arrangement for all concerned, always assuming that a separate choir as such is either practical or desirable – which in many cases it is not.

In conclusion

In conclusion, what might draw this detailed discourse together is the need to discern a theological and liturgical integrity at the heart of everything we are trying to do and to be as communities of faith. For our church buildings, like the music and everything that goes on in them, are there to serve, express and demonstrate the gospel and the mission of the Church and not to compete, to contradict or hinder it. The house of God, the people of God and the worship of God should all be of a piece, expressing the same message and pointing to the same end – namely, the glory of God.

If good worship is an appropriate occasion appropriately expressed, then what makes a church building a good church building is not necessarily something grand or magnificent, but rather whether the building is in keeping in every way with the purposes for which it was built. We are not trying to erect shrines or temples in the sense in which those words are normally used. After all, in designing our homes and houses, the architects often speak of them as being purpose-built. Why not also speak of church buildings as purpose-built?

Ancient church buildings were frankly built for a very different purpose in their day than buildings designed for worship in our own. The mission is a different one. In our day we need to develop these buildings, many of them very splendid, to serve the mission and worship of the Church today, realizing that there will necessarily be a strong element of compromise in the case of structures that are so permanent and solidly erected. Imagination and vision arising out of a strong theological and liturgical awareness are the basic requirements, accompanied by the need to dream unashamedly of what might be possible even in your parish church, now. And all this will only come about if the pastor is teaching, preaching and nurturing the people of God about the sort of people God wants his people to be both in worship and service, in word and deed. God forbid that our parish clergy should become men and women who are primarily interested in buildings for their own sakes, to the neglect of the people the buildings are there to house and serve. Good liturgical practice, however well informed, is no substitute for ministry and mission, and the laity are very quick to spot when a pastor is totally preoccupied with what should always remain as important though secondary concerns.

Yet equally there should be a quality almost transparent in pastors and clergy which will brook nothing less than the best for God – which incidentally is not necessarily the same as the most expensive. Nothing is achieved by clergy speaking irreverently and with loathing about the local church building. The laity often invest a great deal of love for and concern about what they regard as 'their' church – however much that particular building may be, from a more sophisticated viewpoint, something little better than a hideous Victorian monstrosity. In order to change anything or anybody we must first love them, otherwise we shall be little better than all other iconoclasts throughout history, who have reduced visions to causes. For the reordering of church buildings must not be just part of an aesthetic fad or the latest liturgical vogue. It must be rooted and founded upon solid theological and liturgical convictions, so that there is an integrity about both the church as building as well as the Church as the Body of Christ.

11

Worship, service and life

All life as worship

Archbishop William Temple wrote:

> Worship includes all life and the moments spent in concentrated
> worship, whether in church or elsewhere, are the focusing points of
> the sustaining and directing energy of the worshipper's whole life.[1]

We saw from the outset that true worship is a whole way of seeing
God's world from God's point of view in Christ. Although true worship transcends the world, it does not bypass it, and so in that sense
Archbishop Temple in the quotation above is right – 'Worship
includes all life.' The gift of the Eucharist is nothing less than a vision
in which the worshipper sees 'heaven and earth' as 'full of his glory'.
For those with 'eyes to see' and 'ears to hear' glory is woven into the
whole texture of the universe: there is glory under our feet at every
turn in the road. How well Gerard Manley Hopkins expresses this:

> The world is charged with the grandeur of God,
> It will flame out, like shining from shook foil;
> It gathers to a greatness, like the ooze of oil
> Crushed. Why do men then now not reck his rod?
> Generations have trod, have trod, have trod;
> And all is seared with trade; bleared, smeared with toil;
> And wears man's smudge and shares man's smell: the soil
> Is bare now, nor can foot feel, being shod.[2]

But this vision is essentially a very down-to-earth matter, firmly
rooted in the earth and the world of everyday life; within history

while pointing beyond history; spiritual without being cut off from the material. So Christian worship is distinctive in so far as it always begins with what is natural and then moves on to the supernatural. It starts with bread but ends with body. It starts with wine and ends with a life-giving transfusion of blood. Because of the incarnation of Christ, the dynamic of Christian worship begins with the natural plunging into the supernatural – the offering of bread and wine, taken into the sanctuary and placed on the altar as symbols of our whole life, offered to God in just the same way as Mary offers her body to be the tabernacle of the Christ. But that is not the complete story.

For because of the ascension of Christ, worship is completed by raising the natural into the fuller and further environment of heaven and the supernatural. When 'consecrated' the people of God (the Body of Christ) are then thrust back into the world to infect the secular with the sacred and the material world with the further dimension of the spiritual. This whole 'consecration' business is essentially a two-way street. And furthermore, this two-way activity should be seen as one whole dynamic and as the overall perspective of God's purposes for the universe: the slow consecration of all things. So the record of Scripture is right: 'In saying, "he ascended", what does it mean but that he also descended into the lower parts of the earth? He who descended is he who also ascended far above all the heavens, that he might fill all things' (Eph. 4:9–10). So in Christian worship there should be no fragmentation nor rejection of some parts of life as merely secular or profane. This was the supreme lesson Peter had to learn in his vision at Joppa (Acts 10:9–16): the old schizophrenic distinctions between things 'profane' in themselves and things 'sacred' in themselves – that ancient dilemma for God's people – had finally been abolished in Christ.

Indeed, perhaps it is possible to hazard a distinction between Christian worship and other comparable transcendental experiences by demanding that in Christian worship we gather up the fragments that remain in order that nothing may be lost (John 6:12). Worship must lead to holiness, which is the very opposite of fragmentation. Aldous Huxley makes this point most eloquently when he comments on his own transcendental experiences after taking the drug mescalin. Something analogous to contemplation was clearly happening for Huxley when he took the drug, but it is a contemplation and a transcendental experience very remote from the Christian understanding of worship. He writes:

> But now I knew contemplation at its height. At its height, but not yet in its fullness. For in its fullness, the way of Mary includes the way of Martha and raises it, so to speak, to its own higher power. Mescalin opens up the way of Mary, but shuts the door on that of Martha. It gives access to contemplation – but to a contemplation that is incompatible with action and even with the will to action.[3]

Christian worship has always set its face against this kind of fragmentation and regarded it as blatant escapism. A contemplation 'incompatible with action' is not Christian contemplation, for the claim of Christian worship has always been *orare est laborare: laborare est orare*. Each belongs to the other and each is rooted firmly within the other so that in the end 'nothing is lost'. Indeed, in the language of the Jews the word for 'worship' is a derivation from the root *abad*, which basically means 'to serve'. There is in Jewish and Christian tradition alike, no antithesis between the worship of God and the service of the community. So Christians can say with confidence that when the worship is ended the service begins! For worship and service are one.

So William Temple can again write: 'All life ought to be worship; and we know quite well that there is no chance that it will be worship unless we have times when we have worship and nothing else.'[4] Once again he is affirming the principle we have discovered earlier in the book: the route to the universal is through the way of the particular. We need specific moments of worship in order to insure that life at all moments can be offered as worship. So he can boldly and confidently continue: 'Our duty to God requires that we should, for a good part of our time, not be consciously thinking about him. That makes it absolutely necessary . . . that we should have our times which are worship, pure and simple.'[5] It is from these moments of 'pure and simple worship' that we emerge as 'God's spies'[6] with vision equipped to explore and discover that amazing reality that heaven and earth are indeed 'full of his glory'.

Once seen in this way and from this eucharistic and sacramental perspective, there can never again be any dichotomy between the gospel of the sanctuary and the gospel of social concern: yes indeed, 'When the worship is ended the service truly begins!' Again, Temple summarizes this single vision of one world:

> If then the Christian citizen is to make his Christianity tell upon his politics, his business, his social enterprises, he must be a churchman – consciously belonging to the worshipping fellowship and sharing its worship – before he is a citizen; he must bring the concerns of his citizenship and his business before God and go forth to them carrying God's inspiration with him.[7]

There is, for a Christian, no hard line between the secular and the sacred – unfortunately! It would be so much more convenient if there were, because the secular could then belong to a separate compartment of life, free from any possibility of invasion from the sacred. Instead the secular is plunged into the sacred (as at the offertory in the Eucharist) to become the Body of Christ, but precisely in order that in turn the sacred may be let loose on the unsuspecting world of the secular in a million and one indirect, subtle, and mysterious ways through the agency of the other Body of Christ – the Christian, undermining society at its very roots, yet largely unobserved, except by those with eyes to see. This kind of vision makes all the difference in the world because it makes what we sometimes wrongly call a social gospel inevitable without permitting it to deteriorate into patronizing concern; it generates an evangelism that is effective without being self-conscious and rescues stewardship and any concern for environmentalism from legalism and pusillanimous phariseeism.

Worship and the social gospel

The motivation of the social gospel cannot simply be love of our neighbour – neighbourliness. We do not go to others from our strength to their weakness; such a view of care and concern will all too easily degenerate into patronizing and do-gooding. Here, as elsewhere, we need a vision that compels us to go where we would not choose to go, to love those whom we would not choose to love or whom we probably do not like at all, and to share with others whom we would not choose as friends. So in the gospel we have the vision that brings to all service and care for others a single and powerful motivation: 'I say to you, as you did it to one of the least of these my brethren, you did it to me' (Matt. 25:40). It is the same Jesus whom we worship and serve and recognize by faith in the bread and wine at the Eucharist whom we worship, serve, and recognize by faith in the homeless, the hungry, the sick, and the imprisoned. Only if we *recognize* him here in these places will he *recognize* us before the Father. It is that 'recognition' from both sides that brings authenticity to worship and service alike, both in the sanctuary as well as in the slums.

In a single statement, Jesus rescues all our concern for others from anything that could remotely be called patronizing, by focusing worship and service alike in the mystery of the Incarnation: Jesus hidden in the bread and wine, in matter and in every atom, but that same Jesus also hidden in the face of every person in need, poverty, or sickness. So we simply cannot have the one without the other, and in either case to fail to 'recognize' Jesus is to commit that most serious of offences so terrifyingly cautioned by St Paul as 'failing to discern the body' (1 Cor. 11:29). We shall not come to know the full catholic Christ until we learn to recognize him both within what he refused to call secular, as well as in what we choose to call sacred. He is the Lord of both alike. So St John Chrysostom can write:

> Would you honour the body of Christ? Do not despise his naked-ness; do not honour him here in church clothed in silk vestments and then pass him by unclothed and frozen outside. Remember that he who said, 'This is my Body', and makes good his words, also said, 'You saw me hungry and gave me no food', and 'in so far as you did it not to one of these, you did it not to me'. In the first sense the body of Christ does not need clothing but worship from a pure heart. In the second sense it does need clothing and all the care we can give it. We must learn to be discerning Christians and to honour Christ in the way in which he wants to be honoured. I am not saying you should not give golden altar vessels and so on, but I am insisting that nothing can take the place of almsgiving. What is the use of loading Christ's table with gold cups while he himself is starving? Will you make a cup of gold, and withhold a cup of water? What use is it to

adorn the altar with cloth of gold hangings and deny Christ a coat for his back? What would that profit you? Consider that Christ is that tramp who comes in need of a night's lodging. You turn him away and then start laying rugs on the floor, draping the walls, hanging lamps on silver chains on the columns. Adorn the house of God if you will, but do not forget your brother in distress. He is a temple of infinitely greater value.[8]

There should be no fear that by placing concern for well-ordered worship high on the list of our priorities as a Church, we are turning away from the concerns of the inner city, the Third World, or the social gospel. On the contrary, perhaps we should expect that men and women's hearts will grow faint and love will grow cold in these very areas unless the Church seeks also to bring the vision of true worship on to the agenda of social welfare. There have been conspicuous chapters in the life of the Church when beautiful worship and compassionate service have belonged together on the same agenda, when the two could be found within the same streets, and were notoriously contesting for first place at the top of the list of the priorities of the Church, especially in the inner city.

The Christian socialist movement in the late nineteenth century in England was much inspired by what we would call 'high-church' worship, while the Clapham Sect was equally influenced by strong evangelical preaching for conversion. It is Christ who gave to high-church worship and evangelical preaching alike a common concern for the poor and the needy. It was a later distortion of the gospel to see worship and the social gospel as alternatives or opposites or, worse still, as options we can choose according to our preferences and inclinations.

It was the outstanding Bishop Weston of Zanzibar, at the Anglo-Catholic Congress of 1923, who challenged the Church with the words from his address, 'Our Present Duty':

> You are Christians?
> Then your Lord is one and the same
> with Jesus on the throne of his glory,
> with Jesus in his blessed sacrament,
> with Jesus received in your hearts in Communion,

with Jesus who is mystically with you as you pray,
and with Jesus enshrined in the hearts and bodies
of his brothers and sisters up and down the world.

Now go out into the highways and hedges,
and look for Jesus in the ragged and the naked,
in the oppressed and sweated,
in those who have lost hope,
and in those who are struggling to make good.
Look for Jesus in them; and when you find him,
gird yourselves with his towel of fellowship,
and wash his feet in the person of his brethren.

Perhaps it has to be admitted that only where there is a high doc-trine of Jesus and his presence (whether catholic or evangelical), is there a really compassionate vocation to serve the world. Unitari-ans have not in general been conspicuous for a social gospel; and wherever worship is merely an edifying and pleasant aesthetic experience, then historically the Church has tended to retreat into indifference to social ills, political commitment, and social justice and to become the property of the middle classes. In a very telling passage from *Christian Faith and Life*, William Temple points with subtlety to this very issue:

> When we have been absorbed in great music, I do not think we gen-erally feel particularly charitable to the people we meet outside. They seem to be of a coarser fibre than that into which we have been entering. That could never be true of our worship if it has really been worship of God, not some indulgence of our own spiritual emotion, but the concentration of mind, heart and will on him. You will be full of kindness for everybody as you go out from such worship.[9]

Jesus redeems our worship from being just a pleasant aesthetic indulgence by reminding us from start to finish that it was only by reason of his incarnation and ascension that the doors of heaven could ever be open to flesh and blood at all.

Therefore, if we are going to sail on the ticket of his incarna-tion, we soon discover to our cost that it is not a one-way ticket from earth to heaven (a get-away-from-it-all on a long weekend!)

but rather what is commonly called 'a round trip' from heaven to earth and all the way back again, via a stable door, Gethsemane, and Calvary hill. To end up at his right hand or his left hand will almost certainly involve being on his right hand or his left next to that other throne – a bloody cross on Calvary hill. These are not alternatives. They are both centres of a single love and therefore of a single worship, adoration and service. Jesus leads his disciples in every age up the mountain of the transfiguration to catch a glimpse of his glory, yet the same Jesus leads the same disciples straight down the mountain of transfiguration right into the pain of the world, with his face firmly set towards Jerusalem – the place of suffering and darkness. It is the same Jesus we worship and serve from start to finish. As J. H. Newman wrote, 'Praise to the holiest in the heights and in the depths be praise.'

Worship and evangelism

There is another false polarization of alternatives that does not exist in reality: a concern for worship over and against evangelism; kneeling in the sanctuary as opposed to standing on the soap box. The very first apostolic miracle recorded in the book of the Acts of the Apostles recounts how the healed man who had been lame, entered the temple with Peter and John 'walking and leaping and praising God'. It goes on to record that when 'all the people saw him walking and praising God' they in their turn were 'filled with wonder and amazement' (Acts 3:8–10). St Luke shows that this complex of events is a constant theme in the healing miracles: healing and release expressed in worship, with the spin-off of witness and evangelism to others who are standing by and observing the power of that release expressed so vividly in worship. So in St Luke's account of the healing of the blind man we are specifically told that, as soon as he received his sight, he followed Jesus 'glorifying God' and then – almost as an incidental result yet clearly concomitant with that release and worship – we are told explicitly that 'all the people, when they saw it, gave praise to God' (Luke 18:43). Notice, there is nothing self-conscious about the evangelistic spin-off; the healing and worship were not offered for an evangelistic purpose. Far from it. In fact, Jesus is careful in the Gospels to reject that form of evangelism which relies upon spectacular events in order to promote faith. The release and worship are ends in themselves. Nevertheless, they carry with them the almost inevitable result of reaching out to others, causing them either to follow suit or at least to go away asking themselves the right sort of questions.

So, authentic worship is not an alternative to evangelism; on the contrary, it is a necessary and prior ingredient in the total process, laying the foundations for persuasive evangelism. To say this does not suppose, however, that we should regard the Church's worship as primarily for the sake of the newcomer, the enquirer, or the 'man in the street'. The worship of the Church is not intended to take place in the shop window of the Church, commending the goods that are on sale. There was an unfortunate chapter in the history of the Church when we thought that worship had to be made 'understandable' for the sake of the enquirer who might be present for the first time. Not only is this not really practical, it is totally undesirable. In the Early Church it was not possible for the neophyte (the new Christian) to attend the full Eucharist until he or she had been baptized and confirmed. Furthermore, catechumens could only attend worship if they were already receiving instruction. In the present world, and in Western society at least, Sunday morning worship is increasingly for the initiated. It is unlikely that there will be pews full of people who are there for the first time or who have dropped in casually for one of their occasional visits. As we have seen in an earlier chapter, in an age when Christian understanding stands at a long distance from the proverbial 'man in the street', it may be necessary to find a different time, style and occasion for worship which requires only a minimum of church drill, so to speak.

Nevertheless, men and women released through authentic worship will be vehicles of God's love and their lives will speak of the power and the presence of the God they have come to know and love in worship. Furthermore, we can see how evangelists will, rightly though dangerously, use powerful and authentic worship to release people into deeper and more committed discipleship. In evangelistic services there is a real place for singing and adoration, praying and praising; for the creation of an environment in which the mind is stilled *within* the heart, the affections, and emotions, and in which deeper faith is elicited through the powerful preaching of the Word culminating in an act of worship and rededication. Worship and the Word should conspire together to convince and convert. There can be no doubt that it is to churches where worship and the Word are presented with authenticity and care that people are more likely to go. You will not find a full church where worship is badly done, and you will soon find a fuller church where it is well done and where the Word is preached with power. The conclusion is unavoidable. Worship and evangelism belong together and always have belonged together since the days of the first apostolic preaching.

Worship and stewardship

If we need to rescue evangelism from its isolation from worship, we equally need, especially in the Anglican Church, to rescue stewardship from becoming just a thing in itself, a special department in ecclesiastical life.

Of course, it is incontrovertible that in the Bible and not least in the parables of Jesus there is a strong and recurring theme which sees men and women as being called to exercise a responsible stewardship in the use of the world, the environment, the universe, and all its resources. But in the Bible there is a great variety of imagery; no one image is sufficient to tell the whole tale of God's purposes for his world. We are deliberately confronted with a consortium of apparently conflicting images, for this is the only way we can be rescued from idolatry. If we set up stewardship as the overriding image of man's relationship to his environment, we shall end up with a rather mean, legalistic, and even pharisaical view of man's responsibility within the universe. There is something at the present moment about the environmentalists which takes us within a hair's breadth of that most dangerous kind of religion: religion obsessed with the cleaning of the outside of the cup at the expense of the cleaning of the inside (Luke 11:39). So, alongside this image of stewardship, we must also look carefully at the apparently conflicting image of the *prodigality* of God, which runs throughout the whole of the Scriptures. There is an aspect of God that is incredibly wasteful: he is a God who is far too generous by half – a God for whom the waterpots must be filled and filled to the brim (John 2:7) and with whom the grain is always pressed down and running over (Luke 6:38). Man is perhaps most godlike when he is also most generous in going that 'second mile' beyond the first (Matt. 5:41) required by law, in giving his cloak as well as his coat (Matt. 5:40).

So it is with worship. In Christian worship, the offering of ourselves is part of our act of thanksgiving and Eucharist. The woman with the alabaster jar of costly ointment, therefore, is integral to any recounting of the gospel. Indeed, we are specifically told that wherever the gospel is recorded, this story within the gospel must not be forgotten. Her love of Jesus led her, in her generosity, to waste something that could in fact have been sold and the money so raised could have been given to the poor. Yet it was a traitor and a thief who argued that case. For true worship is the vehicle that carries us beyond our cautious selves and inevitably bids us break the limits of mathematical calculation with an overriding generosity inspired by an overwhelming thankfulness.

Stewardship, the giving of money, the free, unsolicited offering of precious objects to the Church, in fact has been an embarrassment for the Church consistently throughout its history. For wherever Jesus has been most conspicuously present in worship, the problem is always what to do with all the money and the gifts showered upon the Church from thankful, praising and prayerful hearts. The rot set in (if you will forgive the phrase) with David in the Old Testament! He was so excessively thankful to God for deliverance from his many battles that he wanted to set up an altar of thanksgiving to express his gratitude. Someone was foolish enough to offer him a free 'threshing floor' for the purpose – something on the cheap! David, in a moment of prodigality and enthusiasm, replied: 'I will not offer to the Lord that which costs me nothing' (2 Sam. 24:24). So from David – hardly the most cautious of stewards – to the woman with the alabaster jar of costly ointment and right through the subsequent history of the Church, we see how worship releases an overwhelming generosity and gratitude.

A worshipping Church, therefore, will never be a poor Church. It is significant that in the Prayer Book of Cranmer, the only place in worship where a collection was mandatory was, in fact, the Eucharist, precisely because that is essentially the right setting for the offering of our money – essentially within the framework of thanksgiving. Furthermore, such offering is made because it should reflect the one great costly offering of love made to the Father by the Son and reciprocally within the life of the blessed Trinity. Wherever men and women have been released into that kind of generous love through the worship of God, they have opened their hearts, their purses and their wallets, and the Church – far from being poor – has in fact been embarrassed by its wealth and riches to the point of being corrupted by them. The Church's greatest, lasting, and only problem has been to ensure that, in its turn, and also with a thankful heart, the Christian congregation has been a responsible steward of its many gifts and riches. In living churches of Word and worship there are no financial problems today, and there never will be till the close of the age, for 'Love so amazing, so divine, demands my soul, my life, my all.'[10]

So all this talk of percentages in giving to the Church is a man-made distortion of what Christians should really mean by alms-giving. It is true, of course, that in the Old Testament you were required to tithe. This was because of the logic and law of the synagogue. A synagogue required a minimum quorum of ten men and it did not require a mathematical expert to realize that ten men contributing a tenth of their income would constitute a living and financially viable synagogue, able to support a rabbi who would receive a living salary. But that is the old law. Christians live by grace, and once you begin to think in those terms you certainly do not get what you deserve – thank God! Grace is neither earned nor distributed fairly as we see in the parable of the labourers in the vineyard. Rather, grace is literally 'amazing' in its abundance. Christians do not need and are not required to give a tenth or a twentieth or any other percentage of their income. It could be said that they are not required to give anything at all – yet it could equally well be said that they are expected to give everything and still know that they are 'unprofitable' servants (Luke 17:10). (Grace is an utterly free, unmerited and unearned gift costing absolutely nothing less than everything!). So, nothing less than grace must be the yardstick by which we measure Christian generosity, and this will only arise from a worshipping and thankful heart. Seen in this way, there will always be plenty with which to pay bills and plenty left over to give away, if grace and nothing less than grace is the measure of our giving, and thankful worship is the context in which all our transactions are undertaken.

12

'With angels and archangels and with all the company of heaven'

Theology and worship

The nuts and bolts of renewal in worship, such as we have been discussing in previous chapters, are intended for no lesser end than the discovery within sinful, yet redeemed humanity, of the capacity for eternity. For true worship is a 'passage' (*pascha*) from time into eternity, from the Church into the Kingdom. Christian worship begins on the earth but ends in the heavens; it begins in the mossy and damp warmth of earth, but its goal is the fresh air and bracing environment of the Kingdom. What we taste, celebrate, and experience even now, as the Church in time, is already realized and fulfilled by the Church in heaven.

So since the very earliest of times, the cry of the Christian Church has been 'Lift up your hearts.' And the response? 'We lift them to the Lord.' In fact that response in its original form would be better translated: 'They are already with the Lord.' So in that sense we simply cannot and dare not speak of the worship of the Church as being simply down to earth. It is down to earth but it is more. It is ironic that it takes ordinary folk who perhaps only go to church occasionally to remind the jaded professionals of liturgy that an act of worship has the power to 'move' people. For so it should, but in a fuller sense than the man in the street so often means. In a full theological appreciation of worship, worshippers enter into Christ's own *pascha* or Passover. They are literally moved over in that passage and are carried with all that they are and all that they have into what is rightly seen as their true inheritance – the Kingdom of light. In many orders for baptism the words are actually used: 'Receive this light, to show that you have *passed* from darkness to light. Shine as a light in the world to the glory of God the Father.'[1]

So although there is a renewal in worship in the churches at the present time, alongside that renewal there is also a liturgical crisis because in many places so much of the worship we experience is neither one thing nor the other. It experiences the worst of both worlds, so to speak. It is neither fully and firmly rooted in the cerebral reductionism of our own age, where it is colourless and meaningless (precisely because it set out to be so meaningful!), nor is it a full expression of truly catholic worship that experiences worship as 'a departure out of the world for a little while, as a "vent" or break in earthly existence, opened up for the inlet of grace'.[2]

There are at least three main reasons for this. Sadly, at least among Western Christians, there has occurred an almost total disconnection between the study of liturgy and the other theological disciplines. This has resulted in the distortion of what should be a single and seamless robe of reality. Theology – again largely in the West and persistently in the English school – has tended to concentrate on the Scriptures, but almost exclusively from the viewpoint of biblical criticism as originating from the German school in the nineteenth century. This has left the study of liturgy to degenerate into a largely historical 'professionalism', akin to archaeology. What matters surely is that liturgy, the work of the people of God, works, engages, nurtures and leads us forward in our relationship with God and each other. It's much more than getting the form and text 'just right'. For theology (and by implication liturgy) is primarily a matter of knowing God and relating to him – the science of 'faith thinking', as P. T. Forsythe calls it. Much Western theology is today derived almost exclusively from scriptural and (even worse) from merely textual criticism, which rapidly degenerates in its turn into a kind of inverted scriptural fundamentalism. There is ever-increasing evidence that the Scriptures themselves were formulated within a strongly liturgical context. It would seem not only that large portions of Scripture were already part of the liturgy as hymns and prayers within the New Testament period, but furthermore, much of the 'scoring' of the New Testament was in a liturgically orchestrated context.

The issue does not end there. We cannot just strip Christianity of its expression through worship and hope to discover pure doctrine or pure anything else – least of all pure Christianity! As Louis Bouyer remarks, 'The Christian religion is not only a doctrine . . . it is a public action or deed.'[3] Christianity grew, developed, and became what it was and is in the context of men and women worshipping the risen Jesus, becoming nothing less than his Body through the overshadowing of the Holy Spirit, and expressing that identity in the liturgy of the Church week in and week out. *Lex orandi, lex credendi*: the norm of prayer is the norm of belief. It is no use trying to find the credentials of the Chalcedonian definition of the Person of Christ exclusively within the pages of the New Testament. Not unlike a good chef, the full doctrine and practice of the Church always has an ear on the comments and experiences of the customers! It would indeed be a strange doctrine of cooking that always relied exclusively upon the written word of the cookery book for the making of a good omelette. (I suppose there might be gastronomic fundamentalists who turn only to documentary evidence for their basic doctrine, but I suspect they would soon be found almost exclusively in museums and libraries and would no longer be in business in the hotel and restaurant trade!) For wherever the Church is really 'in business', and especially today, it is most conspicuously in its worship that we find evidence of living faith and evangelistic witness. Alexander Schmemann comments:

> The liturgical movement has appeared everywhere clearly bound up with a theological, missionary and spiritual revival. It has been the source of a greater realization by Christians of their responsibility in the world. It has been a revival of the Church herself . . . it is a return through worship to the Church and through the Church to worship . . . Christian worship, by its nature, structure and content, is the revelation and realization by the Church of her own real nature. And this nature is the new life in Christ.[4]

Of course, it would be foolish to say that such statements do not also require the checks and balances of other aspects of theology; indeed it would not only be foolish, it could prove disastrous. Today, worship could well be purveyed on the market alongside health cures, personality self-realization, and is frequently packaged as therapy or entertainment. Such a situation already exists and is big business in the United States and is on offer in the United Kingdom and Europe. Liturgy and worship for liturgy and worship's sake is perennially in danger of degenerating at best into a mindless and self-centred therapy and at worst into a demonic force. But all this will inevitably happen if worship becomes a separate department in the life of the Church for those who happen to 'like that sort of thing' or to be 'turned on' by it.

At best, theology and worship belong together as surely as heart and mind. Each will inform, extend, and correct the other in a single environment. In an ideal church it will be the bishop who oversees both areas, for he is both principal celebrant in the liturgy and a responsible teacher in the catechetical work of the diocese. The youthful priest Augustine outraged the African church by appearing to usurp the role of the bishop as preacher when he gave a sermon in the presence of the Bishop of Hippo in AD 393. In the Early Church, the bishop was both celebrant and preacher wherever he appeared, thus holding together in his own person a responsibility both for the worship of the Church and also for the teaching ministry. He was in a real sense the 'Prime Minister' of Word and worship.

The bishop and the liturgy

This leads us to the second reason for the contemporary alienation of worship and theology – the person of the bishop. In the Early Church, the bishop was not strictly speaking a hierarchical figure at all, for he had nothing whatever to do with shapes and sizes, but rather with substance. Especially in the Anglican Church, we tend to regard bishops as being kept for 'big occasions'. Nothing could be further from the image of the bishop in the Early Church. He was literally a substantial figure in whom the fullness of the Church in any one area resided. In his person, he reminded the Church both of its unity and also of its plenitude. (It was a later practice of the Medieval Church to place a seventh candle on the altar when the bishop was present to remind the people of the fullness of his office, and it is in fact perhaps still a useful and impressive symbol of the nature of true episcopacy.)

This did not mean that the bishop himself was everything in the diocese, from liturgical scholar to principal theologian. But it did most certainly mean that many responsibilities in the Church were delegated through the office of the bishop, so that it was clearly seen from the outset that these varying responsibilities were *delegated* by him and not *detached* from him. This meant that all the departments of ministry, theology, worship and pastoral concern related to each other through the office of the bishop and were preserved in a genuine unity and inter-relatedness. The bishop delegated his concerns for worship to the administrator of his cathedral church and he delegated his teaching ministry to his catechists and theologians. But sadly, in later years that delegation became a fragmentation to the point where the dean was 'in charge of the cathedral' and theologians were the property of the university and of scholarly specialization. So the bishop became little more than a peripatetic travelling managing director, either brought in for big occasions (to match the secular equivalent of mayor, senator or president) or to write a pastoral charge that, by implication, was not hard-core theology but dealt with soft-edged pastoral concerns largely directed to the clergy on a purely pragmatic basis, with an ever-increasing emphasis upon canon law. It was surely out of the fragmentation of the bishop's office that the later perversions of prelacy arose.

There can, in fact, be no lasting or substantial renewal in an episcopal church without the renewal of the episcopal office. This is one of the most important tasks facing the Church today. The bishop, at least on Sunday and on major feast days, should be in his cathedral church celebrating the liturgy and teaching the Word. That should be the norm. The diocese should run round the bishop and not the bishop round the diocese! Furthermore, his place in the liturgy of confirmation should not consist of a purely mechanical circuit of confirmations, but rather, in his person, the bishop should embody (though necessarily delegate) the responsibilities for the whole of Christian formation, catechesis and Christian initiation. Only so will he once again be placed where the early bishop belonged and where episcopacy won its spurs, namely, on the cutting edge of the missionary life and risk of the Church. It was for that reason that the Lambeth Conference of 1988 called upon the bishops to become once again 'leaders in mission'.

In a proper understanding of the relationship between bishops and other orders of ministry, local parish priests are literally a localization of the bishop's presence and always act as his delegates, doing largely what the bishop does on his behalf when he is necessarily absent. (In the Church of England, the bishop, when licensing a parish priest, still uses that formula of partnership in ministry – 'Receive this cure which is both mine and yours.') All other ministries derive from the bishop and are free to exercise a wide-ranging and diverse practice of ministry as required by the local circumstances, yet preserving the unity of the whole Body of the Church – a unity which is assured and visible in the person of the bishop. It is the bishop who can thus give genuine flexibility to all kinds of local experiments in ministry and mission. In such a revival of the episcopal office there can be no room for a wrong competition – least of all between liturgy and theology – for both flow within the same chemistry, bringing a fullness and richly diverse plenitude at the very heart of the Christian Church, and not least through its worship and liturgy.

I realize, of course, that such a vision of episcopacy will mean much smaller episcopal areas within our church. The important task, however, will be to multiply authentic episcopacy without multiplying prelacy. We do not need all the trappings of later views of the episcopal office wherever we increase the number of bishops. It is a most urgent and important task facing the Church – not least in America, with its geographically huge dioceses – and one to which the Church should give its urgent attention.

The third and final reason for the alienation of worship from all other disciplines and expressions of Christian discipleship is to be found in the marginalizing of baptism in the Church's liturgy, and in the place it holds in the Church's worship time-table. It is almost as though the whole Church has conspired over the past two thousand years or so to propagate a doctrine of the 'real absence' of baptism from Christian life and worship. Yet nothing could be further from the truth on this front, since in some real sense all true Christian worship consists in making explicit the baptismal status of those present. 'Now are we the sons of God and it does not yet appear what we shall be' (1 John 3:2). For even now we are living out the implications of what it is to be sons and daughters of God our Father and we are already entering upon the promises of the Kingdom. Unless that is the background and presupposition of all worship, then there is no way that Christian worship can lift the eyes (let alone the hearts) of those who are participating, beyond the life of the

Church into the environment of the Kingdom. The Christian lives 'the end in the middle'. In so much contemporary worship there is a total absence of what might be termed a significant point of 'lift-off' – *anaphora* – so that the point of it all is lost in well-meaning exhortations to pray and to sing. For all Christian worship should find its shape and purpose in the shape and purpose of baptism, the bringing of Christ's people through the Red Sea into the Land and Kingdom of Promise. Such a dynamic gives to all Christian worship its purpose and direction. Far from polarizing the Church and the Kingdom, it is essential in Christian worship that we 'passage' and move over from the Church into the Kingdom where Christ's people already belong. 'Our conversation is in heaven' (Phil. 3:20) is no mere pious platitude. It is the scriptural mandate reflected from the earliest Christian liturgies when Christ's people were commanded to lift up their hearts and to which they rightly responded – by the grace of baptism – 'They are already with the Lord.'

Language and worship

Yes, 'our conversation is in heaven.' No study of renewal in worship can be complete without some reference to language in worship. For, in fact, the language of God's people in worship and their identity are essentially bound up together.

As we have already seen, the renewal of all the churches is increasingly evident throughout the whole world as we come to the close of the second millennium. As part of this renewal, in recent years, there has been a marked shift in the location and identity of God's people – 'a people for his own possession' – in relation to the rest of society. Perhaps nowhere is this more evident than in English society and its relation to the established Church of England. Since the days of Hooker and the Elizabethan Settlement of the sixteenth century, until very recently, Church and State were regarded as closely related (not least at a constitutional level), so that the Church of England in its worship represented the spiritual aspirations of a whole nation. Anglican worship was expressed in language formed during the renaissance of English literature, in the age of Shakespeare – language at the peak of its perfection. The beautiful language of the Prayer Book of the Church of England in

1662 was part of a cultural package deal, as surely as Latin had been in the Roman Catholic Church of medieval Europe.

At the Reformation, however, there had been a cry for worship to be in the vernacular and now, in the twentieth century, there has occurred another major shift in the placing of the Church in its relation to society which will have similar implications for the styling of worship in our day. Inevitably this is expressed in a renewed cry for a new vernacular, but this time it is the language of the committed minority, increasingly aware of their distinctive identity as a people for God's own possession, recovering an ever-increasingly 'high doctrine' of baptism. There can be no doubt whatever that all the new liturgies will never again relate so closely to the whole of culture and society as they did in Christendom and in sixteenth-century Western Europe. Today it is very much a case of the Church's book for the Church's people in a language that helps committed church-going Christians to mean what they say and to say what they mean.

This need not in itself constitute a ghetto mentality. Ghettos have nothing whatever to do with numbers. A ghetto is more an attitude of mind and such an attitude should, indeed must, be avoided at all costs and not least in the name of evangelism and mission. Therefore, all Christians need to develop strongly their vicarious consciousness so central to the truly Christian vocation, as being a people called to serve God for the whole world, so that we can become God's people in the scriptural sense in which the many are saved by the few as the few are saved by the one.

Such a Church will be totally engaged with the wider community in which it finds itself, while remaining distinctive from the world in the way in which it lives. Such a Church should see itself as the leaven, the salt, and the light and must lose all its self-consciousness in a deep worship and love of God and a deep commitment in solidarity with the rest of the world. It is important for the Church to recover this sense of solidarity and vicariousness if it is not to retreat into a ghetto. The Church of God is a representative body of people, doing all that it does on behalf of those who are not its members: that is the 'priestly' nature of the Church in relation to the world. St Paul is adamant: the unbelieving husband is 'sanctified' by the believing wife and the unbelieving wife is 'sanctified' by the believing husband (1 Cor. 7:14). From the outset,

Paul's vision on the road to Damascus had shown him the solidarity of the new race of God in Christ, so that he could hear the voice repeatedly accusing him: 'Saul, Saul, why are you persecuting *me*?' (Acts 9:1–9). In order to be such a vicarious and priestly Church, no longer of the world but essentially and always for the world, God's people must always have a consciousness that their citizenship and their conversation are both alike in heaven. They will become a 'bridge people'. Nevertheless, such a consciousness and awareness will involve a break with the culture of that day, which is necessarily secular, and of the age, and nowhere is that break more keenly felt than at the level of language and worship.

Exclusive and inclusive

This tension between being thoroughly *in* the world, while remaining distinctive *from* the world is not an easy identity to recover or to establish. We catch a glimpse of this paradoxical identity of the Church in a short treatise written to a cultured pagan called Diognetus at the end of the second century. The treatise claims that:

> Christians are not distinguishable from other people by nationality or language or the way they dress. They do not live in cities reserved to themselves; they do not speak a special dialect; there is nothing eccentric about their way of life . . . They conform to local usage in their dress, diet and manner of life. Nevertheless in their communities they do reveal some extraordinary and undeniably paradoxical attitudes. They live each in his or her own native country, but they are like pilgrims in transit. They play their full part as citizens and are content to submit to every burden as if they were resident aliens. For them, every foreign country is home and every homeland is foreign territory . . . they are in the world, but they refuse to conform to the ways of the world. They pass their days on earth, but their citizenship is in heaven . . . In a word, what the soul is to the body, Christians are to the world.[5]

In the light of all this it is not difficult to see why in recent years the archaic language of the Reformation prayer books is both everybody's language and nobody's. It's as though you can make it mean as much or as little as you want it to mean. To the secularist non-churchgoer the archaic language is part of a religious environment he is loath to lose and yet to which he pays less and less attention. But to the renewed Christian committed totally to the life of the Church, such language from an earlier age inhibits and hinders any real expression of the new life in Christ and in the worship of God's people. Sooner or later this tension could not hold. Inevitably the break had to come, and when it came in the new prayer books throughout the Anglican Communion we should not have been surprised at the extent of the furore that accompanied it. After all, in one sense the Christian Church was robbing society of its religious department. Threaten to pull down temples and you will soon get yourself crucified, and threaten to rob a culture of its religious dimension and you will certainly provoke a plethora of letters to the newspapers at the very least, or petitions even to politicians above the signature of many who seldom even darken the doors of churches.

But at last the truth is out! People, by and large, no longer occasionally drift to church on a Sunday morning. If you are a member of the Church, the chances are that you really are a fully committed member of the Church, and today that will mean belonging week in and week out, possibly with daily Bible reading and study of the Scriptures, perhaps tithing with a discipline of resources, money, talents, and possibly regularly attending a prayer group, with a refresher course, and an annual retreat thrown in for good measure. If, on the other hand, you are not a member of the Church, then apart from a wistful desire for a return of the old Prayer Book (or the Latin Mass, as the case may be) on occasions of national celebration, you will feel that the Church is out of touch, though – strangely enough – not quite for the same reasons your grandparents thought that the Church was out of touch. In those days they used to say that the Church was out of touch because it appeared somewhat 'holier than thou', but today the complaint is more likely to be that we are not holy enough: too many guitars and not enough thee's and thou's!

All this is inevitable and by no means wholly undesirable, providing that our missionary zeal grows and burns ever more brightly. The opportunity for instruction, learning groups, catechesis, and the present action of the Christian apologetic must claim a new priority in the life of the Church. Increasingly, we must present an apologetic that is able to talk about the truth and to commend itself at the level of truth to readers of *Time* magazine or *The Times*. For too long the Christian Church has pursued its missionary zeal as if it simply wanted to encourage people to come to church and join a club. The result so often is that most ugly and self-conscious feature of the Church – a body of people who are committed but not converted.

The heart of the matter

All the time – and at the same time – Christian worship and inter-cession must be heavily clad with the vision of the Church as representative of humanity: a true priesthood of *all* believers (which is not the same thing as the priesthood of each believer); a people committed to the worship of God in the world and on behalf of the world, matching the priesthood of the One who died for the world, was raised and glorified and whoever lives now to make intercession for all humanity. For in true worship we are co-operating with God and seeking to do the work of God for the world. We are uniting with that one great offering of Christ, which was essentially for the whole universe. That vision, and nothing less than that vision, will prevent a renewed and committed Christian Church from turning its back upon the world and retreating into a ghetto of its own ecclesiastical concerns.

So worship must not be just 'down to earth', otherwise it will be exclusive, worship for those bits of the earth that happen to like that sort of thing. Only worship that raises our prayers and praises and unites them with the prayer of Christ and all his saints in heaven, will necessarily be representative and get to the heart of the matter. In the old Israel, when the Levitical priest entered the Holy of Holies, he wore an ephod over his heart, and on it were the emblems of the twelve tribes of Israel whom he represented. The particularity of the vocation of the tribe of Levi was not an exclusive vocation but a representative vocation. That is always true of all vocations within the whole Body. They are distinctive and different, but never privileged or exclusive. So many discussions about the priesthood have assumed that a distinctive doctrine of the vocation to the priestly life automatically assumes that it is an exclusive and excluding vocation. In the vocation of the tribe of Levi, we see the paradox of the proper exclusiveness of Christians, the Church, and its worship. We must wear the concerns of the world on our hearts, but it is no good to be all dressed up with nowhere to go!

Christian hearts, like the heart of Christ himself, will be heavy hearts, burdened with and if need be broken by the concerns of the world and of society at large. It is those hearts that are 'raised' in worship day in and day out, vicariously bringing the wider community together with its heartaches into the presence of God in Christ through intercession. For that is what the word 'intercession' literally means. To intercede is to go into the presence of a person on behalf of another. If we are before God in Christ, we are in his Body together with all his holy people – visible and invisible, known and unknown. Then we are truly where we belong as the Church and we are truly both serving the world and serving God. The transfigured Christ was with holy Moses and holy Elias. The risen Christ is with his saints and his saints are with him, for they are also the Body of Christ and in Christ we are one with them. All our worship must bring us into the Kingdom and raise us into the fellowship of the saints, together with 'angels and archangels and with all the company of heaven'.

That is the ultimate paradox: only such heavenly worship is any earthly use at all. So, whether it is at the bedside of an old lady who is dying or at the glorious worship of a huge congregation in a vast basilica; whether it is with two or three huddled together in prison on the eve of their execution, singing hymns at midnight like Paul and Silas, or locked up in the basilica like Ambrose with his congregation in Milan; whether in a hospital ward or in a trench before battle; there is no corner of earth and no gathering too insignificant that cannot be raised beyond itself in Christ into the presence of the Father with all the saints, 'enkingdomed', transfigured, and glorified. So we all can become even now (for those with eyes to see) what we were intended to be from eternity and will be in Christ throughout all ages and world without end. As Evelyn Underhill writes, 'In our religion, and in all the worship which is the expression of our religion, we look out towards eternity; and bit by bit, in various ways and degrees, we discover in ourselves a certain capacity for eternity.[6]

13

Epilogue

Now and forever

If worship opens us to 'a certain capacity for eternity' (as we saw at the conclusion of the previous chapter), we must avoid any hint of reductionism within worship that might possibly imprison us within what is merely contemporary. For strangely enough, properly understood, that much-abused word in our contemporary vocabulary, when properly understood, has very little whatever to do with modernity, vogue, or fashion. On the contrary, worship, as we have seen in an earlier chapter, takes us down 'memory lane', powerfully recalling previous experiences that have touched and moved us and re-presenting them to us in the here and now. According to the teaching of Christ that is precisely the work of the Holy Spirit – to bring to our remembrance all that Jesus said. (John 14:26). (The Holy Spirit has this strange power to press the recall button!) For frequently, associated with those former experiences, there have been words, places, times, tunes – even smells. It is this which demands that there should be an inevitable element of conservatism in our attitudes to worship. It is true of course that these associations are so powerful that we are always in danger of mistaking the means of worship for the true objects of our worship. If we are not careful, the church building (including its furniture and fittings) where we worshipped as children, where we were married, where we shed tears in bereavement, may not just be the environment in which we worship, but can become the actual object of our worship. That is just plain, old-fashioned idolatry, and all worshippers need to know the danger of such persuasive and reductive idolatry. It is never very far below the surface in many meetings of parochial church councils, and never more frequently than when liturgy and worship are being discussed!

Yet the clergy and those responsible for fashioning and leading worship need to know a second and perhaps more important principle. Worship is never (on earth) so clean, disinfected and 'spiritual' that it has no *location* and no geography. Worship is rooted in the senses, as surely as love is related to the body. Surgery in either category is likely to prove equally traumatic! Furthermore, because both worship and love belong to a complex of associations, we cannot approach either of them in a totally clean, logical or straightforward way. Most of the *logical* arguments about why one way of doing the service is better than another fall on deaf ears. Logic is only one of many motivations in worship, and it should be freely admitted that it is probably the least powerful.

That is why the advent of a new Prayer Book in the national church, or a 'new service' in the local church can always be guaranteed to open up a whole can of worms. We are tampering with something that goes deeply into the recesses of people's experience, and everyone (including the clergy – and especially the experts and liturgists) will be approaching this subject with all kinds of hidden agenda. You play and interfere with worship at your peril. (If the saying is true, '*On ne badine pas avec l'amour*,' the same, only more so, could be said of liturgy and worship.) Words, phrases, even the tunes of hymns, are overwritten, loaded and heavy with deep associations.

Of course, this does not mean that there can never be changes of any kind in liturgy and worship. Worship is a living response to what is changeless, and worship will always be seeking new ways of expression. So perhaps we need a principle to guide us through this dense and complicated territory, mined as it is with all kinds of unexpected and unpredictable explosives.

The principle is what I have come to call *the principle of gradation*. There are two points in this principle we need to affirm in all liturgical change. The first point is that continuity must be more evident than discontinuity. The second point is that in all new expressions of worship (especially in music) roughly 90% of what is new, will inevitably prove to be unsubstantial and therefore not lasting, while only 10% will 'abide' and become part of the tradition. Let us look at these two points within the principle of gradation and see how they will apply in practice.

Continuity and discontinuity

Continuity and discontinuity are written into life at its most basic level, even into our biological evolution. We evolve by both continuity and discontinuity. There is much about everyday life that is everyday. We get our bearings from the familiar, from things we come to rely upon – from the alarm going off in the morning to the sun setting in the west in the evening. All our senses as well as our nervous system are geared to the regular, the repeated and to the rhythm of meal-times as well as bowel movements, the pattern of day to night as well as the seasons of the year. Yet within those predetermined experiences, we choose to make breaks with previous patterns, to strike out into new and different ways. Always there is both continuity and discontinuity, otherwise we simply would not know who we are or where we are. Our identity and our direction are derived from our past, and much of this feeds us best when it is unself-consciously taken for granted. We do not need to reinvent the wheel (*de novo*) with each new day.

In worship this predictable factor is even more powerfully at work. For properly understood, tradition is by no means a dusty word, imprisoning us in the past. On the contrary, in all evolution it is the dynamic of all life. 'I hand on to you that which I first received' (1 Cor. 15:3). Tradition does not mean getting stuck in the past. Tradition is not sticking to the facts; it is allowing the facts and the record of the past (which we often glowingly call experience) to stick to us! The past sticks to the present, giving it a new potential and enriching it so that we can go with confidence into God's future for us. If, however, we cut off our past, we rob the present of its potential. Ironically enough, it is only those who have a strong tradition who can afford (literally) to be least conservative. Radicals, in fact, have often been defined as those who are so secure at the centre that they can afford to go to the edges of experiment.

It was an unfortunate over-simplification that led the Episcopal Church in America to *replace* the old Prayer Book with the new. In the Church of England the law of the land fortuitously prevented the Church from that form of brutal discontinuity. Legally there is still to this day only one prayer book in the Church of England, and that is the Book of Common Prayer of

1662. The so-called 'new prayer book' is not able to replace *the* Prayer Book of 1662 without an Act of Parliament. So the 'new book' is in fact rightly and legally called *The Alternative Service Book 1980* – and that is precisely what it is. In other words, the old and the new will continue to run alongside and overlap with each other. That, frankly, is the most responsible way of changing worship. (Admittedly, the Church of England should claim no virtue from this situation. It is an accident of law and history, but it has probably prevented the English Church from cutting off its tail and imposing the new book by forsaking or abolishing the old.) In that way contemporary worship will evolve from the old into the new, which itself in turn will become the old.

Yet change there must be – even in language. We know that no prayer book could equal the aesthetic beauty of the English language of the Book of 1662. It so happened that when Cranmer was putting the medieval Latin services into English, he was undertaking the whole exercise at precisely the moment in history when the English language was entering upon its renaissance – its Shakespearean excellence. Technically, no contemporary language of any other age will be able to equal that of the sixteenth century, because that particular period was the high-water mark of the flowering of the English language.

Nevertheless, as a Reformation church, the Anglican Church is rightly and properly committed to the vernacular, and it would be a betrayal of that principle if ever we were to refuse to conduct worship in the vernacular. The time is long overdue for language revision (even of the 1980 Book), for as the preface to the *ASB* says, 'words, even agreed words, are only the beginning of the worship. Those who use them do well to recognize their transience and imperfection; to treat them as a ladder, not a goal.'[1]

It is at this point that the principle of gradation comes into its own. For as that principle urges, we should not cut off our tail, lose all continuity with the past, and start with clean, disinfected language and new words for their own sake. There must be continuity and overlap, especially in those very areas where prayer and worship have become part of the common subconscious, religious experience of a whole generation. The most obvious example of this is the Lord's Prayer, which thankfully occurs in parallel translations in the 1980 Prayer Book. A sensitive pastor would surely never arrive at the bedside of a dying occasional churchgoer and recite the Lord's Prayer in its modern form. It would simply fail to resonate with anything in the person's past experience of God and would therefore be powerless to bring comfort, strength and reassurance. Some 'new Christians' come to mind, however, whose prayer reflex-action would automatically lead them off in the new translation of familiar prayers and responses without a second thought. Generations overlap and the Church has to learn to live with this overlapping, even in an untidy way, for several decades to come and possibly for the rest of time.

For (and this is the second point in the principle of gradation) we need to realize that much of what is new will not wear well. It will simply be found (with experience and with frequent use) to be lightweight. This is especially true with so much generally in the whole art of music and quite specifically in the case of much music employed in worship. After all, there were all kinds of composers in the eighteenth century, many of them remarkably popular in their own day, but it is largely only the music of the Mozarts and Beethovens (probably, in fact, less than one tenth of the total output of the age) that has lasted. So it is frankly foolish and irresponsible to choose exclusively new hymns for any one service. It is encouraging to see that the choice of hymns for the new *Church Hymnal* of the Episcopal Church is wisely based on the principle of gradation:

> As the church itself is continually being made new, so the music of the Church has reflected the life of its many generations. The Hymnal has been and will be an essential part of the record of this life and growth. It should retain classic texts and music which have been honoured by history and are staples for singing congregations. At the same time it should present a prophetic vision that will speak to the Church of the future as well as the Church of today.[2]

Three cheers! After all, we have scriptural warrant for the policy of the wise scribe who 'brings out of his treasure what is new and what is old' (Matt. 13:52). It was in fact not a bad title for a hymn book – *Hymns Ancient and Modern*. That is precisely what all good hymn books should be, though perhaps things are necessarily in such a state of flux in our day, that a loose-leaf folder would serve better than a bound hymnal. For the key phrase in that statement of intention of the American Episcopal Church is, of course, the phrase 'at the same time'. Like the architecture of a great cathedral, the best features of different periods can live happily alongside and in juxtaposition. Don't put all your eggs in one basket – be it old or new – and realize that not all the eggs will prove to be equally good. Hopefully most musical settings to the Eucharist will not survive the decade! They don't deserve to. Yet possibly, and hopefully, one in ten will, and we shall only discover that one by use and through experience and experiment. The new hymnals in all the churches, generally speaking, have a solid staple diet of known hymns that have become the 'folk songs' of God's people. They also include a good selection of new hymns and spiritual songs. Largely speaking, they are to be commended on the balance and content. But let this approach be our approach to all liturgical change and modernization, and then we shall avoid some of the heartbreaks of recent decades and especially amongst the ranks of regular worshippers.

Worship in time and worship in eternity

After the general resurrection there will not be total discontinuity. The risen Christ was 'new' yet still just recognizable, and Paul does not present his doctrine of the resurrection life as though it is or will be a total break with what we have come to know and to be at home with in this world:

> In this present frame we sigh with deep longing for the heavenly house, for we do not want to face utter nakedness when death destroys our present dwelling – these bodies of ours. So long as we are clothed in this temporary dwelling we have a powerful longing, not because we want just to get rid of these 'clothes' but because we want to know the full cover of the permanent home that will be ours. We want our transitory life to be absorbed into the life that is eternal (2 Cor. 5:2ff.).

Never more so than in the case of worship. For it is not only powerful by reason of its many and powerful past associations, but it is in worship that we supremely 'yearn' and reach forward to the perfect worship of heaven with all the saints. When we worship we stand at that point of convergence between time and eternity – the convergence of what is changing and what is changeless. So it is not just a matter of a familiar tune which we have known and with which we may have many associations (though it is that at the very least). It is also at the same time, the 'echo of a tune we have not yet heard'. And somewhere in all of this is a single seamless garment: and it is a deep offence to tear it and divide it into past, present, and future, old or new.

All our worship on earth is intended to prepare us for the life and worship of heaven – where life will be worship, and where worship will be supremely a whole way of life – eternal life, enriched life. God's people in their worship in this world have already 'caught on' to this truth and in turn are 'caught up' by their worship into the life and worship of the saints in heaven, where change is now part of the changelessness and where the new is now overtaken by eternity.

That is the point of churchgoing, and it is a point the laity in the pews, the organist at the console, the choir at their anthem book, the acolytes with their torches, the reader at the lectern, the preacher in the pulpit, and the priest at the altar should never forget. They do so at their peril – an eternal peril. For when worship misses the point it ceases to be anything worthy of our attention – it is like salt that has lost its savour, and we all know what the fate of such salt is. Instead of being an investment in eternity, it becomes simply a waste of time. Yet when time is used for worship, it becomes eternal ('the time simply flew by') – as every lover and worshipper knows from experience. Or perhaps it just stood still. So about all our worship there must always be something of this 'other' and in all changes, however necessary or important they might be in this world, we must never lose what is changeless. The changeless is recognized by its quality rather than by its longevity – just, in fact, like that quality of life which Christ describes both as abundant and eternal. Those responsible for preparing and leading worship need to have an eye and an ear for this quality of the changeless with just the same sensitivity and awareness as those who know a good wine when they taste one or a fine work of art when they see one. Because although everything this book has been concerned with can be and should be discovered within time (where change is inevitable), it can only be fully known and ultimately made our own in eternity. As St Augustine wrote, 'Then we shall be still and we shall see, we shall see and we shall love, we shall love and we shall praise. Behold what will be, in the end, without end! For what is our end, but to reach that kingdom which has no end.'[3]

Notes

Preface

1. S. Tugwell, OP, *Did You Receive the Spirit?* (Darton, Longman & Todd, 1972), p. 104

1 Worship and the human condition

1. Peter Shafer, *Equus* (Avon, 1977), Act 2.
2. Hand, *Saint Augustine on Prayer*, quoted in Ann and Barry Ulanov, *Primary Speech* (SCM Press, 1982), p. 13.
3. Dag Hammarskjöld, *Markings* (Faber & Faber, 1964), p. 64.
4. Michael Mayne, *This Sunrise of Wonder* (London, Fount, 1995), p. 5.
5. G. K. Chesterton, *Autobiography* (Burns Oates, 1937), pp. 94–5.
6. *Centuries of Meditation*, Third Century, 1, 2. (Faith Press), p. 98.
7. W. H. Auden, 'Another Time', in memory of W. B. Yeats (1940).
8. P. Gerhardt, 'The duteous day now closeth', *English Hymnal* (1940), 181.
9. C. Wesley, 'Love divine, all love excelling', *English Hymnal*, 479.
10. Colin Dunlop, *Anglican Public Worship* (SCM Press, 1953), p. 14.
11. *Prayer Book* Collect, Trinity VI, medieval version.
12. Richard Rolle, *The Fire of Love* (London, C. M. Deansley, 1915), ch. 14, 11.
13. *Adversus Haereses*, 4, 20.7.
14. William Temple, *Christian Faith and Life* (Morehouse, 1982), p. 19.
15. William Shakespeare, *Troilus and Cressida*, Act I, Scene III, line 109.
16. A. N. Whitehead, *Science and the Modern World* (Free Press, 1967), p. 23.

2 The nature and characteristics of Christian worship

1. William Temple, *The Preacher's Theme Today* (London, SPCK, 1939), p. 20.
2. C. S. Lewis, 'The Weight of Glory' in *They Asked for a Paper* (Macmillan, 1980), p. 200.
3. Kenneth Leech, *We Preach Christ Crucified* (DLT, 1994), p. 53.
4. Coverdale translation.

5. Henry Scott-Holland, *A Bundle of Memories* (Wells, Gardner & Darton, 1915), p. 61.
6. G. Herbert, 'King of glory, King of peace', *English Hymnal*, 424, v. 3.

3 Worship and the Church today

1. See Andrew Greeley, *The Persistence of Religion* (SCM Press, 1973), p. 1.
2. *Ibid.*, p. 1.
3. Augustine, *Confessions* (Oxford University Press, 1991), VII.xiii.19.
4. Teilhard de Chardin, *Le Milieu Divin* (London, Collins), p. 93.
5. Isaac Watts, 'When I survey the wondrous cross', *English Hymnal*, 95.
6. W. H. Vanstone, *Love's Endeavour, Love's Expense* (DLT, 1977), p. 108.
7. William Temple, *The Hope of a New World* (Macmillan), p. 30.
8. William Temple, *The Church and Its Teaching Today* (Macmillan), p. 15.
9. 1 Clement 10:41.
10. M. de Unamuno, *The Tragic Sense of Life* (London, 1962), p. 33.
11. Brother Roger Schultz, *Festival* (SPCK, 1971), pp. 48f.
12. Colin Dunlop, op. cit., pp. 51f.

4 Unity and flexibility in worship

1. Thomas Merton, *The Last of the Fathers* (Harcourt Brace, 1954), p. 52.

5 Signs, symbols and ceremonies

1. Michael Perham, *Church Times*, 28th July 1995.
2. *Ibid.*
3. Thomas Carlyle, Sartor Resartus (Arden Library, 1981), p. 64.
4. Christopher Bryant, The River Within (Upper Room, 1983), p. 62.
5. The Episcopal *Book of Common Prayer*, (The Church Hymnal Corporation and the Seabury Press, 1977), p. 306.
6. Clifford Howell, 'The Communion Rite – The Deterioration of the Signs', *Liturgy,* No.2 (St Paul Publications,), p. 237.
7. Alexander Schmemann, *The World as Sacrament* (DLT, 1966), pp. 29–30.
8. *Ibid.*, pp. 73f.
9. John Austin Baker, *The Whole Family of God* (Mowbray, 1981), pp. 172f.
10. W. Cowper, 'Jesus, where'er thy people meet', *English Hymnal*, 422, v. 4.
11. T. S. Eliot, *Four Quartets*, from *Collected Poems* (Faber, 1963), p. 215.

6 Music and worship

1. C. Henry Philips, *The Singing Church* (Faber & Faber, 1945), p. 238.
2. Winifred Douglas, *Church Music in History and Practice* (New York, Charles Scribner's Sons, 1940), pp. 9f.
3. Yehudi Menuhin, *Themes and Variations* (Stein & Day, 1972), p. 9.
4. Douglas, op. cit., pp. 28f.

5. *Psalm Praise* (London, Falcon, 1973), p. 49.

6. Betty Pulkingham and Jeanne Harper, *The Sound of Living Waters* (Eerdmans, 1974), p. 64.

7. Anthony Storr, *Music and the Mind* (London, HarperCollins, 1992), p. 39.

8. Phillips, op. cit., p. 238.

9. Michael Perry, *Preparing for Worship: The essential handbook for worship leaders* (HarperCollins, 1995) – a well-produced catalogue of hymns and psalms related to biblical texts and special occasions. It forms an invaluable resource for clergy and musicians in their work of styling the worship and liturgy.

10. Douglas, op. cit., p. 8.

11. 'Cathedrals are Shop windows of the Church of England', *Heritage and Renewal*, the Report of the Archbishop's Commission on Cathedrals (London, Church House Publishing, 1994), p. 17.

12. For further development of this theme, see *Heritage and Renewal*, op. cit., chs 3 & 5.

13. A very full and detailed report is available: *In Tune with Heaven*, the Report of the Archbishop's Commission on Church Music, 1992.

7 Receiving the Word of God: preaching and worship

1. C. Smith, OSB, *The Path of Life* (Ampleforth Abbey Press, 1995), p. 12.

2. R. E. Terwilliger, *Receiving the Word of God* (Morehouse-Barlow, 1960), p. 140.

3. The Episcopal *Book of Common Prayer*, Collect for the second Sunday in Advent.

4. Athanasius, *The Life of Anthony* (Paulist Press, 1980), chs 1–2.

5. Augustine, Sermon 17:1.

6. Augustine, *De Doctrina Christiana*, Book 4, 42:6.

7. Donald Coggan, *Stewards of Grace* (Hodder & Stoughton, 1958), p. 18.

8. Augustine, Sermon 133:1.

9. Augustine, Sermon 19:2 (*Guelfergitanus*).

10. Paul Simon, 'Sounds of Silence' (Eclectic Music Co., 1965), © 1964. Permission to quote gratefully acknowledged.

11. John R. W. Stott, *Between Two Worlds* (Eerdmans, 1982), p. 73.

12. Augustine, Sermons on St John's Gospel 19:9; 1:133.

13. Augustine, *De Catechizandis Rudibus*, 13:19, 209.

14. Augustine, *Enarrationes in Psalmos*, Pss. 36; 3:6.

15. Terwilliger, op. cit., p. 135.

16. Augustine, *De Doctrina Christiana*, Book 4, 12:27, 136.

17. Terwilliger, op. cit., p. 122.

18. *Ibid.*, p. 124.

19. *Ibid.*, p. 13.

20. E. C. Dargan, *A History of Preaching*, Vol. 1, AD 70–1572 (B. Franklin, 1965), p. 366f.

21. D. Martyn Lloyd-Jones, *Preaching and Preachers* (Zondervan, 1972), p. 9.

22. Decree on the Ministry of Life and Priests, Second Vatican Council.

8 The Daily Office

1. *Didache* viii.3.
2. (eds), *Celebrating Common Prayer* (Mowbrays, 1992), p. 677.
3. *Ibid*., Foreword, p. vii.
4. Arthur Schopenhauer, *The World as Will and Representation*, translated by E. F. J. Payne, Vol. 1 (New York, Dover, 1969), p. 251.
5. Quoted in R. W. Southern, *St Anselm – A Portrait in a Landscape* (Cambridge University Press, 1990), p. 96.
6. Thomas Moore, *Meditations* (London, HarperCollins, 1994), p. 44.
7. Quoted in Kenneth Leech, *The Eye of the Storm* (DLT, 1992), p. 89.
8. Bruce Winter, *Seek the Welfare of the City* (Eerdmans/Paternoster, 1994), p. 3.
9. Lesslie Newbigin, *The Gospel in a Pluralist Society* (Eerdmans, 1989), p. 227.
10. (eds), *Celebrating Common Prayer*, op. cit., Preface, p. vii.

9 Alternative patterns of worship for a Church in mission

1. Lesslie Newbigin, op cit., p. 227.
2. John Westerhoff, *Living the Faith Community*, p. 72.
3. *Patterns for Worship* (General Synod, 898), Preface, p. v.
4. *Ibid*., Preface, p. vii.
5. *Ibid*., p. 11.
6. *Ibid*.
7. *Ibid*., pp. 3–4.
8. (eds), *The Book Of Occasional Services* (Episcopal Church, 1979), p. 5.
9. Michael Perham, *Liturgy Pastoral and Parochial* (SPCK, 1984), p. 121.
10. *Ibid*., p. 123.
11. David Jones, quoted in Michael Mayne, op. cit., p. 189.
12. *The Alternative Service Book* (London, Hodder & Stoughton, 1980), the Baptism of Children, p. 245.

10 Reordering church buildings for worship

1. Johnson & Johnson, *Planning for Liturgy* (St Michael's Abbey Press, 1983), p. 74.
2. Paul Tillich, *On Art and Architecture* (Crossroad, 1987), pp. 192f.

11 Worship, service and life

1. W. Temple, *Citizen and Churchman* (Eyre & Spottiswood,), p. 101.
2. G. M. Hopkins, 'God's Grandeur', Helen Gardner (ed.), *The New Oxford Book of English Verse 1250–1950* (OUP, 1972), p. 786.
3. Aldous Huxley, *The Doors of Perception* (Penguin, 1959), p. 35.
4. William Temple, *Christian Faith and Life* (SCM Press,), p. 18.

5. *Ibid.*
6. William Shakespeare, *King Lear*, Act 2, Scene 1.
7. Temple, *Citizen and Churchman*, op. cit., p. 101.
8. St John Chrysostom, Homily, 50:3–4.
9. Temple, *Christian Faith and Life*, op. cit., p. 19.
10. Isaac Watts, 'When I survey the wondrous cross', *English Hymnal,* 337.

12 'With angels and archangels and all the company of heaven'

1. *The Alternative Service Book*, p. 248.
2. Alexander Schmemann, *Introduction to Liturgical Theology* (Vladimirs, 1966), p. 25.
3. Louis Bouyer, *Le Mystère Paschal* (Paris, Les Editions du Cerf, 1947), p. 9.
4. Schmemann, op. cit., pp. 12, 23.
5. *Letter to Diognetus* 5:SC33.
6. Evelyn Underhill, *The Mystery of Sacrifice* (Longmans Green & Co., 1959), Introduction, p. iii.

Epilogue

1. *The Alternative Service Book*, Preface, p. 11.
2. *The New Church Hymnal* (New York, The Church Hymnal Corporation, 1982), Foreword, p. vi.
3. Augustine, *The City of God* (OUP, 1958), Conclusion, p. 463.

Index